NOTORIOUS

THE LIFE AND FIGHTS OF CONOR MCGREGOR

JACK SLACK

JOHN BLAKE

Published by John Blake Publishing Ltd
3 Bramber Court, 2 Bramber Road,
London W14 9PB, England

www.johnblakebooks.com

www.facebook.com/johnblakebooks ⬛
twitter.com/jblakebooks ⬛

First published in paperback in 2017

ISBN: 978 1 78606 406 6

British Library Cataloguing-in-Publication Data:

A catalogue record for this book is available from the British Library.

Design by www.envydesign.co.uk

Printed in Great Britain by CPI Group (UK) Ltd

1 3 5 7 9 10 8 6 4 2

Papers used by John Blake Publishing are natural, recyclable
products made from wood grown in sustainable forests.
The manufacturing processes conform to the environmental
regulations of the country of origin.

Every attempt has been made to contact the relevant
copyright-holders, but some were unobtainable. We would be
grateful if the appropriate people could contact us.

John Blake Publishing is an imprint of Bonnier Publishing
www.bonnierpublishing.co.uk

*For my wife, my parents,
my teachers and my training partners*

CONTENTS

1

STRAIGHT BLAST GYM

Nothing about Conor McGregor's upbringing suggested that he would change the face of the fight business. There was no reason to believe that he was anything remarkable based on his early record in the mixed martial arts game. It would have been perfectly reasonable to dismiss him as delusional when he quit his first job and insisted, after meaningless victories on regional cards, that he was 'the fucking future'. But through stubbornness and self-belief, combined with a remarkable work ethic and an open and keen mind for the intricacies of martial arts, McGregor would come to outgrow the fight game itself and muscle out other famous athletes from more mainstream sports in the headlines of the world's back pages. At every stage of the journey, things could have gone another way, and it wasn't until he was more than five years into a seemingly dead-end career as a fighter that he was able to train under optimal conditions and get off social welfare.

But McGregor's success stands as evidence that world-class facilities are not the only way of producing a world-class fighter. Many of the greatest fighters who have ever lived started their journey in a shed.

* * *

Tom Egan was a normal sixteen-year-old whose hobby was martial arts – more accurately, a karate-inspired form of kickboxing. When a lad from Crumlin joined Egan's school in Lucan, the young Dubliner noticed an unusual intensity in the standoffish newcomer. As it turned out, this new boy, Conor McGregor, was also interested in martial arts. More than interested – perhaps even obsessed. From his earliest days, McGregor had been fascinated by the notion of combat – in the ring, on the street, wherever it might conceivably take place. McGregor's formative years had been spent in Crumlin, where he had joined the local boxing club, but his parents had recently moved to Lucan, uprooting him from his friends, his hangouts and even his gym, which he now struggled to get to as regularly. He was as uncomfortable with the move as plenty of young men would be.

Through his early childhood, Conor had been more interested in football than in fighting, but it was a need for physical activity that spurred him on more than a great love of the teams and players. In an interview with the *Irish Independent*, in 2015, he mused on how some people get 'a little weird', with a tribe-like mentality towards their team. Conor observed that almost everyone he knew in Ireland supported either Liverpool or Manchester United, and while his father spent his early life in Liverpool, the Dubliner reflected that United were probably 'his' team. But by the time his family moved to Lucan, the premiership dreams had fallen away and Conor McGregor was far more invested in the sweet science – the bruising business – boxing. When he was eleven years old, he recounts, he found himself outnumbered by a group of boys who had the intention of roughing him up. To hear McGregor tell it, one lad threw a punch and the young Dubliner slipped it, shuffled his feet and exclaimed 'Muhammad Ali!' Like the great John L. Sullivan of legend, the first heavyweight champion of the world and the child of Irish parents, Conor McGregor has always spun a great yarn. 'I done the Ali shuffle! I'm only eleven years old, I done the Ali shuffle, threw a left hook.' Unfortunately even in his own retelling, our hero fell victim to the numbers. 'It was me versus six of them and I ended up getting my arse whooped.'

By his teens McGregor was an avid boxer, while Tom Egan was involved in karate and kickboxing, but neither was a purist. They both enjoyed the new American reality television show *The Ultimate Fighter*, in which mixed martial arts fighters competed week-by-week to force their way into the Ultimate Fighting Championship – the biggest show in the game. Much of the conversation between the two young scrappers was dominated by the subject of fighting, the Ultimate Fighting Championship and martial arts technique. When Egan's family moved out to Newbridge, his parents allowed him to convert a shed on their new property into a gym of his own. Egan and McGregor would often head out to this shed and, in the words of McGregor, 'punch the head off' each other. Egan, moving on from kickboxing, began training in Newbridge with a Brazilian jiu-jitsu blue belt named Mick Aldridge. Excluding the largely ceremonial red belt ranks, there are only five belts in Brazilian jiu-jitsu: white, blue, purple, brown, and black. They aren't given easily and few academies have grading criteria. You get the belt when your coach feels you deserve it and it could take half a decade or more between belts, or just a year.

Like Conor McGregor, Tom Egan wanted to keep improving and while a blue belt in Brazilian jiu-jitsu was rare enough in Ireland in the early 2000s, Egan began seeking out more experienced teachers. In his search for a coach, one name kept coming up. The name of a man who became responsible in a very large part for the rise of Conor McGregor and mixed martial arts in Ireland: John Kavanagh.

THE GODFATHER OF IRISH MMA

The name Conor McGregor has become inseparable from the notion of confidence. Forthright, unshakeable, borderline delusional self-belief. But the McGregor story starts with another young man, one who had none of that. John Kavanagh was a gawky teen who had never been in a fight in his life and who, like many adolescents, fought a constant battle with his own insecurities. At eighteen years old, Kavanagh and his then-girlfriend were once walking from a bar called The Station in Rathmines when they stumbled upon a cyclist being assaulted by a group of men. Hoping to get the group to move along, Kavanagh suggested that the downed man had probably 'had enough'. The result was that John Kavanagh had seven shades beaten out of him on the Dublin pavement, in the place of the man he had tried to help.

Rescued by a friend who had left The Station shortly after him, Kavanagh had suffered a shattered orbital bone and received little pity, or aid, upon reaching a police station. A fan of Spider-Man since childhood, Kavanagh had received the harsh lesson that – unlike in the comic books – there is a reason why most people keep their heads down when they come across violent or cruel incidents. As an old Japanese saying has it: the nail that pokes up will be hammered down again. By his own account, after the beating Kavanagh spiralled into depression and anxiety, recalling: '[I] was in a constant state of fear. Whenever I did go out, I was always looking over my shoulder.' A keen student of karate from an early age, martial arts had been a big part of his life and character, yet they had done nothing to help him in the one episode of violence he had encountered. To add insult to injury, Kavanagh's girlfriend had witnessed the entire spectacle, a truly emasculating experience for the awkward and timid young man.

Fortunately for the future of martial arts and the fight game in Ireland, John Kavanagh did not abandon his sport just because it had failed to help him in his hour of need. He continued to study, but drifted away from traditional karate and towards the work of street defence guru Geoff Thompson. A doorman from Coventry, Thompson had found time and again that an extensive background in traditional martial arts had failed to prepare him for the harsh realities of real-world violence. Through seminars and publications such as *Animal Day, The Fence* and *Three Second Fighter*, Thompson taught that fear was not only inevitable in a combative situation but that it was a necessary instinct. Fight or flight is inherent in any animal – you run or you throw down.

Geoff Thompson believed that the fight-or-flight instinct had to be embraced and harnessed in order to succeed, and that it could similarly be manipulated in an aggressor to defuse a situation. Thompson believed in the 'fence': essentially a guard, but not in the traditional boxing or martial arts sense, it is an unthreatening posture, usually with the hands open and raised, to keep track of the opponent's movements and obstruct the firing line of their hands. To Thompson, the handling of a situation is more about learning to handle physical abuse and keeping a cool head than the number of 'moves' a man knows. If things start escalating while using the 'fence', and the aggressor begins squaring up to you and getting in your face, a short bump in the chest with the lead hand to push him away can trigger the fight-or-flight response in his brain. With the distance re-established and a slight shock to his system, the aggressor might look for a way out of the situation. On the off-chance that he steps in again, it will be clear that he is ready to fight and at that point Thompson believes the man using the 'fence' should strike first. The pre-emptive strike has been controversial in the traditional martial arts world, but it is also the principle that Thompson places most emphasis on.

The next great moment of inspiration for John Kavanagh was something that inspired so many other successful fighters and coaches in the game of mixed martial arts today. He obtained a tape of the 1993 Ultimate Fighting Championship tournament. Royce Gracie, a member of the Gracie family famed within the martial arts world, entered the contest as the smallest man, and then defeated three opponents in one night to become the tournament champion. Gracie didn't knock anyone out, he didn't muscle anyone around; he slowly tripped them to the floor, got on top of them, moved to their back and submitted them with a choke. To everyone who saw him at the time, it seemed like magic. The core belief in martial arts had always been that technique could overcome strength, but this was not what people had in mind. There were no spin kicks or jumps, there wasn't even much speed or athleticism involved. Gracie won bouts based on his position and knowledge of a whole game that even veteran street fighters did not understand. As the great Brazilian jiu-jitsu black belt Carlos Machado would put it: 'The ground is my ocean, I'm the shark, and most people don't even know how to swim.'

Kavanagh began experimenting with grappling techniques in his self-defence classes but had no formal teacher to show him the ins and outs of the game, relying on trial and error as the Gracie family themselves often had, and as Tom Egan and Conor McGregor would in their own training shed. While there was no chance of getting instruction in Brazilian jiu-jitsu in Dublin, or even across the Irish Sea, at the time, Kavanagh scraped together the money to travel to the United States in order to train with the famous Machado brothers for three weeks. Many of the United States' earliest black belts happened to live in the same neighbourhood as the Gracies and were invited to train with them on makeshift mats in the family's garage. Meanwhile, Kavanagh, who would become Ireland's first black belt, had to travel across the Atlantic Ocean to get even a few days of tuition from a black belt instructor.

In his continued search for improvement as a martial artist, Kavanagh did something that might be regarded as either admirable or reckless. At twenty-one years old, while studying engineering at Dublin Institute of Technology, the young Irishman began seeking out work as a doorman in order to put himself in contact with the aggression and confrontation that had emotionally paralysed him in the wake of his assault. To this day, Kavanagh remains a soft-spoken and thoughtful man who doesn't enjoy the limelight. In an interview with the *Irish Independent* in October 2016, he discussed his inherent anxiety and nerves: 'I don't like a lot of people looking at me when I'm talking,' he revealed. 'I also have a skin condition, a very bad rosacea, which means that if I get nervous at all, this redness comes up around my neck, and I'm talking putrid red. I can actually feel it coming on and that makes me more nervous, which increases it, and it goes on and on until I feel like I'm a beetroot.'

Needless to say, bouncing is a dangerous gig – doormen are considerably more prone to being bottled or stabbed than the majority of the population – but much of a doorman's job involves simply looking imposing in order to convince punters it's not worth causing a scene. Unfortunately, John Kavanagh had never been physically intimidating and this made him an easy target for the drunkard who had just been denied entry or had his advances rejected by a girl and needed to reassert his masculinity. Kavanagh found himself on the receiving end of verbal abuse and threats as often as he expected. As a result, however, the young engineer developed a thicker skin and conquered a great many of the demons that plagued him following his assault. As something of an encouraging bonus, when words escalated to blows Kavanagh found that a little grappling knowledge and practice on top of his traditional martial arts experience made things a lot easier for him than he had expected. As much as every drunk thinks he could have a good crack at a professional boxing career, his fighting is improved by alcohol about as much as his driving and singing.

After graduating from Dublin Institute of Technology, Kavanagh doubled down on his teaching of martial arts. His first gym, known in the Irish MMA community as 'The Shed', hosted many of the coaches now at the head of major teams on the Irish circuit, but it was little more than the name implies. Kavanagh had a so-so career as an MMA fighter at a time when there were few events held in the UK and hardly any to speak of in Ireland. Often, he would pay for his own travel and accommodation and expect no purse in return; these were the dark days when mixed martial arts was an underground sport. Kavanagh's mantra in recent years has been 'We win or we learn' and that optimistic philosophy served him well following a crushing loss to Bobby Karagiannidis in South Africa. Afterwards, a disappointed Kavanagh spent the night drinking with his opponent's coach, Matt Thornton. Thornton had founded the Straight Blast Gym in Oregon and the two became fast friends. Kavanagh's shed soon became Straight Blast Gym Ireland.

After retiring from his MMA career while the sport was still very much in its infancy, Kavanagh moved premises to Harold's Cross on Dublin's south side. The nature of running a gym devoted to MMA or grappling is that you find breezy, bare lots on industrial estates, mat them out and fill them with equipment. If everything goes well, after a few years, you pack it all up and take a risk on a bigger one across town. At every step there is the concern that you will end up with fewer members at the new place than where you started. Whereas boxing gyms typically spring up in down-market areas and the mandatory equipment is fairly inexpensive – with a ring and high-tech kit coming as a bonus if the gym can build up some savings in its coffers – MMA and grappling gyms require space most of all, and then have to mat it all out. Maintenance can also be far more of a burden in a grappling gym because the mats are a breeding ground for staph infection, ringworm and all kinds of other unpleasant maladies that are part and parcel of the grappling game. Cleaning the mats multiple times a day is mandatory at a gym with a high number of sessions and a good number of people on the mats. With a high degree of maintenance and the need for far more floor space, it is tough to find venues that offer an improvement without moving farther and farther out of the city. Often, convenience is sacrificed for square footage. In early 2006, Kavanagh had planned to upgrade location once more to a unit in Tallaght, but when that fell through he was back to teaching part-time in a school hall. Finally, he moved into a unit in Rathcoole, and it was there that Straight Blast Gym Ireland's rise to notoriety on the world stage would begin in earnest.

EARLY DAYS

Whereas John Kavanagh is soft-spoken and spent a good portion of his young life in martial arts, confronting his fears and insecurities, Conor McGregor was filled to the brim with boundless confidence and braggadocio. McGregor would walk into Kavanagh's gym in 2006 with none of its owner's doubts. He had arrived at Dublin's Straight Blast Gym with his friend Tom Egan and the two quickly made a home for themselves under Kavanagh. The latter's account of this time in his life makes it clear that he was entertaining the thought that he might have wasted a good portion of his life on a sport that could only ever aspire to being popular within a small niche. But to hear Tom Egan tell the story, Kavanagh was already a legend in the Dublin fight scene. In an interview with *Severe MMA* in 2015, Egan stated: 'I had met John a few times at different seminars out with the guys I trained with in Athy. To see a guy as good as John back then completely blew my mind. There was this big huge guy training with us in Athy and John would completely tool him. He was a brown belt at the time, and seeing him in action reiterated everything I had already thought about jiu-jitsu.'

Egan began training with Kavanagh at SBG's Harold's Cross and once he had passed his driving test, Egan would bring McGregor along with him. Kavanagh recalls that his first meeting with McGregor was somewhat inauspicious. McGregor apparently set to work sparring with Owen Roddy and dropped the veteran with a blow to the body. When McGregor did the same to the team's first female fighter, Aisling Daly, it was clear that the young boxer was taking liberties and Kavanagh decided to introduce him to the art of 'ground and pound' in the next round. That kind of aggression, though, is only to be expected from an anxious young man who is hoping to make sure that his new gym knows he's serious and can actually fight. McGregor took his lesson, settled down and soon became a regular character at the gym, well liked by those he trained with and competitive without that desperate need to prove himself the tougher guy.

Mixed martial arts was now reaching a point at which specialised gyms were forming in the United States. And these camps, full of top-flight fighters and quality equipment, controlled many of the top spots in the world's MMA rankings. But the barriers for entry to combat sports have always been low. Many gyms with few training facilities can produce decent scrappers out of limited means. For Tom Egan and Conor McGregor, Egan's training shed had served the same role as John Kavanagh's 'shed': they had learned by trial and error and shared experience. McGregor taught Egan to box and Egan taught McGregor to grapple.

Conor McGregor had been competing as an amateur boxer, but in February 2007, with only a short period of formal MMA training, he took his first amateur mixed martial arts bout. Wearing turquoise Hawaiian board shorts, the young boxer was able to quickly drop his man, Ciaran Campbell, with a counter left hand as the latter ran in. Inviting Campbell to stand up, McGregor did it again. As Campbell regained his feet a second time, McGregor swarmed in on him along the ropes with long, wild, loopy hooks and the referee waved the bout off. One thing was clear: McGregor could hit.

This first bout took place in Ring of Truth, a promotion created and run by John Kavanagh essentially for the purpose of giving his fighters some ring experience at a time when there were few opportunities in the Irish MMA scene. Kavanagh chose Ring of Truth as a name because he believed that marketing shows as martial arts events rather than 'cage fights' had a lot to do with avoiding public outcry for this young and controversial sport. Consequently, Kavanagh's promotion used the ring instead of the cage. The major UK promotions Cage Warriors and Cage Rage didn't appear to be worried about this. While the negative connotations of 'cage fighting' might seem worth avoiding, it is rarely worth the trouble of using a ring instead of a cage. If you have ever wondered why MMA has to be in a cage, and feel like it would be far easier to enjoy in a ring, it is worth considering the benefits of the cage and the downfalls of the ring.

The nature of mixed martial arts is that when two men wrestle, one of them will have their back pushed to the boundary. If that is a fence, he can lean on it or be pressed into it. If it is the ring ropes, he risks going through the ropes. If the ropes are not taped together at several points along each side, they will separate freely when pressure is applied against them. In the Japanese promotion Rizin FC, fighters have fallen through the ropes and onto the floor below. Furthermore, the ropes simply serve to entangle the fighters. The rules always prohibit holding onto the ropes, but fighters will do it instinctively or simply get caught up in them as the opponent attempts a takedown. An early MMA fighter (and later fugitive, vigilante, neo-Nazi and human rights activist) named Viacheslav Datsik would use the ropes to the point of being admonished or disqualified. His favourite trick, when an opponent was lifting his hips out from under him, was to swing his arms back over the top two ropes and windmill them so as to entwine himself completely as the opponent heaved in an attempt to take him down; meanwhile, Datsik would be showing the crowd the peace sign with both hands. The legendary catch wrestler Kazushi Sakuraba frustrated Royce Gracie (he of UFC 1 fame) by giving up a back body lock, then poking his head underneath the top rope so that Gracie could not reach Sakuraba's neck while the Japanese wrestler was working on a double wrist lock/kimura. Furthermore, the cage allows many more ways for a fighter on the bottom on the ground to reverse position or work his way back up to the feet. Wall walking – the act of getting the back up to the fence and squirming up – is the most effective means of getting to the feet in MMA. Using the fence as a surface to bridge (raising the hips and arching the back) is considerably more powerful than bridging with the feet on the mat, allowing a fighter to cause a scramble or even turn his opponent over.

Conor McGregor's next bout, his first professional one, was

once again under John Kavanagh's own promotional banner, but this time the cage had been adopted and the name of the contest changed to Cage of Truth. A hunched, shaven-headed McGregor advanced on opponent Gary Morris, swinging blows and fighting off takedown attempts. The bout actually finished with McGregor dropping elbows from inside Morris's half guard in the second round. His next fight was more of the same, a wild McGregor swinging shots and putting his opponents into a defensive shell while his corner desperately shouted for him to 'settle down, Conor!' There was very little indication from McGregor's first three MMA bouts that this scrawny, hunched boy was anything more than a clumsy, wild hitter. There was, however, something relatively unusual about Conor McGregor: he was a true southpaw.

THE SWEET SCIENCE
Southpaw

In the earliest days of bare-knuckle pugilism, most men fighting with their fists would naturally drift towards a stance with the left foot in front. Pick up a sledgehammer – or a baseball bat, or an axe, or a two-handed great sword – and if you are like the vast majority of the population you will feel most natural swinging it with your left foot in front. This is because you are right handed and it is preferable to place that hand and foot in the rear to give maximum force and distance to your strike. Pugilism worked just the same way. If you want to hit with as much power as possible and your right hand is your power hand, you want to swing it through a bigger arc to get more force on it. If you are a rightie and you stand with your right hand and foot forward, though, you will end up prodding and poking with it, with little of the step-in-and-swing that a left-foot-forward stance would permit. The standard bare-knuckle contest consisted of a lot of wrestling, swinging right hands, and 'barring' the opponent's right hand by raising the straightened left arm and shoulder to jam the course of the arm up by the biceps.

If you stand with your left foot forward and your left shoulder leading, and you face someone else doing the same (*Figure 1*), you will find that it is very easy to obstruct the line of their right hand by raising your forearm, or – if you are a decently proficient striker – your shoulder. That means that they can do the same to you. Rear-handed punches travel further and are easier to see coming, but against someone in the same stance they are also very easy to deflect. Watch a masterful boxer like Floyd Mayweather, Jr or James Toney and you will notice that the number of right hands they are caught with are few, even with their lead hand down by their side. Now, the science of boxing developed from an emphasis on straight hitting – to beat looped swings to the mark – and on the lead hand. For the average person, this is the left hand. It is weaker and it is less dexterous in any right-hander, and in an orthodox stance it does not have the momentum and weight transfer that a right hand would – the weight does not transition from the rear leg to the lead leg with a powerful and full turn of the trunk into the blow. But crucially, the left hand is closer and lines up better.

Figure 1

In a standard fighting position, the opponent always wants to keep his left shoulder inside your right shoulder. If your shoulder gets inside his, your right straight has a clear path to his face. Helpfully, by keeping his lead shoulder inside your rear shoulder, the opponent creates the same position for your lead shoulder and his rear shoulder — effectively denying him the quick right straight to the jaw as well. So to land nice right straights, opportunities must be created that sneak the rear shoulder inside the opponent's lead shoulder momentarily without allowing him time to throw his own right hand — but that is something we will touch on later. The crucial thing about this mutual denial of the right hand is that it means the lead shoulder of both men can be lined up with the centreline of the opponent and blows can be snuck through more effectively without a large chunk of bone getting in the way. Against a rightie, the left hand is the keystone punch.

Enter the southpaw. For a long time, boxing coaches would refuse to train left-handers in a right-foot leading stance, instead insisting that they learn to fight with their left foot forward. A great many 'converted southpaws' exist even today, such as Oscar De La Hoya and

Andre Ward in boxing or Semmy Schilt in kickboxing. They are notable for their dexterity and power with their lead hand. The right-foot leading stance appeared to have no advantages to the classically trained boxer. The great heavyweight boxing champion Gene Tunney famously insisted that a man standing in

Figure 2

a southpaw stance – with no lead shoulder to protect him – would be an easy mark for Tunney's straight right hand. Of course, this statement overlooks the fact that the disadvantages faced by the southpaw would be the same for Tunney himself: there would be no major obstruction to his opponent's power hand, the left straight.

In all striking arts there are two forms of stance match-up: 'closed' or 'open guard', sometimes called 'open position'. 'Open' and 'closed guard' are also terms used to describe positions on the ground in mixed martial arts, so for our purposes 'closed' and 'open position' are better suited. Closed position (*Figure 1*) is when the stances match: orthodox versus orthodox or southpaw versus southpaw. Everything discussed above regarding two orthodox fighters also applies to two southpaws. The oddity is open position (*Figure 2*): southpaw versus orthodox or orthodox versus southpaw. The lead shoulder does nothing to protect the fighter from his opponent's power hand, and the lead hands of both fighters often obstruct the path of the opponent's. Sometimes termed 'crossed swords', this means that hand fighting is a bigger part of the open position match-up. This is the process by which both men look to check, control and pull or slap aside the lead hand of their opponent in order to create openings for blows.

Where the keystone punch of the 'closed position' engagement is the jab right down the centre, in an 'open position' engagement both men's rear straight occupy the same path down the centre of the guard. (The rear-handed straight is often called the 'cross' in boxing, but the term cross originally referred to a counter blow that looped across the top of an opponent's straight punch and was a favourite of featherweight powerhouse, and future McGregor rival, Chad Mendes.) The most basic level of strategy for open position engagements sees both men attempting to check their opponent's lead hand, stepping their lead foot outside their opponent's to take themselves past the opponent's lead shoulder, and lining their rear hand up with the chin before throwing the straight down the pipe.

JUST A LEFT HAND

By all accounts, the focus that came to characterise McGregor's career was not always present in his early days. He had big dreams and confidence, but Kavanagh reports that McGregor would also disappear from the gym for weeks at a time, choosing instead to embrace the lifestyle of a young adult in one of Europe's most lively cities. Having fought in March and May 2008, McGregor took a third professional bout in June. This time he was fighting Artemij Sitenkov. Once again, this was under the Cage of Truth banner, so Kavanagh was in charge. Choosing a decent submission fighter, Kavanagh was certainly giving McGregor a problem he hadn't had to deal with so far. The cocky young Dubliner came out, stood in front of Sitenkov and dropped his hands to invite the Russian to lead. Sitenkov stepped in with a right hand and immediately ducked the counter left hand with which McGregor had decked each of his previous three opponents. Sitenkov failed to take McGregor down outright but was locked in an over-under clinch with the Irishman and did something you will rarely see in the high levels of MMA: he pulled guard.

That is, rather than attempting to take McGregor down and end up on top, Sitenkov jumped up and wrapped his legs around the Irishman, falling to his back. Digging his right arm underneath McGregor's left thigh, he began pulling his body around to perpendicular with McGregor's in the hope of attacking an armbar on McGregor's right arm. McGregor postured up and made sure that his arms were in no position to be armbarred, but his opponent rolled all the way around and latched onto a kneebar. As the name implies, a kneebar is an armbar but performed on the leg – the opponent's knee is hyperextended over the pelvis. Kneebars from the guard almost always come when the opponent has already got to his feet because the legs are already 70–80 per cent extended. Attacking a kneebar when the opponent is on his knees means if he can just keep his weight on his foot he can make it impossible to extend his leg.

Conor McGregor was just a couple of years into his grappling training and he had blasted his way through all of his problems up to that point. Attempting to tee off with left hands to the head of the upside-down Artemij Sitenkov, his foot was drawn out from underneath him and he was forced to his rump as Sitenkov extended the leg. McGregor tapped just one minute and nine seconds.

THE SWEET SCIENCE
AN INTRODUCTION TO THE GROUND GAME

John Kavanagh found out about the ground game in the same way that McGregor, Egan, and so many others did: via Royce Gracie's UFC 1 performance. Gracie's run through the first few UFC tournaments confirmed one thing: no one had a clue what they were doing when the fight hit the ground – and the one man who did understand could beat them all, based on his knowledge, regardless of size, strength and reach. It was a lot easier when nobody knew anything about fighting on the ground, but as fighters learned about the hierarchy of positions, the basic escapes, and the principles of submission defence, it became tougher to score submissions in high-level mixed martial arts. That said, it takes the best part of a decade for a fighter to become anywhere near good at grappling and it remains the watershed for an athlete's chances in MMA. Decent boxers and kickboxers do not simply transition over to MMA and mop up the titles against the (admittedly mediocre) standard of striking that is prevalent in the sport, because learning to avoid takedowns and surviving on the ground is so difficult.

Understanding the positional hierarchy is the easiest way to learn to grapple and to comprehend the grappling portion of professional bouts. The best positions to be in are those on top of the opponent, where the weight can be dropped into strikes and used to hold him down and smother him. The optimum positions are those where you are past the opponent's legs, where he cannot influence your posture or control your lower body with his legs, or kick at you effectively. Positions in which the top fighter is past the opponent's legs or 'guard' include side control, the mount and back control. *Figure 3* shows the mount, a position of complete dominance, in

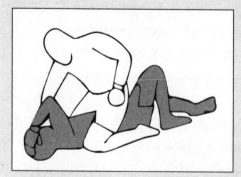 which the bottom man has few means of defending himself, no submissions available to him and no ability to strike effectively.

Figure 3

Positions where the top fighter is in the guard of the bottom fighter include closed guard, half guard, butterfly guard, De La Riva guard and a dozen other variations. If the bottom man's legs are in the way, he can look for sweeps, get-ups, and falter the progress and strikes of the top man. The full guard or closed guard (*Figure 4*) is the most recognisable position of offence from the bottom. It is where the bottom man has his legs wrapped around the waist of the top man. From this position, he is considered to have the advantage in a pure grappling context, being able to use all four limbs to attack while the top player is sitting or standing on two of his own. In an all-out fight, guard is considered to be neutral if the fighter on the bottom

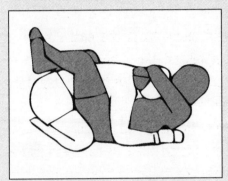

can control the top man's posture as in *Figure 4*. If the man on top can break free and 'posture up', he is able to drop strikes on his man without worrying so much about submission holds.

Figure 4

THE NECESSITY OF ADVERSITY

But young fighters lose, that's how the game works. If a fighter reaches a late stage in his or her career without suffering a single loss, one stumble against truly elite competition can seem a worldview-shattering ordeal that might force them out of the game for good. For most of 2016, it looked like Ronda Rousey, the UFC's biggest star at the time, was ready to hang up her gloves after her first professional loss. When most pundits and fans begin to chalk up a list of their 'all-time greats', the emotional and mental strength to face adversity and come back stronger is one of the most important criteria.

In John Kavanagh's memoir, *Win or Learn*, he speculates

that perhaps there was some part of him that wanted to see McGregor submitted so that he would gain respect for the grappling game and realise how far he still had to go. That was not the matchmaking as Artemij Sitenkov understood it, though. The Russian finished his initially promising career at fifteen wins to sixteen losses, with all fifteen victories coming by way of submission and all but one of those submissions coming in the first round. He was obviously a fighter with a very predictable style. The curious Russian had some bizarre things to say when interviewed by Russian sports blog Sports.ru, once McGregor-mania had taken off, insisting:

> In those days, even if I won, I was supposed to pretend that it was by accident. Otherwise, I would simply not be invited back to fight in the future. I was good at it. At the time, the Irish didn't suspect that I was a good fighter, and John Kavanagh, McGregor's coach, just held his tournaments under the name Cage of Truth […] John thought that McGregor could defeat me. According to his words, I was a fighter who already had experience in overseas performances, was in the rankings and they didn't have to pay me much. I paid for a ticket from my pocket and flew to Ireland to fight.

Conflicts of interest are rife in mixed martial arts, and many coaches and managers will organise their own events in order to give their own fighters experience. Some want experience and that is all, but record padding is an epidemic in mixed martial arts. In certain regional events in the United States, the UK and Brazil, you might see an accomplished amateur wrestler make his MMA debut against someone plucked from the audience. The tip-off is when an athlete is introduced as an 'independent fighter'. Rather than the *dojo*-hopping *ronin* from an Akira Kurosawa screenplay, they are more likely to be some delusional no-hoper who was offered the bout at short notice. Even understanding where Sitenkov's career went after the McGregor fight, that bout does not read like a 'gimme' in any sense. McGregor was 2-0 as a professional, and Sitenkov had the edge in experience with a record of 5-4.

Regardless of whether Sitenkov was the underdog predicted to lose, or the next logical step-up for the young Irish fighter, his account concurs with Kavanagh's at its conclusion. The Russian submission specialist insists that a young McGregor 'cried after the fight. Kavanagh came to him and consoled him.' Conor McGregor disappeared from the gym for weeks, despite owing Kavanagh money from the ticket sales, and the Straight Blast Gym team assumed that was the last they would see of him. It all added up: he had introduced himself as a future world champion, steamrolled his first couple of opponents, and then was suddenly hit by the reality that it just wasn't that easy: champions aren't predestined. The loudest confidence can often prove the most fragile against the first true knock.

For John Kavanagh, it seemed that McGregor was just another young man giving up when things got a little tricky. There are dozens like this who drift in and out of every gym, thinking they have potential to be great but who are not content to take the knocks to get there. It was disappointing, but the SBG coach wasn't in the business of babysitting and you cannot coddle and spoon-feed a fighter to excellence in a sport where a fight can be lost in an instant, and in a hundred different ways. In an interview with the *Irish Independent*,

Kavanagh pointed out that Tom Egan was performing much better than McGregor, Aisling Daly was beginning to have success in the Wild West of women's MMA, and Owen Roddy was beginning to find success of his own. A 2-1 kid who quit at the first hurdle was not the biggest loss to the Straight Blast Gym. Kavanagh even gave up chasing McGregor for the ticket money (almost 500 euros) that the young Dubliner had already spent. Kavanagh was not a big-time promoter – he was just another man in a small, niche sport desperately trying to make ends meet. Half a grand was not a quibbling matter.

The Straight Blast Gym coach credits a mundane coincidence for his change in attitude towards McGregor. He received a phone call from the fighter's mother, Margaret McGregor, asking if he could talk to Conor. Mrs McGregor revealed that the young ex-plumber had lost all direction; he was always happiest when he was training, but that he had been doing none of that recently. So what swayed Kavanagh to make an unprecedented house call on his former student? McGregor's mother shared a first name with Kavanagh's own. A strange thing to grab a man by the heartstrings, but it was apparently enough in this case. Kavanagh had never seen himself as a mentor – he was still a young man after all. But in an interview with the *Independent*, he pinpointed this moment as when he realised that he wasn't the only one dealing with greater issues when he took up fighting; it was also likely that McGregor, Egan, Roddy, Daly and anyone else who crossed the threshold of SBG Ireland was involved in their own battle which extended way beyond a few strikes and a bit of grappling.

At this point in his life, an impartial observer might have suggested Conor McGregor was hardly pursuing any of his options with much vigour, to say the least. He had had a decent gig as an apprentice plumber, a stable career had he carried it through, but he had packed it in after just a year to focus on competing. Knowing what he went on to achieve, it was an admirable decision, but to his parents at the time he seemed to be out of his mind. As different as McGregor and Kavanagh were – the brash extrovert and the cautious introvert – they had this in common: both of their parents were concerned that they were pissing away their youth on a hopeless dream. Kavanagh had a respectable degree in engineering but had zero to show for the last half decade on his *curriculum vitae*. He had come to accept this MMA lark was a dead end.

Conor McGregor, meanwhile, had no qualifications, and his parents were naturally concerned as to what he would do once he had left school. In an interview with RTE Sport, he recalled:

> I ended up getting a trade just to keep them quiet because I used to have a lot of fights with me dad. I ended up getting a trade as a plumber. Literally up in the back arse of nowhere. Up in Wicklow, the Wicklow mountains. That site was one of the biggest sites in Europe, Kilternan. Huge. And now it's just abandoned. Now it's just deserted.

After a cold, wet, miserable day on site months before the Sitenkov fight, McGregor decided that he couldn't do it anymore. He packed up his things, and went home early. A fortuitous call from John Kavanagh enabled him to take his first step as a full-time professional mixed martial arts fighter, for better or for worse: 'John got in touch and said, "I have a show, I'm running a show, I'd like you to fight on it." And then that was it. I packed it in, wouldn't show up.' When he told his parents that he intended to pursue a career in mixed martial arts with everything that he had, they attempted to be supportive while knowing that their son was likely throwing away all future prospects of employment and success. McGregor told RTE:

> I was always getting pestered: 'What are you doing with your life?' They didn't know what it was. They didn't know I could make a career out of it. As far as they were concerned – me ma' and da' I'm talking about – as far as they were concerned, I was just getting into a cage and fighting with some other guy. They didn't know nothing about it. No one did, really! But I knew.

From 2008 until 2014, there was no reason to believe that McGregor could make a living wage from mixed martial arts even if he were the best fighter who had ever lived. When his parents implored him to go back to the site, his response was to sleep in. He recalled that his father, Tony, would come in each morning and 'punch the head off' his son to try to get him to go to work.

Quitting the day job and telling the boss to take it and shove it is a dream for anyone with a more consuming passion on the side. It was the action of someone who is dead serious about fighting. But it just didn't match up with Conor McGregor's behaviour after his first loss – disappearing from the gym without a word. Then again, he was convinced that he was a future champion, and he had just had his illusions shattered by an unrated journeyman from Russia in slightly over a minute. Just as Kavanagh had questioned himself through the numerous obstacles he had run into in the past five years, McGregor was now wondering if he had wasted a good portion of his life chasing his dream of becoming an elite fighter. And the truth was that neither was going to get an answer until they had dug themselves a good deal deeper into the hole.

Conor McGregor returned to the ring one more time in 2008, in December, against a man named Stephen Bailey. It was a characteristically wild and woolly brawl. McGregor came out swinging, tagged his man up with a couple of neat blows and leapt in with a flying knee. Bailey grabbed a hold of McGregor and attempted to take him down, but McGregor stuffed the attempt. A left hook cracked Bailey from the clinch and Bailey attempted exactly what Sitenkov had done just a few months earlier: he pulled guard. This time though, McGregor was nowhere to be found. Bailey fell to his back and threw his legs up but his opponent was already past them and consolidating side control. As Bailey squirmed, McGregor threw his leg over and mounted his man. Chest to chest with Bailey, McGregor waited for the opportune moment to posture up, and when he did, he began to rain down left hands, at which point Bailey quickly turned to concede his back. Bailey continued to roll, but McGregor stayed on him like a backpack; he ended up underneath Bailey. Riding Bailey's momentum, McGregor released his control and came up onto the top of the mount once again at the edge of the ring. This time, McGregor snuck through his left hand before Bailey could roll and Bailey was left covering up. A storm of hammer blows followed and as Bailey hung out of the ring underneath the bottom rope, McGregor continued to pound, himself going between the middle ropes. The referee quickly waved the bout off. Conor McGregor rose from the canvas and ran to the one camera filming the bout at ringside. Leaning through the ropes to press his face right to the lens, McGregor removed his gumshield and announced, 'I'm the fucking future.'

The young McGregor had turned around from a heart-breaking loss and won his next bout in emphatic fashion. Moreover, he had done so on the ground – the area where he, as a striker, had previously been advised not to mess around. He was rounding out his game rapidly and had transformed the loss from what had seemed to be the definitive answer on his potential into a challenge. In an interview in late 2008, one of McGregor's first, the young Dubliner declared, 'My name is Conor McGregor and I live in Lucan. I'm a professional MMA fighter with a record of 4-1 [here McGregor was clearly including his sole amateur fight in the total]. I'm an up-and-coming fighter and without a doubt you will see me in the UFC in the near future. Without a doubt.' But after four fights in the space of a year, Conor McGregor didn't appear on another mixed martial arts card until October 2010, almost two years to the day after his fight with Stephen Bailey. McGregor was in the gym as often as always; he simply didn't compete.

In 2009, something remarkable happened for the Straight Blast Gym team. The Ultimate Fighting Championship, the biggest show in mixed martial arts, held its first event in Ireland. UFC 93 rolled into the O2 stadium (now the 3Arena) on 17 January and featured such names as Dan Henderson, Rich Franklin, Maurício 'Shogun' Rua, and Rousimar Palhares. Whilst not the biggest card in terms of star-power, it nevertheless sold good ticket numbers and drew $1.3 million on the gate. MMA was still largely underground in Ireland, but the UFC wanted an Irish fighter to slap on the card to excite the locals. Their choice? Tom Egan, Conor McGregor's childhood friend from Lucan. The Newbridge lad had been making great strides under John Kavanagh, compiling a 4-0 professional record, and was considered the logical choice to be the first man to represent Ireland in the UFC. Matched with the far more experienced English prospect John Hathaway, Tom Egan took a beating (we'll hear more of that in a later chapter). Never looking as though he was in the fight, Egan was ragdolled around the cage. The fight was waved off as Hathaway rained down elbows on the wobbly Egan with twenty seconds remaining in the first round.

For the Straight Blast Gym team, this was heartbreaking: one of their best men had looked completely out of place in the biggest organisation in the sport. But the SBG credo had always been to win or learn. Kavanagh, who had been in Egan's corner for the fight, was impacted enormously by what he saw that night, but back in the crowd, away from the cage, a young Conor McGregor was changed profoundly. McGregor had a great deal of fun larking around with the best fighters in the world at UFC 93, as immortalised in now legendary photographs with light heavyweight great Chuck Liddell and heavyweight contender Pat Barry. In one of these photos, a shirtless McGregor can be seen flexing and grimacing with a pinkened belly, next to a wide-eyed Pat Barry who had clearly just inflicted this pinkening. But when the jokes and japes had ended, and McGregor was done feeling heartbroken for his good friend Tom Egan, the man who would become 'Notorious' realised something. They weren't that far from it. Those two lads who had started out beating the stuffing out of each other with no guidance in an old shed and who had made the move to a proper gym only very recently. The team of fighters who had zero support from the Irish public, who had to organise their own events just to have fights to train for, and whose training area could still only loosely be called a gym. Those daft kids throwing away their time training under an engineering graduate with a little experience working as a bouncer... they weren't *that* far from the big show.

A reinvigorated Conor McGregor signed for his fifth professional bout and found himself in the ring once again for a match against the 2-1 Connor Dillon. McGregor came out in a low, boxing-like stance, leaning over his lead foot and bouncing around. For the first time in his career, he seemed keen to kick and threw half a dozen high kicks against Dillon's guard. There was plenty of showboating from the Straight Blast Gym charge as he waved his hands, held them out and encouraged 'Done Deal' Dillon to come in on him, or jogged on the spot in front of his opponent. After a couple of minutes of dancing around and jumping in with punches and kicks, McGregor stumbled while throwing a left round kick and fell to the floor. Instinctively, he tried to fight his way up with a takedown, but with his head low he was dragged into a guillotine choke attempt. By scrambling over one of Dillon's legs, McGregor could avoid getting stuck in closed guard and stalled out the choke attempt until the referee returned the men to their feet. The two resumed the trading of clumsy kicks and ineffective punches. As they came to a clinch, McGregor seemed to attempt a shuck to Dillon's back but instead wound up on his back underneath him. But McGregor was rapidly improving on the ground, and quickly kicked his opponent out to range, scrambling up to his feet and avoiding all damage.

Connor Dillon was tiring, but McGregor still seemed fresh – something that the gap in experience could very well account for. Then McGregor jumped in with what was already one of his favourite offensive set-ups. In an open guard engagement, the lead uppercut can be used to raise the opponent's head, as the lead foot is stepped outside the opponent's lead foot. This is usually done with a little jump. The uppercut raises the opponent's head, and the feet ensure that the fighter has a dominant angle and a straight line from his rear shoulder to the opponent's head. (This set-up was a favourite of Marvin Hagler, but really became popular with the English boxer 'Prince' Naseem Hamed. He could box beautifully from four different stances in his youth, as Brendan Ingle had taught him to box both square and side-on with either foot forward. But as Naz became fascinated with his power – he was a rare knockout artist in the featherweight division – he fell back more and more on the southpaw lead uppercut. Hamed's powerful legs, built through Ingle's focus on footwork drills and ropework over roadwork and several years in ballet as a youngster, provided the force for his tremendous hitting.)

The final time that McGregor threw this combination against Dillon, Dillon was well aware of the intentions and ducked low after the uppercut came in, but McGregor's left straight slammed into the side of the tired Dillon's head and sent him backwards.

With his back to the ropes and his gas tank failing him, Connor Dillon threw a hard, low kick – the same kick that had been catching McGregor's heavy lead leg throughout the fight. But this time, McGregor picked his foot up and turned the shin into the kick. Rather than connecting on the tender meat of the inner thigh, Dillon's shin connected high on

McGregor's shin, up by the kneecap. Something in Dillon's shin said 'No mas' and he stumbled to the ropes, desperately trying to keep his weight off the offending limb. McGregor stepped in to finish and the bout was quickly waved off. As McGregor celebrated, Dillon laid down in the middle of the ring to spare his injured leg. With a new love of kicks, some neater movement on the ground and the kind of confidence to throw himself to his back attempting to wrestle with his man, it was clear that McGregor's time off had done him nothing but good. Although his opponent had no real fight experience, with just three fights to his name, this was the first bout where McGregor had begun to look like a rounded mixed martial artist rather than a scrappy boxer in board shorts.

During McGregor's downtime, his relationship with a certain Dee Devlin had been growing stronger. Devlin was a local from Walkinstown in the Southside of Dublin, and was already familiar with McGregor on sight when, one night in 2008, he approached her in a Dublin nightclub. The two struck up conversation and became enamoured with each other. Essentially penniless, and with few prospects, McGregor nonetheless won Devlin over with his wit and charm, and with a caring streak rarely commented on by those who only know him from his professional pursuits. McGregor's career decisions – or rather, his choice to pack in his career to chase a ludicrous dream – would have turned most girls off, but Devlin respected his drive and often helped to spur him on during the moments of self-doubt that punctuated his career. Through the losses and the collection of unemployment benefit, even when he was establishing himself as one of the top fighters in Europe, McGregor was encouraged by Dee Devlin.

Devlin's Peugeot 206 became something of a legend in its

own right among Straight Blast Gym's inner circle, serving as McGregor's only means of transportation while also contributing significantly to his strength training regimen: passengers in Devlin's car were often required to get out and help give it a running start. In an interview in May 2015, once McGregor-mania had begun to sweep the MMA world in earnest, McGregor gave an interview to *VIP* magazine and admitted, 'She'd drive me to the gym, and she'd listen to all my dreams. I wouldn't be doing this if it wasn't for her.' He would later state that his dream had always been to take Devlin out of work and never have her worry about money again, having lived through the leanest of days in a cold flat with a penniless young nobody. While McGregor poured his heart and his soul into his work, into his art, he remained determined to end his career on a beach with Devlin and perhaps some children. While McGregor had once insisted in a television interview that he had no romantic side, he let it slip through briefly and sincerely in the *VIP* magazine feature when he noted: 'I'm doing all this for her.'

IRISH JOE

In November 2010, Conor McGregor got a significant step-up in competition when he signed for his first fight with Cage Warriors, the UK's most successful promotion after the collapse of Cage Rage. To put that into perspective though, Cage Rage was dropped from its spot on Sky Sports in 2008 after drawing in an average of less than twenty thousand viewers. In the context of UK MMA promotion, 'successful' was a relative term. Cage Warriors were to hold their first Irish event in Cork, and they wanted some Irish talent on the card. McGregor was more than happy to get on board and take part in one of Europe's major fight organisations, but his opponent was considerably better than the 2-1 Connor Dillon. McGregor wasn't the star of the show. He was there to fill the slot against the top Irish prospect in MMA, and one of the top prospects in all of Europe: Joe Duffy.

In the interviews ahead of the fight, McGregor insisted that he was dangerous in every aspect of the game now and not just a one-handed boxer: 'At this level I feel I can do anything. I feel like I can fight any way I want.' He continued: 'You can expect to see me pushing the pace, him with his back against the cage – looking for a way out.' Joe Duffy was soft-spoken and understated. Where McGregor was about outspoken confidence, Duffy could only say nice things about his opponent, declaring, 'I've seen a couple of videos of him, he's an aggressive striker. You know, he likes to cut off the ring, likes to push forward, you know, aggressive style. So I'm just going to go out and throw everything at him and, you know, hopefully come out with the right result.' As an interviewee, the man from Donegal was far from entertaining, and had zero showmanship. But Duffy hadn't made a name for himself with his smack talk; he had done it by finishing the first seven men he had met as a professional, each inside one round. The most recent of his opponents, Norman Parke, was Northern Ireland's top prospect and Duffy had choked him into submission in just three minutes. Duffy had previously fought at welterweight (170lb), but the Parke fight was his first at lightweight (155lb).

As the opening bell went, McGregor advanced with his usual aggression. There was only an inch between them in height, but Duffy's upright stance and McGregor's crouched attitude exaggerated this difference. Immediately, Duffy jabbed and attempted to punt the inside of McGregor's lead leg, but was only able to graze it with the end of his foot. The two traded punches, but neither hit anything significant, and Duffy grabbed a headlock on McGregor before he was quickly shucked off into the fence. McGregor circled back to the centre of the cage as Duffy scrambled back to his feet. Duffy lashed out with a jab and McGregor showed his most dangerous asset – the secret of the southpaw – the intercepting left straight as he slipped to the elbow side of Duffy's jab and threaded the left straight down the pipe; it connected on Duffy's left eyebrow and split it open. Duffy took a step back to the fence and McGregor leapt in with a left straight, a right uppercut and a left hook.

But the man who would be 'Notorious' had committed his weight: he had leapt in on Duffy along the fence and his feet were now together and directly under him. The long, low stance that allowed him to drop his weight and sprawl on takedown attempts had disappeared as McGregor grew anxious to push his advantage. And Duffy, like any good fighter should when hurt, had dropped for a takedown. Catching McGregor's right calf, Duffy's head went inside McGregor's knee and his shoulder slammed onto the joint, straightening the leg and forcing McGregor backwards; this allowed Duffy to put McGregor's rump to the mat. A form of low single leg, this type of takedown was a favourite move of the MMA pioneer and catch-wrestling legend Kazushi Sakuraba, but is rarely used at the highest levels of MMA anymore because it involves throwing yourself at the feet of your opponent.

Conor McGregor was on his rear but not flattened out and as Duffy was still holding his leg, McGregor immediately began wrapping over Duffy's head and attacking the guillotine choke. While McGregor's hands were busy, however, Duffy jumped over his legs and into side control. Holding onto the guillotine from the bottom of side control is near pointless for most fighters and often opens them up to submissions from the opponent, so McGregor promptly released the grip. But it was already too late. Defence on the ground is about keeping the elbows tight, but McGregor's were flared out from the moment he attempted the guillotine. As McGregor released the grip, Duffy drove his head to the mat, hugged McGregor's neck with his left arm and slid his knee through to mount the Dubliner. McGregor had been caught in what is called an arm triangle choke.

Triangle chokes can be performed with the legs or the arms, but either way one of the opponent's arms is always 'in' the choke. Rather than attacking the neck alone, triangles and arm triangles encircle the neck on one side and the shoulder on the other. Termed a 'blood choke', the triangle is technically a 'strangle' as it inhibits blood flow to the brain and not the windpipe. This is a key difference, which also means that unconsciousness results much more quickly from a correctly applied triangle than from a choke across the windpipe. In a triangle choke the flow of claret to the brain is constricted on one side by the arm or leg of the man performing the choke, and the shoulder of the victim is forced into the artery to block the flow on the opposite side.

With his arteries closing faster than those of a Glaswegian chain smoker, Conor McGregor bucked, squirmed, turned almost belly down and tried to link his hands to draw his shoulder down and mitigate the pressure, but they popped apart almost immediately. Duffy drove McGregor's left shoulder back towards his head and forced McGregor to tap out. The bout had been a whirlwind of action, and Conor had stunned the best prospect in Europe with that tremendous left hand and made him look bad on the feet. Yet all that would show on the record was: 'Loss (Submission), 0:38, Round 1'. There are no prizes for almost winning and Conor McGregor was now a 4-2 fighter with two submission losses in a minute each. It was clear that with McGregor, what you saw was what you got: a boxer with a cracking left hand, but who was defenceless on the mat. Now he had to go home to the parents who were reluctant to let him pursue this dream to begin with and explain how he was going to be a world champion when for every two fights he won he lost one.

On another timeline, Joe Duffy could have been the man to bring mixed martial arts to the masses of the Emerald Isle. A true world-class fighter in a region whose best fighters boasted chequered records of just four or five bouts at the time, 'Irish Joe' defeated his next three opponents with little difficulty and then Cage Warriors set him up to fight for their vacant lightweight title against Ivan Musardo. Duffy broke his hand on a corkscrew uppercut early in the bout and later succumbed to a guillotine choke in the dying seconds of the fourth round. This was when he made the rather strange career choice to try his hand as a professional boxer. Despite being one of the hottest prospects in European MMA, he jumped ship to a completely different sport. A lover of martial arts since his youngest days, Irish Joe himself put the move down to the opportunity to work with some of the best boxers and coaches in the world. Duffy's boxing career was seven easy fights against journeymen – his opponents were always well below a .500 winning rate – but his hands, footwork and head movement improved in leaps and bounds as he could spend time sparring with boxers as good as Chris Eubank, Jr and George Groves. Despite having his record padded with easy wins, like any promising boxer, Duffy left boxing in 2014, citing repeated hand injuries as his reason for packing it in. But he returned to mixed martial arts just as McGregor-mania was building up a head of steam. Duffy showed he had forgotten none of his mixed martial arts game – in fact, his performances suggested he had missed the more permissive rule set as he choked Damien Lapilus in the third round and knocked Julien Boussuge unconscious with a knee to the head in thirty seconds. In 2015, Joe Duffy was signed by the Ultimate Fighting Championship and he and McGregor would meet once again, on the stage of the 'Go Big' press conference.

2

A BUM
NO LONGER

If Conor McGregor was heartbroken by his thirty-second submission loss at the hands of Joe Duffy, he didn't let it slow him down. The Straight Blast Gym's angsty young boxer was back in the cage in three months: February 2011 saw him facing a Northern Irishman named Hugh Brady. McGregor was 4-2, Brady was 4-1; it seemed like a fair enough match-up. The memory of his bout with Joe Duffy had stayed with McGregor, though. He was anything but reckless as he circled the cage, flicked out jabs at Brady, and retreated at the first sign of his opponent coming back at him. It was the first appearance of McGregor's clever footwork.

Having boxed since his youth at Crumlin Boxing Club, it is reasonable to believe that McGregor's neat feet were not something new in 2011, but the wild and hurried nature of his fights up till then had not allowed him to display any of this craft. Now, a more patient McGregor stayed out of trouble and the mechanics of his sharper punches and the speed of his hands could shine through. That is the way of boxing – the longer a fight goes on, the more the sweet scientist or the ring general is going to come into his own. The economy of motion, the straight line blows taking the inside line on his opponent's arcing or hooked ones, the discipline to return to the guard and stay on top of your feet after each combination – these things outlast the reckless brawler. Though he had power, McGregor had been doing himself a disservice by running out and trying to take his opponent down from the get-go.

Through a couple of minutes of light offence, McGregor could clearly see the shorter fighter's flinches. This is the second reason that technically crisp boxing or kickboxing shines over time and not in the first exchange: good striking science is adaptive. Feints are shown, jabs are flicked out, low kicks are slapped in to test the opponent's reactions. If they haven't been under fire their entire life and they don't have that composure when the bullets are whistling over their head, they are likely to show the same reactions again and again, and that is when the felling blows can be landed. In the first couple of minutes, as McGregor danced across the canvas, he was able to land a couple of long, whipping left hooks on Brady's neck and temple. Brady was slow to react. His forearms came up farther, like goal posts, around his head and he began to hunch into his stance when McGregor stepped in. McGregor shot a long left straight and stepped in behind it with a lead right uppercut that came straight up underneath Brady's chin and jacked his head back. Brady's legs crumbled and he fell forward onto McGregor, whose hands were already in position, pushing Brady off him.

Sugar Ray Robinson recounted in his memoir that in one of his later comebacks he kept having abysmal fights that went to the judges' scorecards until his then-wife asked him why he was trying to knock everyone out. The moment Robinson went back to simply trying to score points and trick his opponent into losing each exchange, the knockouts suddenly began appearing again. His opponents couldn't keep up with him and by building off their reactions and adapting as the bout progressed, Robinson was able to overwhelm them almost without intending to. When Brady hit the deck, McGregor seemed outright surprised that he went down so easily. McGregor leapt on him, quickly secured mount, and then set to work dropping further left hands on his completely helpless opponent. The bout was waved off in 2:31, a positively leisurely time for a McGregor bout, but in that time he had shown the best of his abilities to date.

Mike Wood, McGregor's eighth professional opponent, wasn't able to hang around long enough to test the Dubliner's patience. Wood was caught with the first left McGregor flicked out just seconds into the bout. Without rushing in and tripping over his own aggression, McGregor sent in another one and this one landed more authoritatively on the side of Wood's head. Wood dived for McGregor's hips and McGregor slammed an uppercut in to meet this level change, sprawling beautifully on the takedown attempt. Two more left uppercuts came in on Wood once he hit his knees and the bout was waved off. Sixteen seconds, 6-2. There was no celebrating, no jubilation, and McGregor looked altogether underwhelmed by the fight as he gave his corner a nod.

In April 2011, just thirty days after blasting Wood, McGregor was back in the cage over in Donegal. His opponent, the 4-6 Paddy Doherty, lasted just a quarter of the time. Four seconds was all it took. Did McGregor simply run at him? No, the Dubliner took up his stance in front of Doherty and showed a lazy jab with no apparent intention of doing anything. Doherty responded by immediately rushing McGregor with a right straight into a left hook. McGregor skipped back from Doherty on a slight angle and detonated the left hand on his man's chin. Doherty fell, still swinging his left hook and landed on his side, stiff as a board.

The polished McGregor, with the rounded game to invite an opponent into his money punch, is still a few years off at this point in our tale, though. For much of his early career he was a clumsy brawler with a powerhouse left hand and the odd classy counter amid a storm of swings.

THE SWEET SCIENCE
ON THE COUNTER

Now is the time to talk about Conor McGregor's single greatest weapon: not the cannon that hung from his left shoulder, but a particular moment of time and measure. McGregor excelled at landing a back-stepping counter left hand. Even as a clumsy, swinging, rushing fighter, McGregor had shown glimpses of this technique from his earliest MMA bouts. But first let us consider what a counter is.

In striking martial arts – and even armed hand-to-hand arts – there are three key openings. The Japanese duellist Miyamoto Musashi referred to them as 'initiatives' in his masterwork, *The Book of Five Rings*. In a nutshell, there is leading, there is the delayed counter and there is the simultaneous counter. Leading is the easiest to pick up on day one: it is the act of going forward and attacking. It does, however, tend to expose the fighter to counters from his opponent. Delayed counters capitalise on the moment of recovery from an opponent's failed strike – the opponent swings, misses and is hit with a counter strike in return. Intercepting or simultaneous counters are blows that strike the opponent as he is in the act of throwing his own strike. Simultaneous counters tend to be the ones that knock men unconscious outright: they are rarely braced for a counter when they are in the act of throwing their offence, whereas immediately after missing a blow most fighters will expect a return.

McGregor's counters are often of this simultaneous nature: he would backskip and hammer in the left straight as the opponent rushed onto him. Due to his long stance, he can utilise the standard retreat available to all fighters – push off the front foot and move the back foot first – but he also had access to a back skip. In other words, the lead foot is retracted first, and then the fighter pushes off his lead foot from its new location, creating more distance on the retreat. Kicking the rear leg out behind him into

a stance, McGregor will throw out the left straight, creating a stiff strike for the opponent to run into. This pattern of footwork can be seen in *Figure 1*. Often, McGregor would push forward, pressure his opponent on the fence, and as they struck back at him he would backskip to create distance. Many, many

Figure 1

MMA fighters have the habit of dropping their hands after missing punches or falling short, and of leading with their face when forced to cover a great distance. If they commit these cardinal sins as they chase McGregor, he uncorks the left hand on them as they move into the space he has vacated.

But sometimes, McGregor would look to slip his head to the outside of his opponent's right hand or let it fall short, and return over the top of it at a forty-five degree angle, turning the opponent's head with the blow (*Figure 2*). Many kicking martial arts incorporate the idea of kicking into the 'open side'; well, McGregor punches into the open side. That is to say, against an orthodox opponent his strikes always come in from their right side, so the opponent has nothing to protect his jawline but his forearm. He has no shoulder bone or back to hide behind and could be caught in both the extension and retraction of his longer punch. A constant feature of McGregor's game is his checking the opponent's lead hand with his own, both denying the opponent the ability to jab and inviting him to throw his one free hand. Against less rangy opponents, McGregor often leans and fires left straights down the centre until they reciprocate with their one free hand, at which point he will slip and return fire. It might seem that rule number one of fighting Conor McGregor would be 'don't lunge in with a long right hand', but by smothering

Figure 2

the opponent's lead, picking at them with kicks and long left hands, and retreating from any sign of a return, McGregor can convince even the most disciplined fighters he faces to commit that same mistake.

Conor McGregor's next bout was more remarkable for the setting than for the action in the cage. At *Celtic Gladiators 2: Clash of the Giants*, Conor McGregor and his Polish opponent, Artur Sowiński were both flanked to the cage by a pair of men in Roman gladiator dress, holding battle-axes. Neither McGregor nor Sowiński seemed amped up by their anachronistic entourage, John Kavanagh looked positively embarrassed, while the fans didn't seem to care for it either. The two gladiators and the fighters stood in the cage for the playing of the national anthems – this was the main event and McGregor had been cast in the role of the Irishman taking on the outsider, so the anthems all added to the sense of theatre. Most fight promotions do not bother with national anthems, because it takes long enough in any case to get the fighters into the cage and down to the action.

The cage itself looked to be no more than fifteen feet across. It seemed as though McGregor and Sowiński could stand with their backs to opposite fences and still take a good swing at each other. Sowiński was far from a bum and had eleven wins and just four losses to his name; most of the victories had come by submission. He was everything that had troubled McGregor up to this point and the small cage would only serve to trouble McGregor more. In a striker versus grappler match-up, it is the footwork and movement of the striker that will save him the headache of having to stuff takedowns. A smaller cage or ring limits the space in which he can move and makes it far more difficult to stay off the fence and out of clinches. When he does need to defend a takedown, he requires space in which to drop his hips and sprawl out. In a small cage, his feet might hit the fence as he throws them out behind him, long before he is able to drop his hips and flatten the opponent's forward momentum.

The Irishman struggled to find his left hand early, and when Sowiński moved in and grabbed double underhooks on McGregor, the latter attempted a lateral drop – a tricky throw that relies on anticipation and use of the opponent's momentum. Instead, McGregor landed on his back. He fought his way back to half guard, ensnaring one of Sowiński's legs between his own and regaining a degree of control. Sowiński began attacking a D'Arce choke – a form of arm triangle choke, in which the blood to the victim's brain is shut off by the limb of the attacking man on one side of the neck, and their own shoulder on the other. McGregor looked to be in a tough spot, locked in place underneath the Pole. Less than one minute had passed – it was the Conor McGregor script proceeding as usual, knock them out or get submitted, everyone gets to go home early. McGregor was haunted by the kneebar against Artemij Sitenkov and the arm triangle against Joe Duffy. He couldn't give up another one this easy. As Sowiński drove his weight forward, forcing McGregor's shoulder further into his neck and tightening the choke, McGregor held on to Sowiński's trapped leg in a death grip. If Sowiński freed his leg, he could get McGregor onto his side, step over him, and the Irishman would have no chance of escaping what was already a tight choke. Sowiński drove forward even farther, getting up on his toes and rocking his right shoulder towards the mat. As he did this, McGregor released Sowiński's trapped leg – a tactical rolling of the dice – and freed himself to turn all the way back to the mat and through the choke, relieving the pressure and allowing him to scramble up to his feet. This feat of timing and confidence could have gone horribly wrong, had Sowiński seen it coming and dropped his weight on McGregor. Striker or not, John Kavanagh was drilling some real ground savvy into his young fighter.

McGregor easily shrugged off a shot, but the wily Sowiński turned his back and snatched one of McGregor's legs, rolling under and threatening a kneebar – the other entry on McGregor's defensive wall of shame. McGregor pinned his ankle to his buttock and followed Sowiński through the roll, winding up on top of the grappler. Not this time. The next takedown attempt was easily stuffed by McGregor and answered with a knee strike. And the one after that. McGregor was settling down – even in this half-scale cage, which offered no chance to jog around and slow the pace. But Sowiński wasn't giving up the strikes easily and with two minutes remaining, McGregor closed with a lead uppercut and grabbed a hold of a clinch along the fence. Tripping Sowiński to the floor, McGregor began dropping elbows from the top of the Pole's half guard.

Late in the round the two returned to their feet and Sowiński was clearly slowing. This was where the striking class of McGregor would shine through. Sowiński ate a left straight down the pipe that burst open a raised swelling under his right eye. He lashed out with a right straight but McGregor wasn't there for it, fading away on his usual retreating angle. McGregor returned with a left hand over the top of Sowiński's right as it fell short. The counter cracked Sowiński high behind the ear and sent him stumbling onto the fence (such stumbling as you can do when you're never more than a step from the cage boundary, anyway). McGregor flew past the reeling Pole with a jumping kick. A high kick slapped Sowiński's face as he tried desperately to circle out; the small cage was finally working to the detriment of the grappler. Sowiński survived the last moments of the first round, but McGregor came out swinging in the second, and scored another left-hand counter as Sowiński tried desperately to convince the Irishman that he still had some fight in him. That was the end of the line for the Polish submission artist who fell to his back, was promptly mounted, and suffered a TKO loss at McGregor's hands.

It was at this point in his career that Conor McGregor received another offer to fight for Cage Warriors. Almost a year after his unfortunate first appearance there, he had compiled a streak of four knockout wins between his loss to Joe Duffy and his scheduled return in November 2011. Except this time, he was not in front of his home crowd; he was fighting in Amman, Jordan. A peculiar choice for a night of fights, but Cage Warriors was looking to break into new markets. In what would become a theme throughout McGregor's career, his opponent was forced to pull out within days of the fight and was substituted with a late replacement. That replacement was the 2-1 Aaron Jahnsen. In many respects this was a step down in competition, but last-minute replacements can be a nightmare, as any opponent-specific training immediately becomes useless – or at least considerably less useful. McGregor opened the bout cautiously and was hammered by a few good low kicks that knocked his lead leg out – one danger of the long, mobile stance that he adopted. But from the opening minute it was obvious that Jahnsen was a novice when it came to striking in mixed martial arts. Each time McGregor stepped in, Jahnsen would run straight backwards with his arms extended to keep him away and his chin way up in the air, just asking to be checked with a good punch.

Jahnsen attempted a single leg takedown early and McGregor showed remarkable balance as his opponent lifted him off his feet and had him hopping around on one leg. After some cage wrestling, the two broke and Jahnsen rushed in on McGregor, eating a left hand over the top of the head as he dropped for McGregor's legs again, but this time wound up stuck underneath the Irishman. McGregor beat Jahnsen up on the ground until the Norwegian went to the turtle, whereupon McGregor sprung to his feet and delivered a winding knee to the midsection. He followed with punches for an easy finish.

Now with a foot in the door at Cage Warriors, McGregor joined their February 2012 card in Kentish Town, London, and made the decision to compete as a featherweight. Before the Duffy fight, McGregor had reckoned himself a large lightweight, though Duffy – a former welterweight – seemed to be the bigger man in the cage. Cutting to featherweight took it out of McGregor, who took three attempts to make the 145-lb limit. Steve O'Keefe, the man in the opposite corner, boasted a 6-1 record, hadn't been beaten since his professional debut, and just a few months earlier had bested Conor McGregor's close friend and go-to training partner, Artem Lobov.

Lobov is best known in the MMA world nowadays for his powerful hands, his unorthodox striking, and his comically short reach. Despite owning just a sixty-five-inch reach on a five-foot-nine frame, Lobov was a decent banger and would later be McGregor's travelling training partner through his overseas press engagements. Lobov had done a decent job of roughing O'Keefe up on the feet, particularly with body shots and with uppercuts as O'Keefe dropped level to attempt takedowns. In the third round, O'Keefe had caught Lobov with a right straight as he retreated on a straight line with his hands down – a regular feature of Lobov's game – and sent 'The Russian Hammer' to the canvas. O'Keefe jumped on Lobov's back and sunk in a rear naked choke for the submission victory.

When McGregor met O'Keefe, any struggle with the weight cut was immediately forgotten as the Irishman moved forward and caught the Kent native with a flurry of blows. O'Keefe's reaction under fire was to bend forward at the waist and cover his head, which allowed McGregor to hammer home uppercuts just as Artem Lobov had. Grabbing O'Keefe behind the head with both hands in what is termed a 'double collar tie', McGregor slammed a couple of knees into his opponent's face before O'Keefe grabbed hold of the Irishman's hips and drove him to the fence. Attacking a single-leg takedown, O'Keefe kept McGregor on one foot against the cage, before dropping down and attempting to snatch up the other. After a couple of attempts, O'Keefe was successful and McGregor's rear hit the mat. Within an instant, he sprang back to his feet but O'Keefe was already moving to climb onto his back. With his left foot (or 'hook') in, O'Keefe struggled to put in his right as McGregor kept his side pinned to the fence. McGregor had done a brilliant job of fighting with O'Keefe's hands throughout: one of the first rules of grappling is to deny the opponent any grips that he clearly wants. By snatching away grips and controlling the opponent's hands with one's own, a fighter can make even a much more skilled grappler work for every inch of ground he takes. But as McGregor battled to control O'Keefe's left wrist, O'Keefe freed the hand to hammer him in the head. As McGregor brought up his left arm to defend himself, O'Keefe's arm shot underneath and wrapped McGregor's neck and near shoulder. O'Keefe released his hook on McGregor's leg and wheeled around to face him. An arm triangle choke – a flashback to Joe Duffy once again. McGregor squirmed as they slid along the fence, O'Keefe beginning to squeeze the life out of McGregor's head.

The standing arm triangle is a rare sighting in mixed martial arts bouts, but it remains a powerful position. The great Nova União featherweight Marlon Sandro caught Matt Jaggers in a standing arm triangle and choked him unconscious on his feet. On a later occasion, Sandro snatched up a standing arm triangle on Rafael Dias and tripped him to the floor to finish the fight with the hold. Similarly, each time Cub Swanson placed his hands on the mat to stand up in his UFC bout with Ricardo Lamas, Lamas would dive under Swanson's open elbow and snatch up the arm triangle position as Swanson came to his feet.

O'Keefe exerted himself trying to tighten the choke on McGregor while the Irishman flailed and writhed, until O'Keefe thought it was an opportune time to cut and run, ducking in on McGregor's hips again while his hands were raised. As O'Keefe attempted to pick up the single leg takedown once more, something hard hit him in the side of the head. Then, once again. And several times in quick succession with no respite until O'Keefe was blurrily rising from his knees into the arms of a sympathetic referee. As O'Keefe had been going hell for leather in attempting to drag McGregor to the mat, his head buried on the inside of the Irishman's thigh, McGregor had raised his arm to eye level and slammed the point of his elbow into the side of O'Keefe's head. Pleased with the result, McGregor continued to drop elbows until O'Keefe slid down McGregor's leg like a drunk on a fireman's pole.

The use of downward elbows has long been contentious in mixed martial arts competition. The old story goes that one member of the committee who was designing the rules for mixed martial arts had witnessed a karate breaking competition wherein a karateka had split a block of ice with a downward elbow, and felt that this strike was far too dangerous for mixed martial arts competition. Funnily enough, the vast majority of karateka breaking blocks of ice with strikes in demonstrations are doing so on 'worked' materials. The block of ice is sawn in half, pushed back together and put in the freezer for a couple of hours. Then, when struck, it will split down the break like a table at a professional wrestling event. That said, one of the dangers of permitting 'twelve-to-six' elbows would be that they tended to be thrown in response to an opponent ducking in on the hips and would often land on the back of the head or the spine – prohibited targets.

A high-profile disqualification for downward elbows was the great light heavyweight Jon Jones's only loss. After starching Matt Hamill with this move, Jones was declared the loser owing to his flagrant use of a prohibited technique. However, due to the rule being perceived as somewhat pointless (an overhand elbow can still travel twelve-to-six and is perfectly legal; only when the arm is raised above the head and brought downward is the rule applied), many referees are far more lenient as fighters experiment with new angles on what is essentially the technique that was originally banned. Should an opponent be holding on to a single-leg takedown, a fighter can lean slightly forward and bring a downward elbow into the side of that fighter's head, essentially an 'eleven-to-four' elbow but regarded as a legal technique. UFC heavyweight Travis Browne was one of the first to reintroduce the MMA world to the downward elbow as he starched Gabriel Gonzaga while the latter shot a takedown along the fence. Browne consolidated the effectiveness (and legality) of the technique by stopping the brilliant catch wrestler, Josh Barnett, with the same strike from exactly the same position.

The technique is largely so effective because it is a powerful strike, with an unpadded bone, on an opponent whose hands are occupied, who cannot see the strike coming, and who is in a position where he often believes strikes are no longer a concern and that he is on the offensive. After slamming home nine unanswered elbows to the side of Steve O'Keefe's head, Conor McGregor had taught those in attendance that a single-leg takedown attempt is certainly not a place to rest.

In the space of a year-and-a-half, McGregor had turned his career around. Formerly a 4-2 knockout artist who seemed just as likely to be submitted in under a minute, his record now ran a respectable 10-2, with none of his defeated foes having made it to the final bell. He was exciting and hard hitting, just as he always had been, but now he was defensively sound too. And he was patient: he wasn't afraid to let the fights go on as long as they needed to in order to get the job done. There was very little flailing wild or running in on top of his opponent from the Conor McGregor of 2012. Moreover, whether it was a sound financial decision or not, his choice to abandon his work as a plumber to pursue fighting full time allowed him to spend hours in the gym, whereas many of his opponents on the regional stage would be spending that time working to provide for themselves and their families. Although not the sort of inspirational tale that most parents would want their children to hear, abandoning a seemingly safe career path had given McGregor the time to sink into his passion and to improve at an exponential rate. Natural ability and passion accounted for a good part of that, but being able to train twice a day without worrying about work was something that even many fighters in the UFC at the time were not able to do.

Having shown himself to be a decent fighter and a valuable asset to Cage Warriors, with his entertaining style and finish-filled record (the wins *and* the losses), Conor McGregor was offered a shot at the Cage Warriors featherweight title against Dave Hill. The latter wasn't a slouch by any means – he had a 10-2 record to match McGregor's – but had only one victory in his last three fights. In fact, Hill had actually dropped a decision to McGregor's friend Artem Lobov a year before and had only fought once since then. He was not the incumbent Cage Warriors featherweight champion, having never fought for the organisation. Hill had eight submissions to his name and seemed another test for McGregor's grappling game; he had never been stopped and would prove a great challenge for McGregor's always impressive power and accuracy on the feet. The fight took place on Cage Warriors' return to Dublin in June 2012 and McGregor, though only the co-main eventheadliner, was the man who brought the Irish fans out in force.

Ahead of the fight, Hill was quick to point out that McGregor's opponents hadn't had a great deal of experience and had simply closed up under fire and given in. As far as he was concerned, most of McGregor's knockout losses were due more to his opponents giving up than to being taken out of the fight by a good shot. 'I won't wilt and give up,' he asserted. McGregor, for his part, seemed surprisingly wound-up during the pre-fight hype and at the weigh-ins, where some barging occurred. As the two came together for the referee's instructions, McGregor adopted a fighting stance and jawed constantly at Hill as the referee attempted to reiterate the rules of the contest. Each time the referee's gaze went from McGregor to Hill, McGregor would resume talking over the official. Hill recounts that McGregor told him, 'I'll go all day with you – you look soft. I'll go five rounds if you need to.'

As the timer started for the first round, McGregor ran out, threw his left hand, and suddenly Hill was in on a leg. McGregor attempted to grab a guillotine choke and jump back to his guard, but lost Hill's head on the way, winding up underneath his opponent without the intended choke. It seemed as though the worst side of McGregor had taken control: he had rushed in, swung wide, made a rookie error in jumping on the guillotine and now he was on his back underneath a very strong grappler.

With surprising serenity, however, McGregor hopped out, got to his side, placed down a hand and performed a technical stand-up with little trouble. After some wrestling along the fence, he broke free and got to work. Each time Hill showed a punch, McGregor drew his lead foot in and skipped back, beginning to counter with his left hand before realising that Hill hadn't pursued him. As the first round wore on, McGregor began to get the measure of Hill and the retreats became shorter. Eventually, he was staying just on the end of Hill's reach and battering him with three punches for every one that Hill threw.

As Hill ducked in to take McGregor down, the Irishman

timed him with a left kick to the face, which Hill took flush. To Hill's tremendous credit, he took it with remarkable grit and composure, pulling guard on McGregor to recover but taking a pasting in the process. When the two returned to their feet, a left straight down the pipe sent Hill stumbling and as he swung back in panic, the force of his missed blows threw him to his hands and knees. McGregor swung for Hill's head, but Hill grabbed hold of McGregor's leg. Those terrible downward elbows started to come in and Hill knew he had to keep moving. Driving up from his knees, Hill hooked his left leg behind McGregor's right and drove him over it. Forcing his opponent's centre of gravity past his trapped leg, Hill had McGregor falling onto the cage. But McGregor reached out with his right hand, grabbed hold of the fence and pulled himself around, reversing the takedown and landing in mount. A flagrant and fight-changing foul that the referee noted but did nothing about.

Dave Hill's head coach, Marc Goddard, also happened to be one of the most respected referees in the world of mixed martial arts and regularly officiated at UFC main events. At ringside, Goddard looked on as this outright abuse of the rules cost his fighter a takedown and placed him in the worst possible position, and then saw the referee acknowledge it without punishing McGregor. Goddard was fit to explode, and screamed to the official. Fence grabs are a natural instinct – the hand will shoot out to grab anything it can on the way down – but when they significantly impact the events of a fight, the least a referee can do is stop the bout and stand the competitors back up to remove the advantage gained by the foul. The fight continued, though, and in the last fifteen seconds of the round Hill turned his back to avoid punishment, leaving McGregor fighting to sink in a rear naked choke as the round expired.

The small Dublin crowd was baying for blood by the beginning of the second round as McGregor dashed across the centre of the cage and shot in a good left straight. Hill kept his hands up and his chin down, but as he stepped in, another left high kick pounded through his forearm and slapped against his head, sending him stumbling. McGregor leapt on the fallen Hill and the next four minutes were spent with McGregor on top of his desperately scrambling opponent, controlling him, flattening him out, stuffing his escapes, and dropping heavy leather on him when he stopped moving. Finally, Hill gave up his back and McGregor slid his forearm under Hill's chin to lock in the rear naked choke.

McGregor leapt up from the mat and sprinted for the fence. Bounding over the cage, he ran past the security, who were attempting to hold his friends back, and dived headlong into the crowd to be dogpiled and embraced by his countrymen. Ireland had its first world champion in mixed martial arts. What's more, McGregor had done it by submission, the area of his game that had given the knockout artist so much trouble throughout his early career. Given the microphone, a grateful McGregor was understated, thanking the crowd and insisting that he had envisioned this from the beginning.

Detractors might point to the fact that McGregor was placed in a fight for the vacant belt to sell tickets in Dublin, rather than having to beat any of the previous Cage Warriors featherweight champions for it, but it's the nature of a regional promotion like Cage Warriors that fighters who excel go on to bigger things. Cage Warriors did not have the money or means to keep world-class prospects once the Ultimate Fighting

Championship and Bellator MMA came calling; they were more about the development of European talent. Even then, the field was very competitive: if a champion in a decently sized regional organisation such as Cage Warriors could get a better pay cheque in some other small fight company, such as Japan's Pancrase or Shooto, he might simply vacate the belt. Certainly there are fighters with a number of titles, from moderately sized regional organisations, that look much better on their list of accomplishments than the defence of one belt in a regional promotion numerous times. Although Cage Warriors' belt holders were called world champions, the titles were more accurately indicators of great potential in a fighter. That 'world' was still a world apart from the big stage of the Ultimate Fighting Championship.

The next break in action was a rather long one by Conor McGregor's standards. Cage Warriors sought to use his popularity in their next jaunt out to Dublin on 31 December 2012. New Year's Eve might seem a strange choice for a night of fights in Ireland, but it was a long-established tradition in mixed martial arts. The Japanese mixed martial arts organisation PRIDE Fighting Championship – the biggest fighting show on earth for quite a while – used to treat New Year's Eve as a chance to put on bizarre freak fights and showcase bouts for their stars. K-1, the world's premier kickboxing organization, once co-promoted with PRIDE on these New Year's Eve ventures before launching their own MMA sub-promotion, K-1 Heroes, and hosting their own kickboxing/MMA mega cards on New Year's Eve as well. With major TV deals, and a tradition of staying in to watch television with the family on New Year's Eve in Japan, these events drew incredible viewerships.

For instance, Kid Yamamoto's 2006 return to mixed martial arts against the 0-0 debutant (but Olympic gold medallist in wrestling) István Majoros was a pitiful affair. Yamamoto dropped Majoros like a sack of manure in minutes and felt so bad for him that he simply mimed throwing follow-up punches until the referee stopped the bout. That fight drew twenty-six million viewers. To put that into perspective, it is cause for celebration when the UFC draws between three and four million viewers for their televised UFC on Fox events. The most watched fight in the history of combat sports came in 2003 at a K-1 New Year's Eve show in Japan and was a kickboxing bout between the 300-lb Bob Sapp and the former *yokozuna*-ranked sumo wrestler (and awful kickboxer) Akebono. Fifty-four million people tuned in to watch the giants wheeze, swing, and fall down in a real-life, but disappointing, *kaiju* battle. But the massive audience for combat sports in Japan on New Year's Eve was partly cultural, and partly due to PRIDE and K-1 wrangling deals to be televised on the most prominent television channels. Attempts to hold fight cards on New Year's Eve in the West have typically done poorly.

McGregor's bout at Cage Warriors 51 was supposed to be a defence of his featherweight title against Jim Alers. But when Alers was forced out, the match was changed to a lightweight title fight between McGregor and Ivan Buchinger. Once again, the fluid nature of regional titles was apparent as Cage Warriors had to take the belt from their previous champion, Ivan Musardo, in order to make this bout for the belt. Musardo had bested Joe Duffy in October 2011 and hadn't fought in Cage Warriors since, instead plying his trade in a number of other regional promotions across Europe.

With a 21-3 record, Ivan Buchinger had a huge edge on

McGregor in experience and had been stopped only once. In front of a small crowd of his countrymen, McGregor looked sublime. If you want to see exactly what makes Conor McGregor remarkable as a martial artist condensed into one round, the Buchinger fight is the film to study.

McGregor came out, touched gloves, and immediately pressured Buchinger to the fence. Controlling Buchinger's lead hand with his own, he pounded in front kicks to the midsection before leaping in with the lead uppercut and tagging Buchinger up cleanly. Buchinger ran around the fence to try to escape McGregor, but the Irishman followed, turning his back as if to throw a back kick but spinning all the way through into a 540-degree round kick, something seldom seen outside Olympic taekwondo competitions and kung fu flicks. McGregor immediately followed up with a wild, missed wheel kick and as Buchinger returned with punches, McGregor timed a duck underneath. Conor McGregor, the one-handed boxer, was putting on a taekwondo clinic and had just taken his man down effortlessly.

After Buchinger scrambled back up, McGregor got straight

Figure 3

back to work in his domain. Checking and smothering Buchinger's lead hand, killing his jab, McGregor would lean forward at the waist to flick venomous left straights up the centre of Buchinger's guard (*Figure 3*).

With one hand constantly being taken out of action by McGregor covering it, Buchinger finally surged forward to throw his right hand. McGregor saw it coming a mile off. He ducked and Buchinger continued forward as his fist passed over McGregor's shoulder. In an instant, Buchinger ate a left hand to the liver that had him gasping for air. More front kicks to the body, more flicking left straights down the centre. Buchinger's next charging right hand was countered with a left to the head that sent him stumbling momentarily. McGregor threw out his hands and laughed as he waltzed his panicking man to the fence. As nonchalantly as McGregor flicked out punches and kicks on the advance, he would spring back on a hair trigger when Buchinger returned, looking for the counter left hand. Two more left straights smacked Buchinger right in the nose.

McGregor stepped in with a left knee to the midsection and pushed Buchinger away by the face before he could grab a hold of the leg. Now falling far, far behind on strikes landed, Buchinger shot one more right hand. McGregor rocked onto his back foot and slipped to the elbow side, letting the punch just brush his earlobe as it flew by. Before Buchinger's punching hand could begin returning to his guard, a left straight shot in from forty-five degrees and caught him across the jaw, turning his head around. Buchinger stiffened before toppling like a tree as McGregor bounced back out of range. Buchinger's rigid collapse to the floor and McGregor's lithe, springy movement when the shot was shown in slow motion made for a gorgeous juxtaposition. The knockout became a viral sensation in the mixed martial arts community and, were a fight fan ever to be asked how he could consider the ugly, grinding sport of MMA equivalent to a form of art, the McGregor–Buchinger fight and the knockout as its final act would make a compelling case. An act of violence that bordered on balletic in its grace.

Conor McGregor was handed his second belt and became Cage Warriors' first two-weight champion. Yet he was still destitute. He was still collecting the dole. He was arguably the best fighter in two weight classes on the European scene, but he was still flat-out broke. And as much as the belts meant to him, they didn't mean much to anyone else. Neither of the men he had beaten to take the title had even been an incumbent champion. They were just trinkets from the little leagues, which meant little to the big boys of the sport. The lower levels of each division in the UFC is full of men who have collections of belts from regional fight organisations but who have faltered when removed from their small pond.

The Irish fan base was becoming fond of Conor McGregor, though. On 3 February 2013, it was announced that he had been signed to a five-fight contract with the big show: the Ultimate Fighting Championship. In mid-February, the president of the UFC, Dana White, was in Dublin collecting a 'Gold Medal of Honorary Patronage' from Trinity College and in the course of his Q&A was met with a handful of excited questions about McGregor.

A multi-millionaire who has been asked to stop playing at several of Vegas' casinos after winning millions of dollars in games of blackjack, White is everything you would expect from a man in his position. He is hyperbolic, shrewd and enjoys gaudy displays of excess while concerns still rage in the MMA media over fighter pay. He is also funny and has a disarming charm to him which throws off even the most cynical journalist at press events. But, in these regards, White is nothing out of the ordinary for a promoter in the fight game. In fact, despite his infamously no-nonsense attitude and foul mouth, White was picked to speak for Donald Trump at the 2016 Republican National Convention in place of legendary boxing promoter, Don King. This was because those organising the event observed that for all his quirks, White, unlike King, has never literally stomped a man to death. After hearing the buzz around Conor McGregor from every Irishman he met, Dana White invited McGregor out to Las Vegas and drove him down the strip in his Ferrari. Under the seductive neon glow of the Vegas strip, White witnessed his fierce charisma at first hand, that same intensity that Tom Egan saw in him all those years ago, and he was sold. White would later recall thinking, after meeting McGregor, 'If this kid can throw a punch, he's going to be a superstar.'

3

'I'LL DRAG THEM BACK TO IRELAND'

A LITTLE HISTORY OF THE UFC

The Ultimate Fighting Championship is the premier show in mixed martial arts. To many, it is the *only* show in mixed martial arts. When discussing the state of his payslip in his first interview with Ariel Helwani on *The MMA Hour*, Conor McGregor stated that for a professional fighter, 'It's the UFC or it's peanuts.' Pundits and fans have called the brand a monopoly since it bought out its greatest overseas competitor, Japan's PRIDE Fighting Championship, in 2007, and Strike-force, its biggest United States competitor, in 2011. The UFC is so deeply dug into the heart of mixed martial arts that the sport is often erroneously referred to as 'Ultimate Fighting' by major media outlets. The Ultimate Fighting Championship was the show that popularised 'no holds barred' competition in the United States and which introduced the world to the art of ground fighting, but the UFC's march towards market domination and mainstream acceptance was far from simple or predictable.

The idea of the Ultimate Fighting Championship was seeded by a series of VHS tapes put out in 1992 by the Gracie family, the founders of Gracie jiu-jitsu (now known as Brazilian jiu-jitsu). These tapes, titled *Gracies in Action*, followed members of the Gracie clan through a number of challenge matches with no rules. Taking on karate practitioners, kung fu exponents and bodybuilders, these matches all went the same way. The other man would swing, the Gracie would drag him to the ground, and then the Gracie would mount him. From the mount the Gracie fighter would rain down blows until their victim turned his back, then either strikes to the back of the head or a choke would put an end to proceedings. While the tapes were intended as advertising material for Brazilian jiu-jitsu, a businessman named Art Davie saw them and had the idea to promote these fights on television. Hoping to call the event 'War of the Worlds', Davie and filmmaker John Milius (screenwriter of *Apocalypse Now*) approached a number of pay-per-view providers as WOW Productions and partnered with a young firm called SEG. The remarkable success of the first event saw the *Ultimate Fighting Championship* turned into a series of events that garnered hundreds of thousands of views.

Answering the age-old style versus style question was the supposed point of the events: the 'what ifs' of karate versus kung fu, wrestling versus judo, and so on. Gracie jiu-jitsu seemed to come up trumps in all of them, as Royce Gracie cruised through four tournaments with little difficulty. But most viewers were attracted by the pure, unadulterated violence. In the opening match of the first UFC event, a 460lb sumo wrestler named Teila Tuli had his teeth kicked into the front row while he was on his knees. The viewing public was only familiar with boxing and perhaps kickboxing on pay-per-view; many couldn't understand how this form of fighting could even be legal. That was the downfall of the UFC's first incarnation, though: men such as Senator John McCain took umbrage with the sport and campaigned against it, making it more and more difficult to get the events sanctioned. SEG were forced to sell up to young casino owners Frank and Lorenzo Fertitta, whose excellent business connections made them ideally placed to help the UFC grow to its full potential. Art Davie only resurfaced years later with the idea for X-Arm, a cross between mixed martial arts and arm wrestling. That caught on about as well as you would expect!

Under the management of the Fertitta brothers and Dana White, the UFC was slowly rebuilt. The phrase 'fastest-growing sport in the world' has been slung around with reckless abandon for the past fifteen years, but the rise of mixed martial arts under the UFC banner has been nothing short of remarkable to behold. John McCain ceased campaigning against the sport, major brands such as Budweiser began to sponsor UFC events, and the UFC's sanctioning issues cleared up. By 2015, mixed martial arts competition was legal in all but one US state, one that had been the scene of many of boxing's greatest bouts: New York. Even in New York, it was only professional mixed martial arts competitions that were illegal in 2016 – amateur fights and underground professional events still took place. The hold-out was largely due to union issues and nothing to do with the sport itself. Finally, in March 2016, the New York State Assembly passed the bill legalising professional mixed martial arts in their state. But more important than getting into New York was the UFC's international expansion. The UFC has not struggled with being sanctioned for events in the United States for years now, and their success internationally in recent years has been incredible. Attending the post-fight press conference for any international UFC event, a reporter will quickly realise that few of the questions are directed at the fighters, and there are numerous international journalists there just to ask whoever is hosting the press conference when the UFC plans on coming to their homeland.

By the end of 2008, the UFC had begun including semi-regular jaunts to Canada and England in its schedule, but for the opening event of 2009 the promotion opted to make its inaugural trip to the Republic of Ireland. It may have seemed a curious decision, but it provided a way for the UFC to dip its toe in an international market that had little or no stake in the competition. Great Britain had the middleweight contender Michael Bisping and Canada had the great Georges St-Pierre, but in 2008 there were no Irish fighters in the UFC. Marcus Davis was the closest, and carved out a niche as 'The Irish Hand Grenade', but he was born and raised in Maine. With the UFC wanting a local lad on the card to get the crowd geed up, they picked Tom Egan, Conor McGregor's childhood friend. Egan had just four fights to his name and was the youngest fighter in the UFC when signed for this bout. Yet he was invited onto the biggest stage in mixed martial arts to fight John Hathaway, a 10-0 prospect from London Shootfighters gym. Reflecting on the bout ahead of his own UFC debut, Conor McGregor would later admit, 'We weren't ready... We were just kids.'

Tom Egan and John Hathaway advanced from their corners and there was that usual moment of nervous energy, but it lasted for a few beats and nothing more. Hathaway threw a couple of slappy kicks and Egan showed a jab. Then Hathaway ducked in to clinch Egan and the match quickly found its pace. Grabbing a hold of a body lock, Hathaway drove Egan across the cage towards the fence and Egan attempted to keep his hips away from Hathaway's. But Hathaway killed any space and sucked Egan's hips in tight to his own. With his force underneath Egan's centre of gravity, the Englishman hoisted the Irishman skyward, bringing a knee up to knock the airborne Egan's legs out from underneath him before landing on top of him in side control. Egan got to his knees and moved towards the fence, but Hathaway manhandled him back to the mat. Hathaway placed a hand on Egan's face and turned Egan's head away from him. Releasing the pressure, he allowed Egan's head to snap back towards him as the same arm fell through into an elbow across the brow. Push away and drop the elbow, a technique that found popularity in mixed martial arts with the old-timer Jeremy Horn, but which remains a grinding and effective ploy to this day.

Egan tried again to scramble up and was dragged back to the mat by the 170lb sandbag hanging onto his waist. Rolling to place Hathaway back between his legs and inside his guard, Egan looked up at the clock in panic: 3:50. Seventy seconds had passed. Hathaway was suffocating him. Hathaway stood over him now, dropping punches. Egan kicked Hathaway's lead leg out from below and Hathaway fell on his front for a moment's respite, but the Brit scrambled up to stay on top of Egan. Hathaway advanced to Egan's half guard, sat on top of one of Egan's legs, and continued to drop elbow strikes. Egan bit down on his gumshield and exploded into an attempted sweep, hoping to pull Hathaway over the top of him into what is called 'deep half guard', but succeeded only in giving up his back. Hathaway flattened Egan out, face down on the mat, and began dropping elbows to which Egan was both blind and defenceless. The referee soon intervened to halt the beating, awarding Hathaway the TKO victory and further disgruntling the already uneasy Dublin crowd. In his post-fight interview, the twenty-year-old Egan apologised to his countrymen, thanked them for their support and insisted that he would be back. Tom Egan never got another fight with the UFC; John Hathaway remains in the UFC to this day.

In his first interview with Ariel Helwani in April 2013, McGregor reflected on Egan's big fight and Straight Blast Gym's first experience in the UFC Octagon. For a fighter with four bouts to get a shot in the UFC, especially at Egan's age, was largely unheard of and it seemed to be a transparent attempt to throw an Irishman on a card that, perhaps, he didn't deserve to be on. McGregor had been invited on Helwani's enormously popular *MMA Hour* podcast in response to a flood of demands from Irish fans ahead of his own UFC debut. Helwani noted that McGregor was easily their most requested non-UFC guest in his time before signing with the promotion. Reiterating Tom Egan's inexperience at the time of his Octagon debut, McGregor was keen to point out that he would be making his first UFC appearance in Sweden and so wasn't just a 'token Irishman'.

It was this interview that made many mixed martial arts fanatics outside his existing Irish fan base sit up and take note of Conor McGregor. His charisma was effortless and natural, even behind the braggadocio and one-liners. His cackling, high-pitched laugh served as a strange juxtaposition to the big game he talked – about being able to knock out anyone in the UFC at featherweight or lightweight. Midway through the interview, Helwani asked McGregor if he was single, because he seemed 'quite a catch'; McGregor responded that Dee Devlin kept his head on straight. The interview took place over video chat (which McGregor had trouble operating, admitting he had never used it before) and Dee could be heard shouting from off-screen, 'He *is* a catch!'

McGregor's drive was obvious from this first major interview. His dedication came through, but so did his belief in his own destiny: he simply felt that success was his due. McGregor insisted that in his mind he was already the two-weight champion of the world. In fact, he had been the champion since before he began training, 'since the moment I came outta me mother!' Justifying his statements, McGregor observed that some of the United Kingdom's biggest UFC stars had made their way to the big show through Cage Warriors – including Dan Hardy and Michael Bisping – and none of them ever had two titles.

The confidence McGregor manifested in this interview was a stark contrast to the goings-on behind the scenes since his sensational victory against Ivan Buchinger on New Year's Eve. McGregor had become a favourite among the most hardcore MMA fans – especially the Irish – that night and the knockout had wound up all over the Internet, but he was still barely scraping by; Cage Warriors' first and only two-weight champion was still collecting social welfare. On the trip to the airport before flying out to Sweden, the Straight Blast Gym team was held up by McGregor making a stop at the post office to collect 190 euros to live on. McGregor's coach, John Kavanagh, reported that McGregor had disappeared from the gym and from his teaching duties in the aftermath of the

Buchinger fight, as he struggled to acknowledge that he could be the most famous fighter in Ireland and yet still couldn't scrape together enough money to make a basic living.

At his most candid, McGregor told Helwani and the many thousands of fans watching *The MMA Hour*, 'We're broke as a motherfucker... We haven't got a pot to piss in.' McGregor and his Straight Blast Gym team mates could scarcely get by in their chosen profession. The most successful of the bunch was the Icelandic Gunnar Nelson, who had just had his second fight in the UFC on the infamous 'eight and eight' newcomer's contract: his purse was $8,000 in 'show money' and another $8,000 if he won. Even this was more money than McGregor had seen from his last couple of fights combined. So keen were the SBG fighters to get into the UFC that McGregor and his team accepted the fight in Sweden before even knowing the opponent. McGregor wasn't just flapping his gums: it really was the UFC or peanuts.

In retrospect, that first major interview foreshadows a good deal of what was to come, but perhaps the most significant exchange came as McGregor asked if Helwani knew when the UFC planned to come back to Ireland. Helwani replied that the UFC's international events executive, Garry Cook, had targeted Ireland in eighteen months' time. McGregor wasn't convinced and declared, 'I'll kick the door in and drag them back to Ireland.' Before signing off, Helwani asked the young Irishman how he felt about fighting in front of a stadium full of fans instead of the four thousand or so he fought for on New Year's Eve. 'Make it four million. I don't give a fuck,' came the reply.

Marcus Brimage was the man chosen to welcome Conor McGregor to the UFC's cage. A short featherweight and fellow southpaw, Brimage's sharp left hand and pace had carried him to three victories in the Octagon, all over the distance. The day before the fight, a gaunt McGregor took to the scale in Stockholm in front of a small but rabid group of Irish fans who had made the trip to support him. As Brimage and McGregor came together for the staredown, Brimage attempted to stay stoic as McGregor encroached on his personal space and trash-talked into his face. As their heads came together, the UFC's officials separated the featherweights and the crowd got the weigh-in drama that is expected in the modern fight game.

Come fight time, Marcus Brimage looked anything but stoic as he charged at McGregor, and the Irishman simply circled out. A stiff front kick to the midsection stopped a second Brimage charge in its tracks and sent the smaller man stumbling. As a stern and accurate counter-puncher with neat feet, McGregor was set to have a field day if Brimage continued to push forward at this pace and this carelessly. A reach disadvantage and a height disadvantage combine to form a range disadvantage, as a punch has its maximum reach at shoulder height. Punching upwards results in a loss of reach. McGregor was both taller and rangier than Brimage, who hit nothing but air each time he charged forward swinging upwards.

But McGregor's back-skipping left hand wasn't finding the mark. His opponent's lack of height made it difficult for McGregor to catch him clean, and Brimage's crouching stance, bent at the waist, only exaggerated the height difference. After a few missed counter left hands, McGregor made an adjustment and began to throw the uppercut.

As Brimage chased McGregor around the cage, hunched

and reaching, McGregor looked to take full advantage of his opponent's posture. A knee to the jaw in the opening seconds and an uppercut with the lead hand only served to rile Brimage up. A front kick square to the chin made Brimage take a moment to think. Shelling up, Brimage began to wait on McGregor to lead, figuring he might have a better chance of hitting the elusive Irishman. A faked front kick from McGregor, and Brimage charged straight in, but McGregor escaped out of the side door and allowed Brimage to run past him, cutting an angle at ninety degrees and circling back around to face Brimage on his own terms. McGregor sent in a quick one-two and Brimage pushed forward again as McGregor gave ground towards the cage. With his back foot by the fence, McGregor shot his left up from underneath Brimage's guard. Brimage pushed through it and ate a second snapping uppercut, which raised his head onto two more straight blows and his legs crumbled. McGregor and his team had been confident that Ivan Buchinger was a stronger opponent than many lower-level UFC fighters, but from start to finish it took McGregor just sixty-seven seconds to suss out Brimage, adjust, and render him unable to continue.

The crowd erupted. The interview with Ariel Helwani had made McGregor a minor celebrity with MMA fans, but no one could have imagined that he would back up the image he projected so emphatically. Even those with little understanding of the ins and outs of the strategic side of MMA realised that they were watching something new in this young Irishman. In his movement, his timing, his shot selection. The UFC featherweight division suddenly seemed a more exciting place.

THE SWEET SCIENCE
AN ASIDE ON THE UPPERCUT

The boxing great Archie Moore once gave an interview to *Sports Illustrated* before a scheduled heavyweight title fight with Rocky Marciano. In this interview, Moore gave some rare insights into the style of boxing that had carried him through light heavyweights and heavyweights well into his forties and earned him the affectionate nickname of 'The Old Mongoose'. One of Moore's key observations regarding Marciano was his inaccuracy with the uppercut. This wasn't a secret: Marciano often missed uppercuts, and being one of the hardest and most committed punchers in the history of the ring, it often looked as though he was trying to take out the ring lights rather than the man in front of him. To Moore, the uppercut had to be a counterpunch.

A counterpunch in the traditional sense is a return against an opponent's own strike. A tit-for-tat trade: an eye for an eye and you might knock out a tooth. But the uppercut is a counter to a specific posture. As Bruce Lee pointed out in *The Tao of Jeet Kune Do*, the uppercut is almost a worthless weapon against an upright opponent. When his head is over his body and his chin is down, there is not much surface to strike from underneath with the uppercut. It is when an opponent is crouched and bent at the midsection, with his head ahead of his hips, that the uppercut becomes a powerful weapon. Many boxers, when covering up or 'putting on the earmuffs', will drive their hips forward of their shoulders in order to kill the angle through which the uppercut strikes underneath the chin.

To catch a man with an uppercut as he is deep in a lean or looking down at the canvas can be a fight ender. José Aldo — the man in possession of the UFC featherweight title when McGregor had his UFC debut – made his name punishing wrestlers for attempting to duck in on his hips and take him to the mat.

But the uppercut serves more often as a setup or a deterrent. When a fighter is crouched, the uppercut can return him to an upright position. Frequent use of the uppercut can make a fighter who frequently slips and weaves under punches abandon the method that usually makes him so elusive to the other strikes in the boxing arsenal. A perfect example of this was the boxing match for the world heavyweight title between George Foreman and Smokin' Joe Frazier, held in Jamaica in 1973. Foreman was so terrified of Frazier ahead of the fight that he later admitted he was glad Frazier hadn't looked down during the referee's instructions, or he would have seen his knees shaking. Yet Frazier was a fighter who often bent forward at the waist to get under blows and Foreman's uppercut quickly found the mark. Archie Moore was Foreman's cornerman for this bout and could be heard screaming 'underneath' whenever Frazier began to bob underneath Foreman's jab. A hard uppercut caught Frazier as he dipped forwards and suddenly he didn't want to dip anymore. Standing upright in front of Foreman, he ate hooks from both hands.

As a set-up, the uppercut can be used to lock a fighter into an upright posture momentarily. For this reason, you will see fighters come out of the clinch or infight with a right uppercut, raising the opponent's head for a left hook and a right straight as distance is re-established. From the very savvy boxer, you will see uppercuts 'shown' to put the seed into the opponent's mind and keep him upright, in turn exposing the body to punches. The abdominal muscles are flexed when a fighter is hunched over in a crunch-like position. Standing a fighter up with the uppercut stretches out his abdominals and keeps his mind off them. The brilliant boxer Gennady Golovkin uses his left uppercut to stand opponents up and follows with a sweeping right hook to the midriff.

The main danger of the uppercut is that the fist, at some point, must drop below the opponent's guard. There are two ways to do this: the fighter can bend at the knees, dropping his weight and bringing his whole body up into the blow, or he can send a long uppercut in like a whip from the shoulder. The latter sees the fighter's punching hand leave his guard for the longest period and exposes him to counter hooks on the same side. Joe Frazier's success against Muhammad Ali in their first bout in March 1971 came as Frazier pushed Ali to the ropes, rested his head on Ali's sternum and convinced Ali to drop his right hand to throw the uppercut. Each time Ali's hand dropped in preparation, Frazier nailed him with that wickedly fast left hook for which he was famous.

THE DOLE AND A DICKIE BOW

As McGregor stood in the centre of the cage after the Brimage fight, draped in the Irish tricolour (he had been forced to fight the Swedish commission to even get the flag into the cage), UFC veteran, commentator and on-air analyst [known as a 'colour commentator'] Kenny Florian approached with a microphone. After McGregor had spouted some words about Brimage's attachment to the bout and the importance of fighting without emotion, Florian began to move the microphone away and speak to camera. John Kavanagh reminded his charge about the bonus.

Florian was a relatively new addition to the UFC's commentary team, but he remembered his basic broadcasting training well enough as McGregor lunged to grab the microphone: to Florian's credit, he never let go. Pulling the mic right to his lips, McGregor shouted, 'Dana! Sixty Gs, baby!' The performance and that line snagged McGregor the $60,000 performance-of-the-night bonus, an immediate audience with the UFC's president, Dana White, and a seat at the post-fight press conference – a rare thing for an undercard fighter.

Conor McGregor's career has benefited from his charm and off-the-cuff wit, but just as much is down to planning and foresight. The secret to his success is due more to his behaviour and image outside the cage than in it. Nowhere was this more obvious than in his appearance at this post-fight press conference, for which he had packed his best clothes as well as a dickie bow. The immortal line 'I'm off the dole!' topped off a night of perfection, both inside the cage and outside it. This small, curiously dressed Irishman with a knockout punch and a sack full of one-liners became the talk of the mixed martial arts world.

It was important that the UFC's fan base liked Conor McGregor, but more significant was McGregor's first impression on Dana White. While their relationship would change drastically over the course of McGregor's rise to prominence, McGregor and White's friendship would afford the ambitious featherweight a great many opportunities that simply are not available to most fighters. McGregor might have been charming outside the cage and entertaining within it, but he had been born into his greatest asset. The euro signs must have flashed before White's eyes when he realised that the smack-talking McGregor was the key to a large and previously ignored demographic: the Irish diaspora.

BOSTON'S FIGHTING IRISH

Although combat sports are games that are about the individual, and the teams that fighters train on are cosmopolitan in their make-up, national pride is the most powerful force in fight promotion. One of the first major boxing fights on record took place in London between the 'Venetian Gondolier' and an Englishman named Bob Whitaker. That bout gained notoriety and only took place because the Earl of Bath heard tell of the Gondolier's feats and insisted that he would be no match for a good Englishman; he put up the money to have the Gondolier transported to England in order to take the fight. In the modern era, the UFC had been desperately pushing the American-born Cain Velasquez as the UFC's first Mexican heavyweight champion in order to get into the USA's enormous Hispanic and Latino demographics, which are responsible for much of the money available in boxing. Don King did exactly the same thing with the especially unremarkable heavyweight boxer of Puerto Rican descent, John Ruiz – pushing him to become the first Latino heavyweight champion. It is no secret that from 2012 onwards Floyd Mayweather, Jr – as savvy a promoter as he was a boxer – scheduled his fights on the weekend of Cinco de Mayo (the date of a famous victory by the Mexican army in 1862) and would take on whichever highly regarded South American prospect he felt could shift the most pay-per-view buys.

The tradition goes all the way back to the first great boxing promoter, Tex Rickard. Rickard had Jack Dempsey, the world heavyweight champion, in his charge and desperately wanted to secure boxing's first million-dollar gate. As Dempsey was an all-American rags-to-riches story, Rickard decided to have him fight 'Johnny Foreigner' and play on the patriotism of the American people. The first two boxing matches to draw in a million dollars at the gate were Dempsey versus the French war hero Georges Carpentier ($1.78 million) and Dempsey against Argentina's 'Wild Bull of the Pampas', Luis Firpo ($1.25 million). A fight is just a half-hour of sporting competition between two individuals – it will never really be more than that. But a fight can only be a truly successful business venture when it is built up to the point that people believe it is much, much more than just two poor guys fighting for a purse in gloves and their underwear.

Ireland was not the first target. McGregor would have to wait on dragging the UFC back to his homeland, but the Irish themselves were still a huge part of American life and have been since at least the first half of the nineteenth century, when waves of immigrants sailed from Ireland to the United States. While the population of the Republic of Ireland is just under five million, and the entire Emerald Isle contains around seven million people, around thirty-five million Americans identify themselves as having Irish roots. That is a powerful demographic.

At the height of Irish migration to the United States, the Irish were considered an underclass. The pseudo-science that surrounded race and ethnicity at the time meant that the Irish were often grouped with other 'non-white' groups. They were more closely associated with African Americans in the behaviour that was attributed to them – indeed, one common expression was that Irishmen were 'inside-out negroes'. The infamous sign 'No Irish Need Apply' encapsulated the mistreatment the Irish received in other countries on both sides of the Atlantic Ocean.

It is perhaps strange that the first sporting celebrities of the

United States were of Irish stock. Paddy Ryan was born in Tipperary and considered the best fighter in the USA for a time. Ryan was dethroned by the man who would become the first consensus champion of the world – the 'Boston Strongboy', John L. Sullivan. Few fighters have been as bombastic as Sullivan and none match him for influence on the game of prize fighting. Sullivan was, quite simply, masculinity incarnate. In his earliest days, he became a barroom legend for the immortal line with which he issued his open challenge: 'I'll lick any son of a bitch in the house.' Battering his way through the best fighters and nameless drunks in equal measure, both bare-knuckle and in gloves, Sullivan was peerless. Travelling to London and Paris to fight each country's representatives, and offering a thousand dollars to any punter who could last four rounds in the ring with him, Sullivan reportedly knocked out over four hundred men.

But his greatest foe fought him exclusively outside the ring. Richard K. Fox was perhaps the most significant force for growth in American sporting culture through the late nineteenth century. Fox was not a fighter, but a chancer. Shortly after his arrival in the United States, he began writing the country's first major sports page for *The National Police Gazette*. His pieces resonated with the working class of America, Fox became rich from his writing and soon he owned the publication. 'Sport' was a loose term to Fox, who seemed to regard eating contests and ludicrous world record attempts as equal to the nation's then-favourite pastimes: baseball and boxing.

Fox wanted to promote Sullivan and thought he could make them both rich, but Sullivan wanted nothing to do with the unscrupulous promoter who had a reputation – deserved or not – for fixing contests and making a mockery of the sport. Each time Sullivan addressed his spectators following a fight, he would rub Fox's nose in the dirt by signing off with 'Yours, always on the level, John L. Sullivan.' Most people considered John L. Sullivan the champion and the man to beat after he defeated Paddy Ryan. (The story goes that Ryan was so impoverished when Sullivan met him that Sullivan split his purse with Ryan out of kindness.) Fox, hoping to punish Sullivan for his snubs, declared his own man, Jake Kilrain, the champion of the world and had a championship belt made up for him while Sullivan was in Europe. When Sullivan later battered Kilrain, in 1889, his own claim to the title was beyond dispute: he was the man. The Irish residents of Boston, many of whom were no better off than old Paddy Ryan, gathered a collection of $10,000 to create a world championship belt for Sullivan that had his name spelled out in diamonds on the front. Moved by the love of his fellow Bostonians, Sullivan announced that though he had won the belt that Fox had given to Kilrain, he 'wouldn't hang that thing around the neck of a goddamn dog'.

Boston has produced heaps of other top-quality boxers in the century and a bit since that bout. 'The Boston Tar Baby' Sam Langford was a boxer so successful, and a knockout artist so prolific, that he was close to becoming the first black man allowed to challenge for the world heavyweight title. The middleweight great, 'Marvelous' Marvin Hagler was a black Bostonian as well. Then there was the legendary 'Brockton Blockbuster' Rocky Marciano, the son of Italian immigrants and one of only two boxers to retire undefeated as the heavyweight champion of the world. 'Irish' Mickey Ward was from Lowell, Massachusetts, but every bit as popular a few miles down the road in Boston. Each of these men boxed their way out of the ghetto, but none compared to Sullivan as a force for change in society. In the nineteenth and early twentieth century, when the general attitude towards the Irish, and to Catholics in particular, remained sour, Sullivan was lauded in the papers as 'The Noblest Roman of Them All'. Black, Irish, Italian – fighting has always been the greatest means of social mobility.

Steve Collins, the Irish electrician who boxed up Chris Eubank and Nigel Benn twice each and who the great Roy Jones, Jr never quite got around to fighting, referred to Boston as a second home for an Irish fighter. When Conor McGregor showed up late for his third video-call interview with Ariel Helwani on *The MMA Hour*, wearing an expensive new pair of Ray-Bans and bragging about all the money he had gambled away on fights, Helwani surprised him with a call from Collins. The latter had nothing but kind words to say about the city of Boston, and more importantly about McGregor. For his part, McGregor had made regular training trips to Collins's brother's Celtic Warrior Boxing Gym and clearly felt strongly for the Collins family. When Steve Collins announced to the viewers that he believed Conor McGregor had everything necessary to be a great champion, the young Irishman could be heard getting emotional behind his sunglasses. 'You're the greatest, I'm the latest,' retorted McGregor.

Another heart-warming aspect of McGregor's Boston debut was the return of Tom Egan to the UFC, albeit in a different capacity. Now living in Boston, the Irish expatriate trained with McGregor in the lead up to the bout and then took a spot in his old school friend's corner. Short videos of them training together in the UFC's Boston gym made it apparent that the surroundings had changed but the two knew each other's movements very well.

While John Kavanagh made it clear that Egan's presence was not a game changer, remarking that 'the training was done in the 10 years leading up to this [...] I've done most of my cornering on my own so the fact we have Tom there is a luxury', McGregor was keen to have Egan there and Tom was able to show Kavanagh and McGregor the sights and sounds of Boston during their visit. The UFC, already putting great stock in McGregor, gave him a special entrance with lighting and music, and as the young Dubliner walked to the cage with his two friends, Tom Egan could be seen behind him, loving every moment of it.

Conor McGregor's spot on the UFC's second Boston event in August 2013 was once again on the undercard. He was capturing the public imagination already, but he wasn't receiving any special treatment just yet. McGregor was matched against Max Holloway in one of those fights that has become far more significant in retrospect, because of what both men went on to do. After a rough loss in his UFC debut in 2012, Holloway had pushed his record to 3-2 in the UFC. Watching Holloway during these early days made it abundantly clear that he had talent – he could jab, work the body and use his reach excellently when he remembered to. But Holloway was just as likely to swing wild and repeatedly jump in with flying knee attempts, just to be an entertaining fighter for the spectators.

Although McGregor had a couple of inches of reach on Holloway, his opponent's height made him more of a challenge than most featherweights, whom McGregor was usually punching down upon. Certainly, going from the five-foot-four and crouched Marcus Brimage to the five-foot-eleven and upright style of Max Holloway was a trip to the extremes of physique in the 145lb division. Holloway's solid striking game would prove a real test for McGregor. More importantly, though, this fight marked a clear development in McGregor's all-round game.

While McGregor had always been a fan of the left round kick and the left front kick, the Holloway fight proved a turning point in his development as it began a move towards a more kick-centric game. Starting as a one-dimensional boxer, McGregor was to become one of the most prolific kickers in the UFC. While kicks in mixed martial arts tend to be of the Muay Thai and kickboxing variety – swinging round kicks and the occasional pushing front kick – McGregor's kicking game was much more heavily influenced by traditional martial arts such as taekwondo. Disciplines in the taekwondo and karate mould tend to focus on chambering kicks and hinging at the knee to develop a 'snap'. Most important to the Holloway fight was a classical technique that the MMA world barely appreciated at the time: the side kick.

THE SWEET SCIENCE
AN INTRODUCTION TO THE SIDE KICK

The side kick will be familiar to anyone who has seen a kung fu movie at some point in their life. The leg is chambered in front of the body and then thrust out to the side, often on the end of a skip in toward the opponent. It was a favourite move of the American kickboxer (and one-time personal trainer of Elvis Presley) Bill 'Superfoot' Wallace. Wallace's right leg was injured before he took up kickboxing, so rather than focus on practising equally on both legs and still being near useless with his right side, he focused all his effort on practising kicks with his lead leg. Bringing his hook kick, round kick and side kick all from the same chamber – side on and with his lead knee coiled up in front of his chest – Wallace could make the three kicks indistinguishable from each other; invariably, by the time an opponent worked out what was heading his way, it was too late to do anything about it. Known for his flashy high kicks, Wallace actually picked up the majority of his knockouts in kickboxing by pumping the side kick into his opponent's bread basket while their guard was nailed to their head in anticipation of the head kicks.

The problem with the side kick in mixed martial arts was the same as with any other kick. MMA fighters looked at it and thought, 'That will get you taken down in an instant by a good wrestler.' It is a real concern. The side kick can easily be deflected with a parry or the elbows of the target, or even connect slightly off line and be deflected past the opponent. If a side kick passes the mark so that the target is on the calf side of the kick, the kicker has just given up an easy path to his back. The threat of the kick being caught is not nearly so severe as the threat of missing the kick slightly and being well out of position to get the hip square, recover the leg and fight off a takedown attempt from the opponent.

As the name implies, a side kick is thrown to the side of the kicker and not directly in front, where a fighter concentrates most of his efforts. In order to side kick, a fighter must get himself to a side-on angle in front of the opponent. This involves taking a more bladed, side-on stance, which carries a few significant disadvantages. It places more distance between the rear hand and the opponent, it removes the threat of an immediate lead hook by placing the body almost in the finishing position of the hook and it exposes the lead leg to low round kicks. That particular point would become enormously important in one of the toughest fights of McGregor's career a few years on.

The potential of the side kick was hinted at in 2010, when then-middleweight champion Anderson Silva met one of the greatest grapplers in mixed martial arts history: Demian Maia. Silva was terrified to engage with anything that might get him tied up in a grappling exchange with the Brazilian jiu-iitsu savant, and so resorted to throwing kicks exceptionally low on Maia's legs. The round kick to the thigh traditional in kickboxing and Muay Thai can easily ride up the target's leg and all a fighter really needs do is run through into a takedown attempt. The low line side kick attacks the front of the opponent's leg, forcibly straightening it, and is considerably more difficult to grab hold of. Later, Jon Jones, the light heavyweight great, would use low line side kicks to jam his opponent's advances on him.

In dealing with Holloway's height and reach, McGregor found the side kick to be an excellent weapon, one that prevented Holloway from stepping in on him. This was

Figure 1

confirmation of one of Bruce Lee's theories: the low line side kick's value is like that of the jab in boxing – in that it is the longest weapon and closest to the opponent – but has the added bonus of being aimed at a nearer target than the opponent's head. Over the course of two rounds, McGregor would pump the side kick at Holloway's lead leg whenever it looked like Holloway wanted to step in and get his offence going (*Figure 1*).

But the key to the science of striking is in forcing adjustments from the opponent and immediately capitalising on the changes they have made. Soon, McGregor began building on this low line side kick, just as any good boxer will build upon a jab that is finding success.

With Holloway struggling to step in, McGregor still had to address the issue of the distance between them if he wanted to land his vaunted left hand. To do this, he began utilising a jumping switch kick or 'bicycle kick'. McGregor would pick his lead leg up and hop in as if to stomp down with the side kick on Holloway's lead leg once more, but instead would jump off his supporting leg and throw a rear leg round kick at Holloway's head or body (*Figure 2*).

Figure 2

As he came back to the mat from the jumping kick, McGregor would control Holloway's lead hand and throw his left straight down the guard. It was that same southpaw 101 strategy of getting the lead foot outside the opponent's and lining up the left shoulder with their centreline but hidden behind a flamboyant jumping kick, which was more than enough to occupy Holloway's mind and often forced him back onto the fence before the left hand shot through and hit him.

In an uncharacteristic move, McGregor took Holloway to the ground and controlled him there for some of the second round and much of the third. He picked up a safe unanimous decision victory on the judges' scorecards, and McGregor's march towards the top of the division continued. But something was awry. Midway through the fight, after having taken Holloway down, McGregor began to pass the Hawaiian's guard, beginning a knee slide through to side control. Holloway managed to hold on to quarter guard – this is simply the last possible layer of guard, where the passer's ankle is trapped between the bottom man's legs. It can be seen in *Figure 3*.

Figure 3

McGregor maintained an underhook with his left arm, keeping it underneath Holloway's armpit so that he was pinned and prevented from coming up to attack McGregor's back. Holloway began trying to laterally pressure his opponent's knee by using his thighs to pull McGregor's ankle backwards – this movement can be used to unbalance the top man and fight back to a more defensively sound guard. But during a moment of movement, McGregor's trapped leg was straightened and Holloway's hips served as a fulcrum against the side of McGregor's knee. Something popped. As soon as round three started, McGregor immediately took Holloway down and kept him there for the rest of the fight. McGregor won a comfortable unanimous decision victory but soon found out that what he had felt was his anterior cruciate ligament tearing. A blown-out ACL is quite common in the sporting world, but the lengthy recovery time, and the fact that it is worryingly easy for an athlete to repeat the injury, can result in a drastically changed product returning to the ring or field.

In a return to *The MMA Hour* in the aftermath of the injury, Conor McGregor seemed restless. He had been in Los Angeles without his family or team for weeks while working on rehabilitating his knee. 'Don't have no family, no friends, I'm here in a little room on my own,' McGregor told Helwani, giving the audience a good view of the offending leg on his webcam and insisting that to have such muscle definition back in such a short space of time was unheard of: 'ACL, MCL, PCL, all the fucking "CLs".' McGregor didn't reveal the extent to which this injury had impacted him mentally. John Kavanagh reports that on hearing the news, McGregor had disappeared in his manager's car until the Straight Blast Gym leader was able to get in touch with him from Ireland and talk him around. Months later, McGregor announced that the UFC had booked the O2 arena in Dublin provisionally for May but that they would be willing to push an Irish event back until he was healthy. McGregor's obsessiveness and competitive spirit shone through as he recounted the exact number of weeks that it took UFC welterweight great Georges St-Pierre to recover from a similar injury. The Irishman had clearly sat down and done the math: he insisted that while St-Pierre was technically out for ten months on the calendar, it was closer to a year in weeks. McGregor was being treated by the same surgeon as St-Pierre, had the same rehab programme and team, and was determined to break another record – even in injury.

Though he was forced to do much of his rehabilitation in the United States, away from his friends and family, McGregor returned to Dublin in December in order to be present for the opening of John Kavanagh's newest incarnation of the Straight Blast Gym, on Naas Road. McGregor's presence brought in hundreds of spectators and helped Kavanagh drum up interest in training at the new facility. In his memoir Kavanagh recalls wanting McGregor to stay in the US until he was given a clean bill of health, but McGregor's appearance at the opening of his mentor's new headquarters reflected the remarks he made throughout his career about loyalty. McGregor had started with Kavanagh, and whether he was a failed plumber or an emerging star, he planned to continue repaying the kindness and encouragement of his friend and mentor.

While it didn't happen in May 2014 as originally planned, the UFC finally returned to Ireland in July. Unheard of when the UFC had last visited Dublin, Conor McGregor was now top of the bill. Going from a preliminary card fighter to a main eventer in just two fights is a rare feat, doubly so in the lower weight classes, which do not typically have the drawing power of the middleweights, light heavyweights and heavyweights. McGregor was booked to face Cole Miller – an interesting challenge, as he was a skilled grappler and McGregor had only met strikers in his UFC career so far. McGregor's two famous losses came by way of submission, so Miller – while not the best all-round fighter out there – seemed like an intriguing test of McGregor's ground game. The two exchanged heated words in a phone interview with Ariel Helwani. Miller pointed out that McGregor often just repeated the same material over and over in his interviews and yet was being lauded as some kind of trash-talking genius. McGregor insisted that 'Many a man's mouth has broken his nose.' The rivalry was hard to buy into, but the stylistic match-up was a good one.

As it turned out – and in what would become a tradition for McGregor – his opponent was lost in the run-up to the fight. In the first week of June, Miller pulled out with a broken thumb and was replaced by Diego Brandão. For McGregor, this was a good switch-up. He had been demanding a top ten opponent since the Holloway fight and while Brandão was a very limited and reckless fighter, he was respected in the division. Dustin Poirier (whom McGregor referred to as 'Pea Head') had just broken into the top ten by knocking Brandão out. McGregor went as far as saying, in the months of rehabilitation after his victory over Holloway, that he should have been fighting Brandão on the night that Poirier did and that Poirier's spot in the top ten was his. Brandão was a Brazilian jiu-jitsu black belt and an accomplished grappler, but he was a loose cannon and often preferred to wade in swinging, rather than doing something that would bring the fight down to the mat and into his area of expertise.

As the opening bell sounded, McGregor moved across the cage to meet Brandão. Immediately, he threw the jumping switch kick from the Holloway fight. Clearly, he still had confidence in his knee. McGregor turned away from Brandão and his rear leg swung around in an attempt to knock the Brazilian's head off. A wheel kick. This wasn't unusual for McGregor, who regularly attempted flashy taekwondo and capoeira kicks in the cage. What was unusual was that he immediately returned to his stance and – as Brandão moved in to punish the seemingly wild, missed kick – that famous left straight struck him down the pipe and wobbled him to his boots.

Brandão quickly shot for a takedown and McGregor fought it off, winding up in a clinch along the fence. As Brandão seemed to secure a trip, McGregor used the momentum to carry his opponent over the top of him and landed in the guard of the Brazilian. McGregor broke free and stood over Brandão on the mat. He got quick control of Brandão's ankles and pushed them back over his head in an attempt to run around the jiu-jitsu black belt's guard, but Brandão freed one leg and threw it across McGregor to prevent the pass, grabbing McGregor's nearest leg and turning upside down underneath him, hunting for a knee bar. It was the same position from which McGregor had been submitted by Artemij Sitenkov six years earlier. McGregor dropped to his knees and kept his weight on the leg, refusing to allow Brandão to extend it. Realising the chance was gone, Brandão stopped fighting for the leg and McGregor shook free. The O2 arena filled with a sigh of relief for the Irishman, but it was short lived, as McGregor immediately dived back in to attempt to pass Brandão's guard again, and Brandão once again got a hold of the leg. Now McGregor showed his hours of experience rolling with John

Kavanagh and Gunnar Nelson as he flattened Brandão out along the fence and began to drop stiff elbow strikes on him. Brandão eventually kicked McGregor off and scrambled back to the feet, eating a stiff left hand on the way up. He'd tasted the power and he knew he had to get on his bike.

Having taken McGregor's left hand as he rose from the floor, Brandão frantically tried to recall his training and circled away from McGregor's left hand. Spiralling clockwise around the cage, attempting to avoid further jolting straights, Brandão ran directly onto a wheel kick that struck him across the neck and jaw like a clothesline. Trapped along the fence, the reeling Brandão fell to the floor on the end of a long left hand and the referee mercifully jumped in to stop the fight.

It is difficult to think of a fighter who has done so much in the UFC in such a short period of time. Conor McGregor was a superstar within his first two fights with the promotion, was forced out with what could have been a career-changing injury, and recovered to headline an event and take out a top fifteen ranked featherweight in just his third UFC fight. More importantly, he had done exactly what he had set out to do and what he had promised in that first interview with Helwani. He had kicked in the door and dragged the UFC back to Ireland. The McGregor–Brandão card also saw appearances from McGregor's friends and Straight Blast Gym training partners: Gunnar Nelson, Paddy Holohan and Cathal Pendred. McGregor really was sharing his success with the people who had helped get him there. Coach Kavanagh would later write in his memoir that the UFC's return to Dublin was the greatest night of his life in the fight game, going on to say: 'Nothing has topped it since, and I can guarantee nothing ever will.'

Yet the real work had only just begun. Now that Conor

McGregor was a proven star, everyone in the division wanted a piece of him. But he was on his way up and now it was on to the top ten.

THE SWEET SCIENCE
AN ASIDE ON THE WHEEL KICK AND RING CUTTING

McGregor's use of the wheel kick from the Brandão fight onwards significantly advanced his game. Previously he had thrown it on a whim and achieved little, but as he became more aggressive in his ring craft and looked to back opponents onto the fence rather than counterpunch on the back foot, his wheel kick became a powerful herding tool.

When a fighter walks his opponent towards the fence, he removes the most common form of evasion – retreat. With only two directions left to move, the man on the fence must circle either left or right, or stand still and eat strikes, or be pressed into the fence at his opponent's leisure. As McGregor is known as an almost entirely left-sided southpaw, most of his opponents have spent the months or weeks up to a fight with him working religiously on circling away from his left hand and past his lead foot. The issue that McGregor faced was that as a more side-on fighter, he had no real threat to keep an opponent from circling in that direction. A fighter using a more square-on stance might utilise the lead hook to keep the opponent from circling past his lead foot, but McGregor's in-and-out, left-hand-heavy style demanded a longer, more side-on or 'bladed' stance. Circling away from McGregor's lead hand was an excellent way of complicating his task in the cage. He had to figure out a way to deal with this.

The traditional boxing arsenal let McGregor down in this regard.

He could not throw a decent punch when his opponent was able to get ahead of his lead shoulder. But his love for self-development and martial arts experimentation allowed him to develop an alternative means of punishing his opponent's lateral movement. As opponents circled past his lead foot, they would shorten the path of his turning kicks, both the back kick and the wheel kick. Where a fighter would normally need to perform a 180-degree rotation or more on their pivoting leg, the opponent circling into the turn would shorten the technique, making it faster and more difficult to see coming. Additionally, the act of circling into a strike can often amplify the effects of it. Think of driving your car into the back of someone as you both speed down a main road, and then think of a head-on collision – that is the difference between moving into a strike and being hit while moving away from it.

The difference between the taekwondo wheel kick and capoeira's *meia lua de compasso* is that the hand is placed on the ground

Figure 4

during the spin. The capoeira wheel kick involves bending deeper at the waist in order to do this. In Figure 4, the *meia lua de compasso* is shown on the left and the more common wheel kick is shown on the right. McGregor enjoyed throwing out both in his fights, but the wheel kick became a more reliable move for him.

The great Swiss kickboxer Andy Hug was also a southpaw and famed for his dexterous and powerful kicking techniques. In several of his fights, he was able to capitalise on opponents who were circling into his spinning kicks. In one bout, Hug recognised that his opponent would parry with the lead hand circle past his lead foot whenever he jabbed. After testing this reaction a couple more times, Hug flicked out a jab and turned into a spinning back fist. His left fist smashed into the left side of his man's head as the latter circled towards it, his left hand (the one that would have been in the way of the back fist) still out to parry the jab that was no longer there.

Where McGregor had been a one-handed threat on the feet and struggled when opponents circled around to his right, with the addition of his spinning kicks, running away from McGregor's left hand was no longer an option.

4

CHASING
THE CROWN

While Conor McGregor's standing in the public eye was going from strength to strength, and he was winning over as many fans with his humour as with his punches, his next opponent was far from a laughing matter. A native of Lafayette, Louisiana, Dustin Poirier was just twenty-five years old and had already won the most victories in the history of the UFC's featherweight division. With eight victories and five finishes in the previous three years, Poirier was as active a fighter as the UFC had on its roster. His two defeats in the UFC were not to slouches, either. Poirier had fallen short in battles with Cub Swanson (the consensus number three guy in the division) and 'The Korean Zombie' Chan Sung Jung, who had most recently challenged José Aldo for the belt before disappearing for mandatory military service.

The Irishman was on his usual form as he took questions at the press events during the week of the fight. Appearing in finely tailored trousers and a waistcoat, with the sunglasses he now always adopts, even indoors, McGregor captivated the audience and upstaged the main eventers: light heavyweights Jon Jones and Daniel Cormier. McGregor announced that he had no ill feeling towards Poirier and that the Louisiana native was just 'a quiet little hillbilly from the back arse of nowhere'. Poirier was understatedly confident, assuring the crowd that while many believed McGregor was the next big thing, he was there to prove that this wasn't the case. McGregor's most cutting lines came when he insisted that, 'Dustin thinks it's all talk. When he wakes up with his nose plastered on the other side of his face he's going to know it's not all talk.'

Even as McGregor's next opponent stood in front of the crowd, those in attendance waited with bated breath to hear what McGregor had to say about the rest of the division. Chad Mendes? He was a blown-up bantamweight, essentially just a bodybuilder now. 'I have eight inches reach on him... I would tower over Chad.' José Aldo? He had gotten to a point in his career where he was just happy to maintain his skill set, he wasn't growing or improving, said McGregor.

The UFC's Q&A events, particularly in Las Vegas, have always been more of a chance for fans to come out – often intoxicated – and to 'stir the pot', or even smack talk to their favourite fighter's opponent. One fan read a quote from German featherweight Dennis Siver regarding the rankings. It seemed as though Siver was not impressed with McGregor's number nine ranking, based on the fact that neither Brandão nor McGregor was a top ten fighter at the time of their bout, and the Irishman had leapfrogged the number-ten-ranked Siver in the rankings. In response to this, McGregor cut straight to the heart of the matter: he was not celebrating being ranked number nine in the world. To him, it didn't matter. It was number one or nothing, and in his mind he was already the greatest featherweight alive. This insight didn't leave his mouth without a snub for the offending party though: 'He's a midget German steroid-head.'

Going on to attack Poirier's record, McGregor drew attention to the fact that the German's last opponent was a '*TUF* reject'. By this, he meant that Akira Corassani, the Swede, whom Poirier had just laid out, had made his way into the UFC through an unsuccessful stint on its reality television show *The Ultimate Fighter*. Hilariously enough, McGregor would go on to coach on the show and his friend and training partner, Artem Lobov, would make his way into the UFC through the show. But McGregor's trash talk, while flamboyant and repetitive, was brutally honest regarding one crack in Poirier's armour. McGregor observed that in the fight with Corassani, 'He got wobbled forty times... His chin is deteriorating.' Going further, McGregor scoffed that any time he ate a punch Poirier would 'hit one knee' and that a strong gust of wind could have Poirier doing 'the chicken dance'.

Poirier had never been stopped, but there were certainly some legitimate questions over his hardiness after that last bout. Akira Corassani was not an especially sharp or technical striker, but Poirier's impatience and sloppy punching got him clipped far too often. The southpaw Poirier would throw his left straight, leaning well forwards at the waist to do so, and expose his chin in the aftermath as he moved in behind the left hand, which would subsequently drop to his waist rather than return to his guard. Midway through the first round, Poirier opted to step in with a long, rear-handed uppercut, with no attempt to conceal it. A long uppercut with no set-up is just an invitation to counter and Poirier was met with a jab to his exposed face, which knocked him off of his feet. It was only a case of Poirier's hand hitting the mat before he rebounded back up to continue contesting the striking portion of the bout. The next few times Poirier stepped in, he ate a counter and his feet shifted underneath him in that famous 'chicken dance'.

It was only through Poirier's tremendous hitting power that he had been able to pull himself back into the fight. Forcing exchanges on the feet, he took blows but split Corassani's brow open. As the latter ducked down to shield himself from a combination, Poirier snapped him down into a front headlock. From here, Poirier threatened with one of his specialities: the D'Arce choke – the same choke that Conor McGregor had found himself in very early on against Artur Sowiński. Corassani flattened himself out on the mat to kill the choke before Poirier could set his grips, but the technique tired the Swede and bought Poirier some time to recover from the counterpunches.

In the second round, Poirier ran in even more recklessly than in the first, but found the mark with his punches. A lead hand uppercut on the end of a running combination jacked Corassani's head back like a Pez dispenser. The Swede hit the fence and the 'quiet hillbilly' poured on the punishment against the cage until Corassani fell and the bout was waved off.

At first sight, Dustin Poirier versus Conor McGregor seemed another simple case of brawler versus counter fighter. Poirier relied on volume and aggression to get to close the distance – often breaking his stance and running to do so – and falling back on his tremendous hitting power and slick jiu-jitsu to cover for these defensive shortcomings. McGregor had, until recently, been all about moving forwards until his man struck out at him, then giving ground and looking to score counterpunches. On paper, it seemed as though Poirier's aggression would play right into McGregor's hands. But that is why we have the bouts: things are rarely as simple as they might appear in the prelude to a fist fight.

The fact that Poirier was a fellow southpaw made him a particularly interesting opponent for McGregor. Traditionally, the southpaw carries a natural advantage into fights because he has seen and worked against a great many more orthodox fighters than his opponent has against southpaws. It's just a numbers game. Those long, powerful lefts can be chucked in from unfamiliar angles and the simple but subtle battle of lead-foot placement is something an orthodox fighter cannot replicate against orthodox training partners.

Because southpaws are far less common than orthodox fighters, the southpaw versus southpaw match-up is the one that you will see least often in the ring. However, when both fighters are fighting from a southpaw stance, the engagement is the mirror image of a standard orthodox versus orthodox engagement. A reflection of stances – orthodox versus orthodox, or southpaw versus southpaw – is termed 'closed guard' or 'closed stance'. The second is preferable for our purposes in mixed martial arts, because 'closed guard' also refers to a position on the ground. A mismatch of stances on the feet – which can only be orthodox versus southpaw – is termed 'open guard' or 'open stance'. As we discussed in the first chapter, the key strike in an open stance engagement is the rear-hand straight of each man. It is a higher-stakes game than a closed stance engagement, in which the jab is the keystone punch that lines up with the centre of the opponent's guard.

The interesting thing about closed stance engagements with regard to McGregor is that they make it much more difficult to land the left straight. For a disciplined opponent, the lead shoulder can always be kept in the path of the opponent's rear straight. While a Floyd Mayweather, Jr, James Toney, or Ezzard Charles would be comfortable leaning slightly away and ducking down behind the shoulder alone to narrowly evade even the most powerful right hands, a less comfortable fighter can raise his forearm or elbow to make a more complete guard for his head and a more complete barrier for the rear-handed straight.

Poirier came out surprisingly calm and reserved, whereas McGregor skipped up and immediately attempted to hook kick his opponent's head off – with little success. Next, Poirier retreated towards the fence and McGregor pursued in his usual long, narrow stance. Poirier circled along the fence, away from the left hand of McGregor, who then spun into a back kick that struck Poirier in the chest and sent him back into the fence. McGregor attempted the same kick again, but was met with a Poirier low kick that knocked his standing leg out and left him on the mat for a moment. McGregor quickly recomposed himself and stepped in to punch, but another low kick thudded against his thigh, knocking him out of his stance. While McGregor asserted that no one else in the game moved like him, the downside of his fleet footed style was that the more a fighter moves his feet the less time his legs – his support struts – are braced for an impact. Moving the feet means taking the weight off them, which in turn means they can be knocked wildly out of position if they are impacted in this window.

The banger from Lafayette, Louisiana, stepped in for McGregor, lunging with his left hand and McGregor slid away. McGregor returned with a crisp one-two, but found himself punching directly into Poirier's raised lead forearm (*Figure 1*). That closed stance position was taking away McGregor's favourite weapon. Within seconds, though, McGregor had recognised this and began adapting.

Figure 1

Strikes typically come in two forms – circular and linear. Linear strikes – like the jab and the straight – are quicker to the mark. Asked how he beat his man to the punch time and time again, the great boxer Joe Gans would reiterate 'straight hitting gets boxers' plums'. But circular strikes are for stopping an opponent as they circle out, and for circumventing guards and particularly blocks.

If a blow cannot be evaded it will usually be either parried or blocked. Blocking a strike means, quite simply, disrupting its path to its intended target. As a general rule, the earlier that path can be disrupted, the less danger of damage. The least effective means of blocking strikes is covering up: if you place your hands or forearms against your head and then the opponent punches them, he is still free to punch with full force. Blows will sneak through or simply strike the guard into the defensive fighter's head. The most effective means of blocking is smothering: if your opponent loads up to throw his power hand and you push your palm into his biceps, you are going to stop the strike before it even gets near you. Most blocks are in the middle ground – at some point the forearm or shin is put in the path of the strike. By changing the path of his strike, a fighter can circumvent the block.

When McGregor shot in the straight, Poirier's lead arm came up high to block its path. So McGregor immediately began trying to capitalise on Poirier's defensive adjustment. The Irishman sent in a long left to the body, narrowly escaping retaliation. Then he swung a long left hook, but didn't have his distancing down, clipping only the side of Poirier's guard. Another attempt and McGregor ate a left hand in return – shaking his head in disdain as he did whenever he was hit. A circular blow has a shorter reach than a linear blow and McGregor needed to swing around the obstruction of Poirier's

guard (*Figure* 2). He would have to step in deeper. Another spinning back kick to keep Poirier's mind moving. McGregor's lead hand was proving more active than usual, and he sent in a couple

Figure 2

of jabs. Another jab and McGregor stepped in deep, his left hand swung in a wrecking ball hook that whipped in behind the crook of Poirier's elbow and turned the Louisianian's head around by the jaw. A visible wobble and Poirier circled frantically across the cage.

Fighting is an art, built around several sciences, but the most important moments of a bout are instinctual. Brilliant technique and tactics only hold up as long as discipline does. The first drain on a fighter's discipline is fatigue – there aren't many other endurance sports with so many strategic considerations – but the second test of discipline is being hurt. It is frightening to feel that pain, but more importantly it throws a fighter back to his instincts. Fight or flight. Some will run wildly around the cage or ring and others will bite down on their mouthpiece and start lashing out like a wounded tiger.

Dustin Poirier is the latter type of fighter when hurt. Just as against Corassani, being stunned gave Poirier the excuse he needed to start opening up in combination. As Poirier lunged in with left hands and low kicks, McGregor gave ground and escaped unscathed, repeatedly stepping back in and pressuring Poirier towards the fence. As Poirier came close to the wall of the cage, McGregor flashed the jab again. Poirier's right forearm came up to its usual position, but he ducked in as McGregor threw the hook. The blow glanced across the back of Poirier's head, high behind the ear, and Poirier collapsed to his hands and knees. McGregor followed with a pair of hammer fists to his downed foe and the bout was done.

McGregor swaggered into the post-fight press conference, immaculate in an ivory three-piece suit accompanied by an emerald tie and pocket square – and sunglasses, of course.

Often boxers will opt to wear sunglasses after their bouts to hide the swelling around their eyes, but McGregor had gone largely untouched.

The main event between Jon Jones and Daniel Cormier had been forced off the card due to injury, but Demetrious Johnson, the UFC's flyweight champion, was still on the card. Yet it was McGregor who was the talk of the post-fight media presser. Immediately, he was questioned about the legality of the shot that put Poirier to the canvas. McGregor insisted 'Watch it again… It's a legal blow', but admitted that he wasn't happy with the strike – he felt as though he had lost control of his weight and 'fell into it', and had wanted to find the same mark as the punch that had hurt Poirier just before. The final punch became something of a controversy very briefly in the aftermath of UFC 178, with some particularly kooky fans even convinced that Poirier had taken a dive – something that could be instantly refuted by a slow-motion replay of the blow. The disbelief and frustration was understandable, though: fans expected to see McGregor tested and forced to show something new, but the fight had ended – rather anticlimactically – inside two minutes. That said, had McGregor stuck to the usual darlings from his toolbox, he would have been forced into a longer fight. It was his quick assessment of Poirier's defences, and swift adaptation to them, that had allowed him such an easy victory.

McGregor once again broke his character straight after the bout. In a moment of real insight, he asserted that he could never hate his opponents: 'How can I hate a man who has the same dreams as me?' As much as fans gobble up McGregor's insults and trash talk, he would never keep it up after the fight except to set up the next pay day, and used it exclusively to 'push the fight, push the numbers'. As McGregor put it, he was 'professional inside the cage and professional outside of it' and that undoubtedly underlined his value to the UFC. A silent killer is interesting. Like the great Russian heavyweight Fedor Emelianenko, or the Kazhakstani knockout artist of boxing Gennady Golovkin. But that doesn't move pay-per-view buys. Meanwhile, two of the UFC's better pay-per-view stars were Chael Sonnen and Tito Ortiz – smothering wrestlers who rarely finished a fight and could still get people to tune into their fights based on their behaviour outside the cage.

There was already talk of matching McGregor up against the upper echelon of the division. The top four featherweights were already booked in matches and it was assumed that McGregor would have a good case for fighting the winner of either of those bouts. The former lightweight champion Frankie Edgar was booked to fight the division's previous most exciting knockout artist, 'Cub' Swanson. Meanwhile the American wrestler Chad Mendes had earned a second shot at José Aldo's world title. McGregor, however, stressed his desire to stay active as much as possible. He had only returned in July from ten months of inactivity due to his ACL tear, but had taken two fights in that time. Two bouts against decent competition and two first-round knockouts, no less. 'Would you doubt me? You probably did. But would you doubt me now?'

It seemed as though it would only be big fights for Conor McGregor from then on. He needed it to be – the Irishman was living a flashy lifestyle beyond even his growing means. In an interview with Ariel Helwani following the Marcus Brimage fight, McGregor revealed that he had been gambling away much of his money on fights and that he would happily bet on almost anything. 'I have a gambling problem,' admitted McGregor, 'I'll gamble on the weather if you give me the odds.' In addition to the suits and the watches and the Ray Bans which made him look the part of the gaudy million-dollar fighter, McGregor was splashing out on gifts for his loved ones. McGregor buried the memory of Dee Devlin's Peugeot 206: the little banger with 'smoke coming out of the engine' which used to 'shake down the road' was gone and in its place McGregor gifted Devlin a Range Rover. In an interview with the *Irish Mirror*, McGregor reflected, 'My first paychecks, I just wanted to get myself a hell of a lot of nice clothes and I got my mother something, I got my coach something, I spoiled my girlfriend.' McGregor continued: 'I got a 645i BMW, and I got my girlfriend Dee a Range Rover, but they were probably stupid things.'

It was extravagant and it seemed to be foreshadowing the fall from grace and trouble with taxes that seemingly every major earner in boxing has fallen victim to, but it pushed McGregor to keep working and to keep chasing the money, and in the process it allowed him to thank the people he loved. This would continue through the coming years. In 2017, Tony McGregor recounted Conor calling a meeting with his accountant and the McGregor family: 'We walked out of there and we all had BMWs.' As much as Conor McGregor loved his suits and watches, he seemed to have more money than he needed and rather than hold onto it he wanted to spend it on the people who were most important to him. McGregor's father, who was a taxi driver in Dublin for twenty-five years, quickly found his mortgage paid off by his son and can now be seen cutting a fine figure in suits of his own at each of Conor McGregor's bouts.

All of this extravagance and momentum was the reason that it threw the MMA world for a loop when McGregor's next opponent was announced to be Dennis Siver. Siver wasn't badly ranked, but it was assumed that McGregor was beyond that fight. At one point, Siver had been famous for his back kick, being among the first to use it with any effect in the UFC and picking up two wins as a direct result of hurting his opponents with it. In recent years, however, Siver had been uninspiring at best and shown up at worst. He hadn't finished an opponent since 2010, he had been stopped twice in recent memory, and even his victories were becoming close affairs. Worst of all, his 2013 victory over Manvel Gamburyan was overturned due to a failed drug test for hCG, a hormone used to mitigate the negative effects of anabolic steroids on an athlete's testosterone levels.

DRUGS AND THE UFC

While hCG itself is not a performance-enhancing drug, it is a banned substance because it can be used as a masking agent. In recent years, the Ultimate Fighting Championship has gone to great lengths to tackle the use of such illicit advantages in the sport – especially when compared to other professional leagues or many of its competitors in the mixed martial arts business. When drug testing within the UFC was taken care of by the state athletic commissions, it was minimal and rarely random. As Victor Conte, the man at the centre of the BALCO drug scandal – in which the Bay Area Co-operative, claiming to be a developer of nutritional supplements, created and distributed designer steroids such as Tetrahydrogestrinone to athletes at the highest levels of competition – would observe, a scheduled drug test is just an IQ test. It's simply a case of scheduling, which an athlete could work out alone but for which he will more often have the help of a coach, a nutritionist, or whoever is procuring the substances for him.

As much as it might hurt the average sports fan to hear it, the chances are that more money will be put into research and development on the 'dark side' of sports than into testing by commissions and committees. For a good many non-fans, MMA is still two 'roided up' guys trying to beat each other to death. Hoping to change this perception, in June 2015 the UFC announced a partnership with the United States Anti-Doping Agency (USADA). Since late 2015, USADA has been able to randomly test the UFC's athletes at any time, taking both urine and blood (the latter a much more reliable indicator of performance-enhancing drug use). Fighters are expected to give USADA notice of any movements away from their home gym, and a fighter returning from retirement cannot compete without notice well in advance in order to be placed back into the 'testing pool'; moreover, they will only be allowed to fight once they have been in this 'testing pool' for four months. While this has been a brilliant move for the transparency of the sport, it has also raised important questions about the relationship between a fighter and the UFC. In 2016, the UFC's fighters are expected to wear uniforms and be subject to drug tests at all times, but cannot form unions because they are independent contractors.

At the time that Siver was caught using hCG, none of USADA's extra testing was in place. He failed a urine test administered by the Nevada State Athletic Commission and argued, ineffectively, that he had been using hCG drops that he had bought over the counter for weight loss. At that time, no over-the-counter hCG product had been approved by the United States Food and Drug Administration and hCG was likewise unavailable over the counter in Siver's native Germany. Effectively, Siver had been caught dead to rights on a scheduled test that put him in a rough position in this fight. Conor McGregor could put Siver on blast and drag his name through the dirt in public because he had been caught using hCG. Unlike any previous McGregor opponent, Siver could not argue back and resigned himself largely to silence.

As a mixed martial artist, Siver was peculiar to say the least. An orthodox fighter, almost all of his best offence came from his lead side. His left high kick was more traditional martial arts style than a kickboxing technique, as he picked it up straight from his stance and snapped it out in the style you would see in a Jean-Claude Van Damme movie. Siver had drawn a good deal of attention in his early days with the UFC through his spinning back kick, a technique that was barely used in mixed martial arts at the time. Rather than coming out of a long, narrow stance as McGregor did, Siver would jab into a long, side on stance and rely on the jab hiding the advance of his left foot into pivoting position. It is worth directly comparing Siver's back kick to McGregor's. The Irishman's came directly out of his stance, with no need to step across himself before turning, and was most often used as a counter to the opponent circling towards his back side. Siver's back kick was the more basic jab-and-spin variety. The task in the back kick has always been getting the lead foot across so that the fighter can turn for the kick. From a basic, squared stance like Siver's, a big step is necessary. Siver concealed this with a jab – throwing the long lead as his front foot stepped forwards and he turned his stance side on, setting up the spin. *Figure 3* shows this set-up: Siver's jab takes him from a squared stance to a bladed stance, with his feet in line and ready to spin.

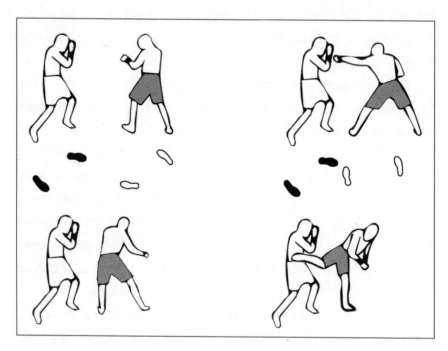

Figure 3

Siver's money punch was a counter left hook, which he would throw over the top of his opponent's right hand or in answer to their jab as they stepped in, dipping down to his right side as he did so in order to avoid his opponent's punch. This reliable dipping to his right side, combined with Siver's short stature and wandering right hand, could be readily exploited. Against Donald Cerrone, a six-foot lightweight, Siver had been stunned numerous times by a left high kick. Being an orthodox fighter, Cerrone's take on this move was a switch kick: he would switch his feet on the spot to get his left leg behind him and prime his hips for a power kick. Siver ducked into this kick numerous times in their bout before Cerrone took the reeling German's back and choked him for the submission victory.

Siver had been a short, stocky lightweight and had often conceded reach and height to his foes, but had recently begun cutting to featherweight. Looking completely emaciated by the time he stepped on the scales, Siver rehydrated to be one of the most muscle-bound fighters in the 145lb division. While he struggled to cut to featherweight because of his thickly muscled frame, McGregor's cut to featherweight was even more arduous because he had a much larger frame – he was variously billed as five-foot-nine or five-foot-ten to Siver's five-foot-seven, and had four inches of reach on the German. The match seemed like a strange, not to say obvious, 'gimme' designed to make McGregor look good and keep him active while the division's top four sorted out the pecking order.

Fans and media had begun to pick up on McGregor's favourable treatment. Not so much the practice of building cards around him – he was legitimately a star and even his most fervent detractors would begrudgingly admit that. It was the fact that Conor McGregor, despite competing in a division stacked with talented wrestlers and takedown artists, had never fought one of even marginal note.

THE WRESTLER DILEMMA

While rankings give a tangible order to the fight game, they are not really indicative of anything but previous performance. Fighting is a uniquely one-versus-one sport and the styles of specific fighters can match up awkwardly with others. The number three guy in a weight class might be completely perplexed by the skills that a fighter from outside the top twenty brings to a contest. This is why the most overused –

but accurate statement – in combat sports may well be 'styles make fights'. Conor McGregor sat in the middle of the UFC's featherweight top ten, and was surrounded by relentless takedown artists whom he had never had to fight. Not just the men at the top of the division such as Chad Mendes and Frankie Edgar, but the heaps of wrestlers lower down such as Clay Guida, Dennis Bermudez, Nik Lentz, Tatsuya Kawajiri, Darren Elkins and Hacran Dias.

The history of Western Europeans in the UFC (those nations without strong wrestling pedigrees) had been one of high-level strikers coming into the UFC, impressing the fans in their early performances, perhaps being protected for a while, and then falling woefully short as soon as they ended up underneath a high-level wrestler. Michael Bisping had struggled with Rashad Evans and then been kept on a steady diet of brawlers for a few years. Arguably the hardest-hitting welterweight in the world, Paul Daley, had set the fan base on fire with his left hook, but soon found himself stuck underneath American wrestler Josh Koscheck and unable to get up. So frustrated was Daley by the end of the bout that he sucker-punched Koscheck and was expelled from the UFC for life in spite of his continuing excellence in the cage. Dan Hardy had been rushed into a title shot with the welterweight legend Georges St-Pierre before he met a top-flight wrestler, and spent most of the fight on his back as a result. Ché Mills barely had a chance to be the next big thing before he met Rory MacDonald and was ground into a TKO loss.

It was true of early mixed martial arts competition that 'every fight goes to the ground'. That is what the Gracie family set out to prove in the early Ultimate Fighting Championship events and they were able to, dragging every opponent to the mat either underneath them or, in the more difficult cases, on top of them in the closed guard. That isn't so simple in the upper echelons of MMA today, but there is a similar rule that still applies: it is extremely difficult to completely avoid the clinch. You can see this in any boxing or kickboxing or MMA match: a missed strike, a mistimed attack, even a perfect connection that doesn't knock the man outright, all can easily end up in the clinch. Nowhere was this more apparent than in the career of Ronda Rousey, the UFC's biggest superstar through much of McGregor's early tenure with the company.

Rousey was a world-class *judoka* who could throw almost anyone from the clinch with her brilliant *harai goshi* hip throw. Despite never developing anything close to decent ability with her boxing, head movement, or footwork, she could reliably get the clinch early in every fight she had. The genius of throwing from the clinch into a dominant position was that Rousey never had to contend with her opponent's guard on the mat, where so many fighters get tied up. Falling into the scarf hold – basically a headlock on an upward facing opponent, but controlling their near elbow so that they cannot turn into the pinning fighter and escape 'out the back door' – Rousey could immediately attack an arm or move to mount her opponent. Through twelve professional fights, no woman was ever able to even go the distance with Ronda Rousey.

Her reputation simply served to aid her rush to the clinch, as every woman she faced decided the best course of action was to try to get off their hardest right hand as early as possible. This is the ticking clock of the takedown artist – fear of the takedown makes the other fighter overcommit, rush his or her blows, and give up the clinch much more easily. Throwing the rear hand only serves to square the hips to the opponent, whereas stabbing with the longer, less powerful jab keeps the body bladed and makes the clinch more difficult to attain. When Rousey did eventually lose, it was to a beautiful performance from Holly Holm, a skilled boxer who spent the early part of the fight simply circling away from Rousey's advances rather than trying to knock her out straight off the bat. But even Holm, whose game plan was perfect and whose execution was damn close, found herself in a couple of clinches with the *judoka* by accident.

To see how tough it is for even world class strikers to avoid falling into clinches a fight fan could watch any Floyd Mayweather, Jr bout. When Mayweather threw his right hand, he would often fall straight into the clinch deliberately to avoid a retaliation. When he got hurt or surprised, he immediately stuck to his opponent. And if Mayweather's opponents wanted to clinch him, he would project an elbow or his forehead and use his footwork to counter their attempts. His mastery of boxing was just as much a mastery of tie-ups. Similarly, Muhammad Ali's later career relied heavily on how easily he could tie up opponents when they started firing in punches. Once Ali's legs were shot, he couldn't dance around the ring as consistently and energetically as he had done as a young man. Instead, he would jab and dance beautifully for a round, and then hold for a round or two, usually leaning on the ropes as he recovered the pep in his step. A thirty-eight-year-old Larry Holmes was able to tie the young Mike Tyson up for four rounds simply by taking a grip behind Tyson's head and one on his biceps whenever Tyson began to open up along the ropes.

Conor McGregor had already found himself in the clinch plenty of times in the UFC. He was able to take Max Holloway down and reverse an attempted takedown from Diego Brandão, but the wrestling chops of those men were nothing next to those of many of the competitors in the featherweight division, whom McGregor had been carefully steered clear of. McGregor was perhaps the most interesting stylistic match-up for José Aldo, on paper, but he seemed horribly unsuited to many of the wrestlers competing for a shot at Aldo. Siver was decent at muscling guys to the mat, but he was not anything special in that regard. It seemed as though McGregor was being given a tune-up fight to wait for a shot at Aldo. Or perhaps, as this was a return to television for the Irishman, the UFC's broadcaster Fox had asked for some of that McGregor magic on the ratings before he moved into a title fight that would be another pay-per-view.

As Dennis Siver and Conor McGregor met in the centre of the cage to receive the referee's instructions, Siver looked irritated and McGregor appeared raring to go, towering over the stocky German. McGregor extended a fist to touch gloves with Siver, a concession that all the talk had simply been done to hype the fight, but Siver was having none of it. The UFC's usual five-second delay paid off as the camera cut away, hiding McGregor's flip of the middle finger to Siver – to a raucous response from the crowd.

One of the few interesting moments of the bout came early on, as McGregor immediately began stamping on Siver's knee with the low line side kick. Many fighters when met with this will return it, even if they have never shown it in their fights before, hinting at their frustration. Max Holloway threw a couple back at McGregor, but Siver began throwing them back straight away and often. McGregor seemed momentarily perturbed by this and some in the crowd cringed as the side kick came in on his knee, bringing to mind the ACL injury that had kept him out for ten months. Fortunately, McGregor's damaged knee was in the rear of his stance and his lead knee was healthy – or as healthy as a professional fighter's joint can ever be.

Siver was on his bike and circling constantly towards McGregor's right side, escaping the heavy left kicks and punches. McGregor looked for the wheel kick early, and landed a glancing back kick to the body about a minute in. A low kick from Siver knocked McGregor's standing leg out as he attempted his own high kick; getting knocked off his feet by timely low kicks was becoming a common feature in McGregor bouts, just because of the number of kicks he threw and the amount of time that he spent on one leg. Throughout the early going, McGregor was aiming to utilise the same jumping switch kick he had employed against Holloway, but to land a kick or knee to the head of Siver rather than against the body. One such kick flew completely over Siver's head and had McGregor hurrying to get back to fighting position.

Conor McGregor avoided the issue of retreating onto the fence by spending much of any fight as the aggressor. By walking his opponent towards the fence, when he did retreat to let the opponent fall short or to look for his counter left, he rarely even came to the midline of the enormous UFC Octagon, let alone the fence.

Dennis Siver and Conor McGregor were polar opposites in stance. McGregor's long, bladed stance allowed him to push off his lead foot to create a chasm between himself and Siver as he retreated. McGregor could even retract his lead foot into his stance and then drive off it to create even more distance. Siver's shorter, more squared kickboxing stance left him struggling to cover distance to pursue McGregor and left him an easy target for the left straight down his centreline. McGregor could explode in and out, and all Siver could do was reach and fall short. Siver had few weapons that could even approach the distance McGregor had put between the two men.

After a minute-and-a-half of largely ineffective work, following Siver around the cage, McGregor began to adapt. Siver pumped the side kick too often and too inaccurately. Each time Siver kicked, McGregor removed his lead leg from striking distance and returned it to step in while Siver was still on one leg. As Siver recovered from a missed kick and attempted to circle away, McGregor put in his first good left straight, which snapped Siver's head back as he sidestepped. The low line side kicks stopped and Siver started trying to box with McGregor, moving his head to try to make it a more difficult target. Suddenly, McGregor raised his lead leg and jumped in with a left knee to the head – that jumping switch kick – but the knee caught Siver leaning.

The fight had found its dynamic. When Siver ducked to avoid the left hand, McGregor would kick him in the head. When Siver stood up with his right arm braced for the high kick, McGregor would snap a left straight down the middle. Siver bounced between a rock and a hard place as McGregor tagged him up. Soon, it was McGregor following a wounded Siver around the cage and letting off combinations of jumping kicks, wheel kicks, and left straights. As Siver found himself on the fence again he lunged in with a left hook, but ate a left high kick as he did so, which sent him clutching for McGregor's legs. McGregor's rump hit the mat for a moment before he based his hand and dragged himself up again. No respite for Siver. A high kick came in, then a body kick, and Siver was fading badly. His footwork wasn't clever or graceful, but at least his predictable wheeling around to McGregor's lead side was keeping him in the fight and preventing his opponent from keeping him in one place long enough to finish him. Another jumping knee, this time against the fence, and McGregor rattled off a quintet of punches on the wounded Siver before being tackled to his rear again for just an instant. The klaxon sounded the end of the first round as McGregor ravenously pounded Siver's head and body in combination and the two went back to their corners.

The second round picked up exactly where the first had left off. McGregor walked Siver towards the fence, Siver would lash out and come nowhere near McGregor; McGregor would throw a left hand from well outside of Siver's reach and crack him clean. A quick 1-3-2 – the jab, lead hook, rear straight – sent Siver to the mat a minute-and-a-half into the round and McGregor showed some surprising versatility on the mat as he followed up. Dragging one of Siver's legs past him and driving his knee over the top of the other, McGregor crossed Siver over himself in a guard passing position known as the leg drag.

The leg drag was largely made popular in competitive jiu-jitsu by two brothers, Rafa and Gui Mendes, but had been used by plenty of competitors such as Léo Vieira and Fernando 'Tererê' Augusto before them. What makes the position so powerful is that it can be entered in numerous ways – from simply dragging one of the opponent's legs past you to passing guard completely to one side before hopping over the opponent and walking back into the leg drag position on the other side. The other strength of the position, with the bottom man crossed over himself and his bottom leg pinned to the floor under the passer's weight, is that the bottom man is given the choice between giving up his back or side control. McGregor used a common but intricate transition from the leg drag to the mount by switching his knees over, stepping over Siver's dragged leg before reversing direction to climb up to the mount.

Dropping shots from the mount, McGregor was soon stopped by the referee. He had seen more than enough and so had the fans. The Irishman stood to free Siver, then made a dash for the fence. Vaulting over the cage, McGregor ran to the audience. Dee Devlin, turned out immaculately in a glistening scarlet dress, rose to meet her long-time partner – but that wasn't McGregor's intention. Standing next to Devlin, understated in a leather jacket, was José Aldo, the featherweight great and face of the division. Undefeated for a decade, a man who dragged himself up from the *favela* and came to be recognised as pound-for-pound perhaps the finest fighter on the planet. As McGregor pressed his chest into the arms of the stadium security workers separating him from Aldo, Devlin looked concerned. All José Aldo could do, when faced with a screaming, blood-smeared Conor McGregor in front of a sea of Irish flags, was to laugh in his face.

The Siver fight was decried by many journalists and fans for the obvious showcase match-up that it was, and the build-up to the fight mostly showed the worst side of 'selling a fight'. McGregor had called Siver a Nazi and offended many German fans. Siver, not being a fluent English speaker and not having much to say that McGregor couldn't counter with some variant on 'you failed a drug test', was quiet through the build-up. It seemed as though he was just a canvas for McGregor to work on, both in the promotion and the match-up.

McGregor's independent pulling power was on display once again as the UFC returned to Boston, with the Irishman topping the bill. Televised on Fox Sports 1, the McGregor vs Siver card drew in the highest ratings since the UFC's deal with Fox began in 2011. The peak viewership? The last fifteen minutes of the broadcast, as McGregor knocked Siver all around the cage, garnered over three million viewers.

José Aldo versus Conor McGregor was unavoidable now. McGregor would get the fight he had been asking for and the shot at the belt that he believed he already deserved. For better or worse, fans would see whether McGregor was the superstar to carry the UFC into the mainstream, or just another pretender to the throne of Aldo about to be knocked back into line like all those before him.

THE SWEET SCIENCE
AN ASIDE ON DISTANCE

There were several factors that made Conor McGregor a stylistic nightmare for Dennis Siver, even before you consider where they were in their athletic careers. But the difference between McGregor and so many of the opponents he had bested in the cage came down to one word, and it is the word that governs all fighting arts: distance. Part of distance is range, the effective range of techniques being governed by height and reach. If your arms are shorter than those of your opponent, you could be at a disadvantage. If you have to swing up at your opponent and he is punching level with his shoulder, you are definitely at a disadvantage. But more important than the range of a fighter's techniques can be the distance he can create and cover with his footwork.

Before the Dustin Poirier bout, Conor McGregor uttered the now oft-repeated line, 'They don't move like I move', and it quickly became a theme. He described everyone else in the division as 'basic' or 'stiff' and professed to have some kind of method that made him completely unique. He had a point, though. While mixed martial arts was considered an amalgamation of all fighting arts, often gyms gravitated towards the same plodding kickboxing style on the feet. McGregor's in-and-out boxing/taekwondo hybrid was a breath of fresh air. Over and above specific techniques, many of McGregor's opponents simply could not move linearly nearly as fast or effectively as him. Most footwork in striking martial arts is done in 'push-pull' fashion. To move towards one direction, the opposite foot pushes first, allowing the foot nearest to the direction of movement to step, then the foot that provided the drive is pulled back into the stance underneath the fighter in his new location. So, to move right you drive off your left foot, and vice versa.

The body moves most effectively in directions directly opposite the driving foot. If you stand with your feet level and side step, you can cover more distance, and faster, than if you were trying to move laterally in a long, bladed stance. But in that stance you can advance and retreat far faster than when taking a more square-on attitude. You don't see many defensive linemen or baseball fielders adopting a stance with one foot far in front of the other, and you don't see fencers standing with their feet level. Long stances like those used by Conor McGregor are most useful to a fighter who wants to move in-and-out on a straight line as a fencer would, rather than a fighter who wants to circle the cage.

There isn't a single technique in any unarmed fighting art that cannot be killed by creating enough distance. By fighting at a more exaggerated distance, a fighter can also create a longer window in which to react to his opponent's movements. Attempting to react and counter in exchanging range is difficult, takes years to get proficient at, rapidly fades as a fighter's reactions slow and can even fail him simply because his timing just isn't 'on' that night. Often the best defence is simply to skip back and re-establish the distance.

That said, one of the cardinal sins of boxing is backing up on a straight line. The second step is always cut at an angle to begin circling away from the ropes. Each retreating step a fighter takes puts him nearer to the ropes, where he can be trapped. A double or triple jab from the opponent and if your only defence is retreating you will soon be on the ropes with nowhere to run. Distance is significantly greater in sports that allow kicks than in boxing, but the principle remains the same – back up too readily and you can run yourself onto the fence and into a whole mess of trouble.

Top-quality boxers gauge the proximity of the ropes by their distance from the centre of the ring, or from the opposite ropes, and are taught never to take two steps in direct retreat. In mixed martial arts, it is rare that fighters are so alert to their ring position, and some fighters such as Stefan Struve, Junior dos Santos and Martin Kampmann will retreat onto the fence from the other side of the cage when under attack. However, Holly Holm's masterful handling of Ronda Rousey was aided enormously by her refusal to take more than one step back before circling out.

5

THE GREATEST
FEATHERWEIGHT
OF THEM ALL

The name José Aldo was synonymous with the featherweight division in mixed martial arts for almost a decade. In fact, even in the wake of Conor McGregor's march through the 145lb ranks, it still is. He was almost faultless through nine years of fights. Many observers thought that by challenging Aldo, McGregor would bite off more than he could chew.

In the United States, World Extreme Cagefighting had been one of the first promotions to realise the potential of the featherweight and bantamweight divisions. While the Ultimate Fighting Championship had its pick of the litter on all mixed martial arts talent in the United States above welterweight, and could easily outbid the small WEC, the UFC was not going to go to the effort of building and advertising two new divisions just to steal the WEC's featherweight and bantamweight rosters. That would be a far more significant financial commitment than simply outbidding the little guy.

It seemed like sound logic, but the WEC was so successful with its early forays into the lower weight classes that Zuffa LLC, the parent company of the UFC, opted to buy WEC outright and use the organisation to focus exclusively on bantamweight, featherweight and lightweight fights, with the intention of incorporating these growing divisions into the UFC at a later date.

It is worth noting that the second prong to World Extreme Cagefighting's attack on weight classes that the Ultimate Fighting Championship did not have was a less-well-thought-out attempt to cultivate a super heavyweight division. Proving the obvious shortage of legitimate super heavyweight talent, Ron Waterman won the belt against a 208lb opponent, weighing under the regular heavyweight limit as he did so, then went off fighting around the world. Two years later he actually defended his belt against the overweight and long-past-his-prime Ricco Rodriguez, who still came in under the regular heavyweight limit. When Zuffa bought WEC, they applauded the establishment of the lower weight classes and immediately cut the super heavyweight division, never to revisit the idea.

The designated 'villain' of Conor McGregor's story was for a long time the hero of the featherweight division. It was José Aldo who would provide the immovable object to test McGregor's irresistible force. It was Aldo whom McGregor's denouncers would retreat to after each McGregor victory, scorching the earth as they went. When McGregor met Aldo, *then* we would see what he was made of. Aldo had suffered just a single defeat in his entire career, had bested world champions as a pure grappler and put on a kickboxing masterclass against many of the best strikers of the division. He was the stick by which mixed martial arts fans would measure McGregor. So to fully appreciate the impact of Conor McGregor, we must also understand the significance of José Aldo.

SCARFACE

The largest city in the Amazon rainforest, Manaus grew up along the banks of its river, becoming of tremendous importance to the world with the growth of the rubber industry. Brazil monopolised the rubber trade by the late nineteenth century and the isolated Manaus was the country's biggest producer. The city was wealthy enough to rapidly urbanise, and even install electric street lighting; it had an electrical grid ahead of many first-world cities. But Manaus's position as the most industrially developed city on the South American continent was short lived and the whole enterprise came crashing down when an Englishman named Sir Henry Wickham procured almost a hundred thousand seeds from Brazilian rubber trees and shipped them off to various colonies of the British Empire to explore their feasibility for intensive farming. The tree found greatest success in South-East Asia and in plantations built from scratch with the sole purpose of harvesting rubber, as opposed to farming it from the thinly spread trees that already grew in the Amazon rainforest. Furthermore, intensive rubber farming on plantations proved impossible in Brazil, where diseases and pests could ravage acres of trees in close proximity. Such problems did not exist in areas where the rubber tree was not native. Manaus's economic boom sputtered and fell into a nosedive. Today home to two million Brazilians, landlocked and hundreds of miles from anywhere of note, Manaus is a concrete jungle within the world's largest rainforest. And it was here that little José Aldo, the bricklayer's son, was born.

His family often struggled to scrape by and to put food on the table. When his elder sister accidentally allowed the infant José to fall onto a barbeque he was left with the scarring along his jawline and cheek which would earn him the nickname 'Scarface'. At an early age, José Aldo, Jr developed a passion for football. Two years older than Conor McGregor, while that young Dubliner was sprinting around the garden in a Manchester United kit, José Aldo was dreaming of playing for the Brazilian national side. Both grew up as the middle child, between a pair of sisters, and both boys had big dreams. By all accounts Aldo was a very competent player, but decent young footballing talent is not hard to come by in Brazil. The chances of Aldo breaking out of poverty through the sport were unlikely, so football was put on the backburner. After his parents separated, Aldo was sent to live and work with his father. It was during this time that he began to play with the *capoeiristas* of Manaus.

Capoeira is a Brazilian martial art that is sometimes called 'dance fighting' by the layman. In performance, two practitioners perform extravagant kicks and cartwheels to the music of the *berimbau*, a Brazilian single-stringed instrument. The history of capoeira is unclear, with one of the earliest accounts being of a pair of black slaves in Brazil taking it in turns to lunge with their head into their opponent's sternum, attempting to knock him off balance. How that became the whole-body, acrobatic art of today is hard to fathom. Whatever the case, capoeira was wonderful for Aldo, because it was both a social exercise and something that could be practised alone when he couldn't afford classes.

Aldo was introduced to Brazilian jiu-jitsu by a black belt named Marcio Pontes who allowed him to train for free because of the talent he saw in the youngster. Aldo excelled in competition and eventually the Manaus government paid for a plane ticket to let José compete in the world championships in Rio de Janeiro. Aldo performed well but was hit square between the eyes by Rio itself. The young man from the landlocked river city of Manaus had always declared that he wanted to see the ocean, but it had seemed unlikely that he would have the means or the reason to get away from his isolated hometown. Shortly after arriving in Rio, he had abandoned his team mates for a walk along the beach. He was infatuated. When he was back in Manaus, Aldo made the decision: he would move to Rio de Janeiro. In this pursuit he was aided by his friend and training partner, Marcos Galvão, who had spent some time in Manaus but was now returning to Rio de Janeiro to pursue a fighting career under the tutelage of the legendary André 'Dede' Pederneiras.

As a teacher, Pederneiras has to be considered one of the best in the world. And as a force for change in the *favelas* of Rio de Janeiro, he is almost unequalled. Pederneiras has produced over a hundred top-quality Brazilian jiu-jitsu black belts, numerous world champion grapplers and a handful of mixed martial arts world champions in the UFC, WEC and Bellator. But his greatest accomplishment is using martial arts to enable social mobility. Sleeping on the mats of the gym, and subsequently moving in with teammate Hacran Dias in the *favela*, Aldo began his transformation into a fighter.

In June 2008, a couple of weeks before Conor McGregor was easily submitted by Artemij Sitenkov, José Aldo got the call up to the big leagues from World Extreme Cagefighting as a tune up for featherweight legend, Alexandre Franca 'Pequeno' Nogueira. Over one-and-a half rounds, José Aldo made Alexandre Franca Nogueira look like a fool. Aldo's performance did exactly what fight fans hate: it screamed in the face of tradition. There are no points for time served in fighting: no one will go easier on you because of your reputation, and that is what Nogueira was finding against Aldo. Nogueira was coming off the first knockout victory of his career and had to consider that his striking was getting crisper. Aldo didn't agree. Boxing the smaller man up with ease, Aldo proved himself a vastly superior striker and more multi-faceted fighter than Nogueira, shucking off every takedown attempt with ease. Moreover, Aldo towered over Nogueira. He was not only a testament to the improvements in technique and strategy in younger mixed martial artists, but also a shining example of how important weight cutting could be to a fight. Pequeno was always a small featherweight, while Aldo – like Conor McGregor – emaciated himself to make the weight, eventually giving himself kidney stones as a result.

Each time Nogueira charged at Aldo, the latter would perform a pivot around his lead leg that took him off the line of attack perfectly, and leave Nogueira either charging past him, or turning back into a punch of Aldo's own.

THE SWEET SCIENCE
THE PIVOT

The point of a pivot is to turn around the ball of one foot. Most fighters use it to turn and face an opponent who has side-stepped them. What José Aldo did with his pivots, however, was break the line of attack. Closing the distance, whether by running combinations or by a deep stepping double jab, is usually done on a straight line towards the opponent. Aldo's management of distance was near perfect as he kept his opponent on the end of his kicking range and invited him to either lunge with blows or dive for a long, easily rebuffed takedown attempt. As opponents rushed in to close the distance, Aldo would step out to his left side with his lead foot, moving the pivot point off the line of attack, and then pivot ninety degrees around it. Should the opponent be rushing desperately to close the distance, he might run straight past José Aldo, as Frankie Edgar did numerous times through their two bouts. But most would stop as they passed Aldo. While running straight by Aldo as he pivoted off line was embarrassing and consumed energy, stopping in the space he had just vacated left the attacking fighter stationary with Aldo on a ninety-degree blind angle. Now he had to turn as he

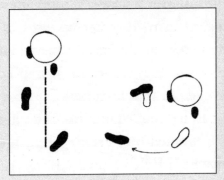

was free to hit. It was genius, and a method that punishes the normal behaviour of the disciplined fighter even more effectively than the reckless one (see *Figure 1*).

Figure 1

Each time Nogueira advanced on Aldo, Aldo pivoted off line beautifully and went back to work picking at the Brazilian legend. By the second round, Nogueira was in desperation mode. Shooting a reckless takedown attempt, he was shucked off again and Aldo immediately jumped on top of the old-timer. Pinning Nogueira's right arm under his knee, Aldo used both hands to control Nogueira's free arm, pinning it to Nogueira's chest and dropping elbows with his left arm, slicing Nogueira's face wide open and battering him to a brutal TKO stoppage.

THE WAR IN MARACANÃZINHO

To understand Aldo's brilliance you have to break away from the traditional archetypes of 'striker' and 'grappler', terms which are used to distinguish between fighters in mixed martial arts bouts. What Aldo has always done best is beat up wrestlers. Shucking off and defending takedowns is one thing, but punishing them was the business in which Aldo always excelled. Against wrestlers, Aldo would snap out some low kicks, stuff the first couple of takedown attempts and then begin looking to land intercepting knees as the opponents ducked in. Aldo would often push out a lazy jab, well above the opponent's head, inviting them to dive on his hips. As they did, he would switch feet before pounding in a brutal left knee to the sternum. These crushing knees destroyed WEC champion, Mike Brown. Pushing out that lazy, high jab, Aldo encouraged Manny Gamburyan to level change and met him with a low uppercut which crumpled the wrestler, face first into the floor. When caught in the bodylock of Chad Mendes, Aldo separated Mendes's wrists, turned to face his man and, before his eyes even found the opponent, threw a blind knee strike, which met the challenger with tremendous force and knocked the challenger out.

Aldo won the belt in 2009 and hadn't shown a moment of weakness since, but fan infatuation with him didn't last. When opponents couldn't be tempted to dive after takedowns, he was content to stand back and pick them apart on the feet in contests, which only really interested the aficionado. By 2013, Aldo was out of favour with much of the UFC's audience. He was still an incredible fighter, near untouchable. But no one could argue that he had lost his fire: that killer instinct that carried him through the WEC. If you don't talk trash and you can't or won't finish fights, you have lost your two main attractions as a fighter. Fans at large, whether they admit it or not, want to see a fighter decisively stopped, or they want to see a braggart shut up. Wherever Conor McGregor excelled as a promotional powerhouse, Aldo faltered. Quiet confidence was eating away at his buy-rates and his fan base. Aldo on cruise control just wasn't what people wanted to watch.

In October 2014, a month after Conor McGregor had emphatically starched Dustin Poirier, José Aldo was set to defend his title against Chad Mendes in a rematch. When Mendes had challenged Aldo the first time he was just a wrestler, but in the intervening years he had developed into a monstrous puncher and a decent enough ring general. No one could have predicted the shape of the fight to come, though. Mendes came out more mobile than ever before, showing Aldo angles and attacking the champion with low kicks that seemed to irritate the Brazilian. There is a peculiar thought process in mixed martial arts which says that if a fighter is good at something it would be suicidal to try that thing against them. The truth is, however, that fighters often build their offence on techniques that they find troubling to deal with themselves. You don't want to build your offence around mundane, easily defended moves, after all. Mendes found success against Aldo with low kicks just as Frankie Edgar had, and rather than kick back Aldo started swinging. As he threw a long right uppercut that hit Mendes in the chest, he was struck with a left hook on return. Long, naked uppercuts leave the jawline completely exposed to the hook. But this time, fans were surprised by a sight that they hadn't seen throughout Aldo's tenure in the WEC and UFC combined: Aldo's legs buckled.

It was only for an instant. He rebounded to his feet and kept punching. But everyone had seen it. The dynamic of the fight changed instantly as Mendes began to stalk Aldo and the two threw pot shots from directly in front of each other. A hard one-two snuck through for Aldo and Mendes attempted to laugh it off. Aldo threw a long right hand to the body again, and immediately ate a counter left hook to the chin. It was apparent that Aldo wanted to work Mendes's body, but every time he did so he was close enough to eat counters, and Mendes's counterpunching was looking sharper than ever. Hell, most fans didn't even know he could counterpunch with a good striker and here he was busting up the greatest featherweight in the game. By the last minute of the round, the champion's face was already beginning to bruise and the right side of his nose had torn at the nostril and begun to bleed.

Over the next four rounds, both men came close to stopping each other and neither was able to escape punishment for long. Aldo used his jab to draw Mendes's parrying right hand forward in anticipation, exposing his right jawline. Aldo would step in as if to jab, then hook with the same hand instead, looping it around Mendes's right and catching him clean. Mendes, meanwhile, continued to switch stances, hack at Aldo's legs with kicks, and land slick counterpunches when Aldo committed to his right hand. All this from the

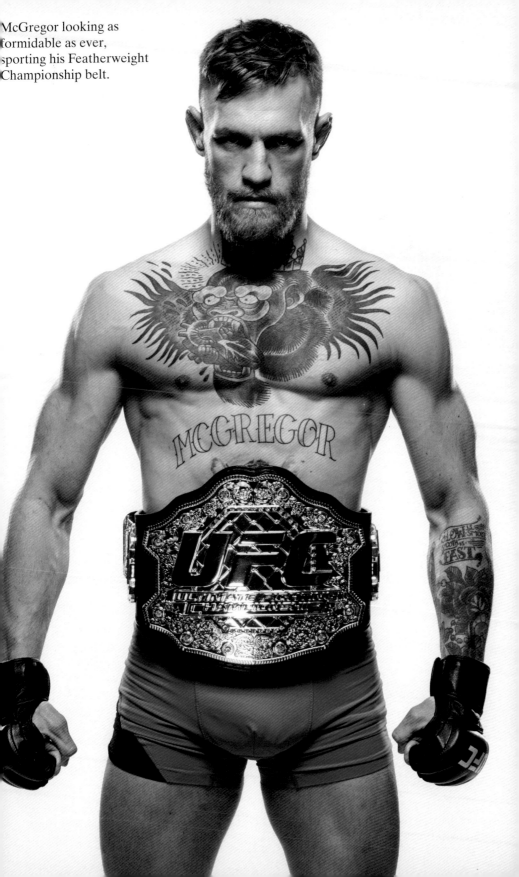

McGregor looking as formidable as ever, sporting his Featherweight Championship belt.

Above: McGregor shows no beginner's nerves at the weigh-in for his UFC debut in Stockholm, on 6 April 2013.

Below: Despite an aggressive opening from his opponent Marcus Brimage, McGregor paves the way to his first Knockout of the Night award, beating Brimage in the first round after barely one minute.

Above: McGregor takes on and takes down Diego Brandão in front of a lively crowd of over 9,000 people at the O2 arena in his hometown of Dublin. 2014.

Below: Out of the Octagon, McGregor takes a seat on the couch for *Jimmy Kimmel Live*.

Above: McGregor takes no prisoners during an open training session in Las Vegas.

Below: Never one to shy away from the crowds, McGregor takes the stage and steps onto the scales at the UFC 189 weigh-in.

Left: Even the toughest fighters love a hug from their mothers: McGregor celebrates with his family after defeating Brazilian José Aldo.

Right: Sky-high celebrations: McGregor becomes the undisputed UFC Featherweight Champion and the first Irish-born champion in UFC history.

Left: McGregor receiving a congratulatory headlock from Dee Devlin.

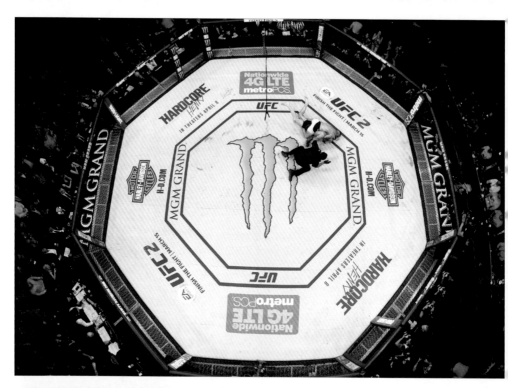

Above: A birds-eye view of the stage upon which McGregor suffered his first ever UFC defeat, after being submitted by Nate Diaz.

Below: The ultimate 'cheat day' treat – a birthday cake that even McGregor may struggle to take on.

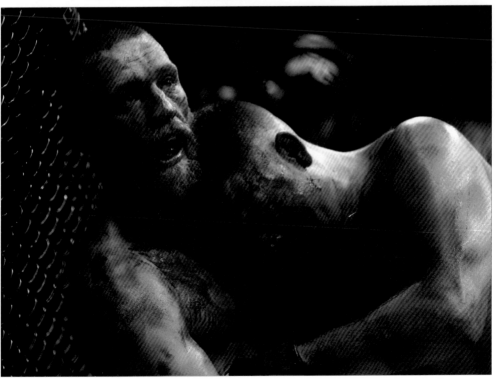

Above: Raring to get in the Octagon, McGregor at his weigh-in for UFC 202 as he gets ready to face Nate Diaz once more.

Below: A bloodied McGregor and Diaz clinch near the bitter end. McGregor beats Diaz by majority decision.

Above: No matter how many hits to the head he takes, McGregor has ensured he never need worry about forgetting his own name…

Below: Now the UFC Lightweight and Featherweight champion, McGregor celebrates his victory over Eddie Alvarez in Madison Square Garden, NYC.   *All photos © Getty Images*

wrestler who had done nothing but dive for Aldo's legs in the first bout – and when Aldo was asked about Mendes's improvements before the second fight, the champion would say that all he saw was a right hand. At the end of five rounds, the judges deemed Aldo's performance worthy of retaining his title, but his face told the full story. Bleeding from above and below the left eye, both cheeks swollen, a torn-up nose, Aldo was not the untouchable colossus of the featherweight division anymore.

ALDO VERSUS MCGREGOR: THE WORLD TOUR

In the week leading up to UFC 183 in January 2015, Conor McGregor took the stage at a UFC Q&A event in Las Vegas to break the news. Looking far from his usual dapper self, the Irishman wore bright red trainers that clashed violently with a pair of blue jeans, themselves sitting underneath a plain brown T-shirt with plunging neckline. The UFC 183 card was headlined by a strange match-up between long-time middleweight champion Anderson Silva and the faux middleweight, actual welterweight Nick Diaz, but McGregor still drew the crowds on his own. Megan Olivi, the hostess, apologised to the crowd for starting late but teased that McGregor had been busy finalising a business deal. At this point McGregor announced that he would be fighting for the UFC featherweight title against José Aldo on 11 July at the MGM Grand as the headline act of the UFC's yearly International Fight Week. This event normally consisted of two or three UFC cards over one weekend, during which time multiple press and fan events as diverse as UFC pool parties and UFC charity bowling tournaments take place around Vegas. The culmination of the weekend would be a major pay-per-view event. It was Olivi who had to remind fans of International Fight Week, though, because McGregor was focused on one thing: 'I'm going to rip that Brazilian's head off.'

By this point it was clear to fans that McGregor was the man that UFC brass wanted as the featherweight champion. He was obviously more fan friendly, already being one of the biggest promotional stars in the UFC even without a belt, while José Aldo's undefeated decade of unerring excellence didn't move pay-per-views and his often cautious attitude to even the most overmatched opposition did little to build anticipation for his title defences. Obviously, McGregor's appeal in Ireland helped, with much of the nation becoming mixed martial arts fanatics overnight because of him. But most importantly, McGregor was a company man. He repeatedly made reference to 'collecting heads' for Dana White, Lorenzo Fertitta and 'Uncle Frank' (meaning Frank Fertitta III) and, when asked about future match-ups, would insist that it was his job to turn up in shape and finish whoever those men deemed fit to put in front of him. Aldo, meanwhile, had repeatedly spoken out about the need for better fighter pay, which one supposes might not have endeared him to his paymasters. McGregor seemed the perfect replacement for Aldo and, as a truly remarkable striker, he seemed a better test than anyone else coming up through the ranks.

The UFC's promotion of its fights has always been in the same mould: a couple of press conferences with staredowns between the fighters in suits, maybe a morning television appearance, a late-night appearance on a major show for the biggest stars. But for Aldo versus McGregor, the UFC booked its first 'world tour'. From 20 to 31 March 2015,

Aldo and McGregor appeared at both open and closed events for fans and media across five countries. Starting in Aldo's hometown of Rio de Janeiro, the two travelled to Las Vegas, Los Angeles, Boston, New York, Toronto, London and finally Dublin. The crowd at the Dublin Convention Centre were near riotous when McGregor made his way to the stage and the first media question had to be repeated three times before the reporter's microphone could be heard over the noise of the crowd. Aldo was asked, having been confronted by the Irish contingent in both Boston and Dublin, whether he thought McGregor's raucous compatriots would affect his performance. A moronic question that no fighter would ever answer in the affirmative, but par for the course at a press conference. In fact, most of the questions asked at this press conference, as with the later 'Go Big' press conference, seemed to be entirely for the inquirer to get the approval of the crowd. Amid the jeers of the Irish contingent, Aldo quietly and calmly responded in Portuguese. His translator, the only man on the stage who wasn't Dana White, Aldo or McGregor, slowly converted the response into English. 'I am the king of Dublin. When I got here it was raining but I brought the sun with me.'

The partisan crowd erupted with boos, jeers, incredulous laughter and the odd cheer. The chant of 'Who are ya? Who are ya?' went up and McGregor shouted into his microphone: 'Yeah?! You're looking at him! You're looking at the king of Dublin!' At this point, McGregor lunged across Dana White's central podium and grabbed Aldo's belt from the desk in front of the champion. McGregor hoisted the 'ten pounds of gold' aloft as the spectators struggled to contain themselves. Aldo was held back from McGregor by Dana

White as security and stage managers rushed in to return the belt to its proper place and restore order. The rest of the show was the usual repetition of prepared material and pandering questions from journalists, but the headline had already been written. Every MMA news outlet and a few major sports pages around the Internet had the photograph: McGregor triumphantly hoisting the title as José Aldo strained to reach it around Dana White.

The press tour was an enormous success and the excitement for the fight was reaching fever pitch when in late June, José Aldo was revealed to have suffered a rib injury. Originally thought to be a fracture, the injury was revised to be a bruised bone, with which Aldo could theoretically still fight. A week later, however, he withdrew from the bout. There was plenty of speculation in the press and among fight fans over whether Aldo's rib was broken or 'just' bruised. The truth of the matter is that both injuries make competing significantly more difficult and, more than that, would affect Aldo's ability to slim down and actually make weight for the bout. UFC 189 seemed to be in decent shape even without McGregor versus Aldo, though, with Robbie Lawler defending his welterweight title against Rory MacDonald, but the UFC knew that McGregor was the ticket mover. Chad Mendes had been approached when news of the injury first came out and was asked to be ready in place of Aldo should the champion be forced out of the fight. McGregor apparently received word that the fight had been switched when John Kavanagh woke him. All the challenger had to say was, 'They're all the same.'

But nothing could be further from the truth. That was a lesson McGregor would be made to learn the hard way down the road. José Aldo was a fighter who had an exceptional grappling pedigree, but who liked to work on the feet. Chad Mendes was a stellar wrestler who had a cracking punch but would almost certainly look to take McGregor to the ground at the first opportunity. The match-ups could not have been more different, especially when one recalled how obviously McGregor had been steered clear of the great American wrestlers to get to the title shot. Mendes had been brought into a video call with McGregor some months earlier while hyping another fight and Mendes had pointed this out, asking when McGregor planned to fight a wrestler and what he intended to do once he had been taken down. McGregor's response was, 'I'll "wrest" my balls on your head.'

Chad Mendes was as dangerous a fighter as the featherweight class had to offer. Not only was the squat wrestler a tremendous takedown artist, he had landed more meaningful blows on José Aldo than the champion had likely absorbed in the previous decade. He had bruised Aldo's aura, and he had rebounded from that close decision loss to outright starch Ricardo Lamas. After a couple of minutes of circling the cage, Mendes pressured Lamas to the fence and slipped a panicked right hand to land a right hand of his own, which dropped the mohawked Lamas. The latter spent the next minute or so stumbling around the cage and diving after Mendes's ankles as Mendes looked to land opportunities for another big punch. A final punch came in underneath Lamas's armpit as he was turtled and he slid out flat on the mat, face down. A top ten competitor taken out in just a few minutes. But two enormous question marks were raised over Mendes's chances against McGregor. The first was how well conditioned and prepared he would be, given that he got the call just a couple of weeks out. The second was how he would be affected by the loss of his coach, Duane Ludwig. Ludwig had transformed Mendes from a right-hand-obsessed swinger into the switch-hitting Muay Thai machine who fought Aldo in the rematch. He had also turned the one-dimensional wrestler TJ Dillashaw into one of the slickest strikers in mixed martial arts – and, in due course, the UFC bantamweight champion.

All was not going swimmingly for the Straight Blast Gym team either. A mishap had taken place while Conor McGregor had been travelling for the world tour with his close friend and training partner, Artem Levin. When the two were in Toronto, Levin called John Kavanagh to report that McGregor had severely injured his knee – the same knee that had put McGregor out for ten months and made him consider giving up on his dream just as he had begun to make progress. While training wrestling with Rory MacDonald, an enormous welterweight who would be challenging for the title in UFC 189's co-main event, the bigger man had landed on McGregor's leg and now McGregor was struggling to move with any of his usual agility. When facing a truly top-level wrestler, footwork is one of the most valuable assets a fighter has. It is footwork that controls the distance, it is the legs that provide power for punches in the stand-up, and getting out from underneath another man without having the confidence to bridge powerfully with both legs is near impossible.

When the two entered the cage, each knew that they had a ticking clock on them, a limited time until the other man would realise what was wrong. McGregor's feet were not nearly as quick as they had been, and Mendes's gas tank would likely not hold up for the full five rounds. It was McGregor who took the initiative, running across the cage and back-kicking Mendes. A step-in knee from McGregor was immediately caught and the Irishman was placed on his back. McGregor managed to keep his feet on Mendes's hips, though, and kicked the wrestler away in order to scramble back up to his feet. Mendes ploughed into a clinch with McGregor on the fence and scooped up the taller man's hips again for another takedown attempt, but McGregor maintained his balance and Mendes withdrew from the clinch. McGregor threw out his hands with a smile and a shake of his head; he could be seen to say, 'Ta-dah!'

A small victory does not signal the end of a bout, though. McGregor's feet were too slow to evade Mendes's rush with an overhand right and a left hook that turned the Irishman's head around. As elusive as he had been in previous bouts, fans were getting to see that McGregor had a chin on him. But how would it hold up? McGregor repeatedly pressured Mendes towards the fence and dug in back kicks and front snap kicks to the body, scoring the occasional left hand to the dome of the wrestler. Yet each time Mendes rushed forwards, McGregor failed to time his skip-back counters. He couldn't get out of the way fast enough and ate Mendes's blows flush. It was the most aggressive McGregor had ever been, but it was also the ugliest. Defensively, he was almost clumsy without his beautiful footwork to take him out of the way.

While he did 'tower over' Mendes, as he had always suggested he would, McGregor's upright stance and low hands made him an easier mark for the overhand if he couldn't maintain distance with his feet. Three minutes into the first round, an already tired Mendes penetrated deep on McGregor's hips and hoisted him airborne, landing on top of McGregor in his closed guard. An elbow came in and split McGregor's left eye open. McGregor kicked away and began to stand up against the fence, his feet again slow and unsure, and Mendes battered him with heavy leather as he did so. McGregor's defence was nowhere in sight; it was his durability that was saving him. Returning to the centre of the cage, McGregor attempted to time Mendes coming in with his back skipping left, but ate an overhand that sent him stumbling. McGregor got in with a one-two, but again could not retreat in time to avoid the overhand. Moments later, he had been taken down again. The last minute of the first round was spent with Mendes striking McGregor from on top of him, appearing to smother McGregor's mouth with his hands whenever possible, and seemingly digging his fingers into the cut that was opening around McGregor's eye – an illegal move that certainly had McGregor screaming at referee, Herb Dean, to act on.

The second round began with some more front snap kicks from McGregor and continued body work, but Mendes quickly drove through the Irishman and had him on the mat again. The next four minutes was a gruelling, ugly grind in the trenches. Mendes was exhausted and attempted to hold McGregor down with underhooks, but this left McGregor free to bring elbows down on the top of Mendes's head. Mendes protested vehemently to Herb Dean, but Dean insisted that elbows to the top of the head were legal. So Mendes began to put his arms over McGregor's in an attempt to stop the elbows, and began to land his own. Always with his hands on McGregor's mouth or his head driving underneath McGregor's jaw. Suffocating and unpleasant. McGregor appealed to Dean, insisting that Mendes was not doing enough and the fight should be returned to the feet as Mendes was stalling. But Mendes kept dropping in hard forearms and punches and

Dean was not interested in the appeals of either man, in what was becoming a dirty, brutal bout. McGregor clearly had very little to offer in offence from his back.

The break in the lines came as Mendes saw a chance to advance. Pushing to half guard, he began to look for the signature Team Alpha Male guillotine choke. McGregor bucked his hips and Mendes fell to his back to attempt to finish the choke, but McGregor rolled his back to the mat and all the way through to scramble up to the feet. The exhausted, bloody, sweat-soaked Irishman wasn't talking anymore as he gasped for air, but he nodded at Mendes. Another front kick dug in. A left straight. A combination of blows. McGregor was pouring it on. Mendes dived for another takedown, but this time McGregor was able to shake the waning wrestler off. He nodded again, more assured. McGregor shellacked the American with another left hand and ate a right hand in return, but shook his head emphatically. No, not now. Mendes came off the fence for another right hand and McGregor timed it perfectly. The skip back and the left hand pierced through Mendes's guard, snapping off his forehead. Mendes went into a shell and three more punches came in to his head. A kick to the liver. Another front snap kick and Mendes's hands were dangling by his waist. His mouth open, the American walked away from McGregor's left hand – but not quickly enough. A one-two and the long left caught Mendes flush on the jawline on the way out, sending him to the mat. McGregor followed with punches to the prone, fatigued wrestler and Herb Dean waved the fight off. McGregor was the interim featherweight champion. 'Interim' meant nothing: to him it was the title.

Conor McGregor, the young lad from Crumlin, the amateur

footballer, the almost plumber, climbed the fence and screamed into the Las Vegas night. The Straight Blast Gym team draped him with the Irish tricolour and John Kavanagh climbed the fence from the outside to embrace his charge and protégé atop the Octagon. It was not just Conor's dream, but theirs. Team Alpha Male had won titles, most of the UFC title-holders in the organisation's history had been Americans, but Ireland had won nothing. The small team that had started in a banged-up hovel of a gym, described by Kavanagh as somewhere more suitable for storing old paint cans, had won the biggest title in the fighting world. As McGregor had always insisted, 'We aren't here to take part, we're here to take over.' Returning to the cage, McGregor collapsed to his knees and wept into the flag. As the doctor attempted to attend to the gash around his eye – the handiwork of Mendes, which was streaming into the flag – McGregor's face crumpled with emotion and he covered it with his hands. Chad Mendes extended a hand to help McGregor off his knees and the two embraced. 'You're a legend,' said McGregor, raising Mendes's hand. 'Aldo, he's a juicehead pussy!'

As McGregor walked straight past an impressed Lorenzo Fertitta, his eyes found Dee Devlin. Dee – who had run him to practices in her run-down old Peugeot 206, who had met McGregor just weeks before he turned professional, and who had remained with McGregor when he was collecting the dole and his ambitions of being the greatest fighter in the world were seen by most as youthful bravado or downright delusions of grandeur. The interim featherweight champion of the world embraced Devlin and sobbed into her shoulder. A visibly ecstatic Dana White approached McGregor with the belt and one of the UFC's new Reebok-sponsored 'champion uniforms' – a black T-shirt with gold writing, often with the name of the fighter misspelled. McGregor scarcely looked at White, gasping for air between exhaustion and sobs, and took the shirt only to throw it aside. As he was interviewed by Joe Rogan in front of his team and his family, the interim champion insisted that the injuries he had gone into the bout with were far more significant than José Aldo's bruised rib. 'He's gone running,' he said, dismissively.

It was nearly impossible to deny that Conor McGregor had been funnelled towards the featherweight title from the moment that Dana White and Lorenzo Fertitta realised his drawing power, but the last-minute replacement for Aldo would have seen many fighters pull out. Worse than that, Aldo's stand-in was a stylistically horrible match-up for McGregor and did exactly what most in the know expected him to: took McGregor down and pounded on him relentlessly. With a knee injury that obviously affected his mobility and saw him eat far more shots on the feet than he ever had before, McGregor still showed up and got the job done. It wasn't by any means pretty, and the notion that he was some kind of unbeatable superman had been thoroughly dented, but he had done it.

Tony McGregor, who was stood behind his son through his emotional post fight interview, would later sum up the journey up to that point. 'I didn't approve of Conor's job choice initially, because I just couldn't see the career in it.' The two had exchanged cross words throughout Conor's early MMA career and had fallen out badly over Conor's abandonment of a career in plumbing. In an interview with the *Irish Independent* in 2016 Tony McGregor gave Conor perhaps the highest praise he could hope for when he reflected: 'He was able to prove me wrong, which has made me so proud.'

THE SWEET SCIENCE
AN ASIDE ON FRONT KICKS

Many onlookers were surprised by how quickly and easily Mendes seemed to tire. In the coming months, the notion that Chad had 'come straight off the couch' did the rounds. Certainly it is unreasonable to expect that a fighter with a few weeks of preparation would be in better shape than one at the peak of his training, but equally it is unusual for a fighter of Mendes's level, training with any degree of regularity, to tire within five minutes of a fight. The key to Mendes's fade-off was McGregor's effective body work. The spinning back kick proved effective on occasion but the front snap kick was the difference maker.

The front snap kick is a day-one technique in traditional martial arts. Little boys and girls in white pyjamas practise them in dojos and dojangs across the world, but you scarcely saw them in professional combat sports until very recently. More common was the Muay Thai-style front kick: this is a pushing or thrusting motion. In the Thai-style front kick, the knee is raised high – then the kick is thrust in. It can be a damaging strike, but it has a tendency to be slow. More often in kickboxing and Muay Thai, you will see top-quality defensive fighters such as Saenchai and Giorgio Petrosyan bring their leg up quickly and not fully coiled, with the intention of simply prodding the opponent with the ball of their foot. It is a distance preserver and a means by which the fighter can knock his opponent off balance when they attempt a more powerful round kick.

In the traditional front snap kick, the heel is pulled tight to the buttocks and the leg is coiled well below the line of the target, then the knee is raised and the kick swings in behind it in one motion.

This 'chambering' of the kick high or low is the main difference between a pushing or snapping kick.

The value of the snap kick is that it is a fast, damaging action, like the round kick, but it occupies the straight line between the fighter and his opponent. Just as the jab is to the looping right hand, the straight line strike is longer and has a clearer path to the target. If the attacking fighter uses distance correctly, he can often perform much of the initial motion of the kick in what in karate is called the 'blind angle'. This is the area below an opponent's vision when he is focusing on the eyes or upper chest of his opponent. A textbook example of this would be the first major front-kick knockout in the history of the UFC: Anderson Silva's title defence against Vitor Belfort. Staring Belfort straight in the face, Silva snapped the kick up from underneath him, through the blind angle, and straight between Belfort's high forearms – a hindrance to most high kicks. Belfort's legs stiffened momentarily then collapsed in a controlled demolition as he fell in on himself.

But the focus with most fighters has been on the immediate results of Silva's kick: the outright knockout rather than the front snap kick as a weapon of attrition. The power of snap kicks is that they use the ball of the foot – delivering force through a smaller surface area compared to the full shin of a round kick. Connecting with the end of the foot and along a linear path from one body to the other, front kicks are also considerably longer. Just as reach is maximised on a jab by punching level with the shoulder, kicking as close to hip height as possible maximises the range of the front kick.

When matched up with an orthodox opponent, the left front kick to the midsection can be put in to the solar plexus. The latter is one of the most valuable targets in combat sports, not only for its vulnerability but also for the difficulty an opponent will have in guarding it. The chin and floating ribs can be hidden, but from any standard guard the solar plexus is naked. Consistent use of a body jab can be enough to get opponents dropping their hands and puffing for air; a full front kick to the solar plexus is considerably more damaging.

Conor McGregor pounded front kicks into Chad Mendes's solar plexus time and time again through their two rounds, often along the fence, sending Mendes back into the cage wall when he connected. The danger of kicking against wrestlers has always been that they will grab hold of the kick once it has landed and immediately dump the kicker on his back. With a round kick that would be true, but with a front kick the knee or often the entire length of the leg separates the wrestler from control of their opponent's hips. Mendes repeatedly caught McGregor's left foot after receiving a kick and would attempt to take advantage, but McGregor would push his foot into Mendes again to prevent the wrestler from closing the distance and then kick his foot free.

The front snap kick to the midsection is perhaps the most consistently undervalued strike in mixed martial arts and kickboxing. In every fight in which it makes an appearance, it seems to affect the result. Eddie Alvarez, who won the UFC lightweight title in 2016 and who will make an important appearance later in McGregor's tale, had tremendous difficulty with a relatively unknown Japanese fighter named Katsunori Kikuno because the latter was exceptional with snap kicks and went to them so frequently that Alvarez struggled to get in and use his vaunted boxing. Semmy Schilt, a Dutch seven-footer, won more heavyweight grand prix events than any kickboxer who ever lived by mastery of a front snap kick off his front leg. Schilt's height meant that this linear kick made him almost untouchable by many shorter opponents, but the kickboxing world felt that the kick only worked because of Schilt's build. The truth, of course, was that while Schilt was indeed a giant, he had mastered a technique that even the highest-ranking kickboxer rarely ever had to deal with.

Most intriguingly, while fighters such as Stephen 'Wonderboy' Thompson and Kyoji Horiguchi will also display this technique from time to time, they come from traditional martial arts backgrounds. McGregor is a man who came from a boxing background but who has become a pioneer in traditional martial arts techniques and underutilised kicks on the biggest stage in the fighting world.

THE ULTIMATE FIGHTER

Conor McGregor had won the world featherweight title, in his eyes at least, and wanted nothing more than to go home to Dublin but the UFC had one more favour to ask of him. The UFC's flagship reality television series *The Ultimate Fighter* was suffering from diminishing returns on its ratings and had been for years. The format was stale and – while far from a long-term solution – the addition of McGregor would inject some much-needed life into the brand, even if just for one season. The opposite coach? The UFC's favourite company man, Urijah Faber. Traditionally, the coaches of *The Ultimate Fighter* would fight each other at the conclusion of the season, giving some weight to the rivalry between the two on the show. But Faber hadn't won a fight as a featherweight since 2010 and had been competing with mixed success at bantamweight. It was a fight that made no sense to anyone. The solution? No fight at the end of the season.

Simple enough, but this left the show with none of the weight that the early seasons had held. McGregor, to his credit, attempted to create the 'beef' that fans love, repeatedly pointing out to the Team Alpha Male leader that he had 'whooped' his team mate, Mendes. Faber laughed this off and pointed out that Mendes came off the couch to batter McGregor for two rounds while puffing for air. So McGregor turned to the inner-camp politics that were tearing Team Alpha Male apart, by referring to TJ Dillashaw – whom Faber had brought in as a guest coach for his team – as a 'snake in the grass'. This was because Dillashaw owed his UFC bantamweight title to Duane Ludwig, the striking coach who turned Team Alpha Male's abilities on the feet around. Under Ludwig, Dillashaw had battered the great Renan Barão twice, and Chad Mendes had put on the crispest performance of his career against José Aldo, utilising footwork and strike variety that noticeably vanished over his next two bouts. The rumours were that Dillashaw was going to leave Team Alpha Male to work with Ludwig in Colorado – and the rumours turned out to be true.

Aside from that single morsel of juicy gossip, however, the season was relatively tame. Faber spent much time laughing at McGregor for wearing suits in the heat of the Nevada desert – suits which he happily sweated through and even tore during the course of the show. McGregor's dumbbell sized watches and sunglasses looked just as ridiculous inside a windowless gym, sitting on bleachers amid two teams of fighters in tank tops and shorts. But McGregor was there as a favour to the company, he didn't want to be there, and so was in full-on promotional mode, or as McGregor would say 'all business'. Really McGregor wanted to be back in

Dublin where he spent much of his time on the couch or walking the dog in tracksuit bottoms. He wanted to be celebrating and recuperating with Dee and with his family, working in his own gym and surrounded by his own people. As Tony McGregor would say about his son in a November 2016 interview, 'He likes his downtime, his hometown and his own time. He's very private as well. Conor is very loyal to his close people and you got to remember they all rose from nothing as well. His coach, his team members. They just rocked up to the gym with a backpack on their back and that's all they had.'

But McGregor was there as Conor McGregor the product, and he played the part of opulence well, from the many fast cars he drove, to the Vegas accommodation he rented in the build up to the ill-fated first José Aldo bout. Dubbed the 'Mac Mansion' this had six bedrooms, an infinity pool and its own spa and gym. In fact the UFC used their official YouTube channel to advertise the Mac Mansion and paint McGregor in the same light as the flamboyant Floyd Mayweather.

It proved harder to invest in the show after it became obvious that McGregor didn't really care about the role of coaching his team, aside from his long-time Straight Blast Gym training partner Artem Lobov. McGregor initially skipped morning training sessions and only visited his team for the evening training sessions, while Faber made both. McGregor made it clear early on that he didn't want to get emotionally invested in his team and that fighters shouldn't need their hands held. In the third episode of the show, as Team McGregor's fighter, Sascha Sharma, dropped rounds en route to a decision loss, McGregor was furious at cage side.

Each time Sharma was able to fight his way back to his

feet, he would make a bizarre strategic decision such as jumping on a guillotine and flopping to guard, bringing all his work to naught. McGregor paced around the outside of the cage swearing, chastising his own charge as a 'pussy', and throwing his sunglasses against the fence. As the decision was announced, McGregor sat disgusted and dejected, his beige shirt and cream trousers soaked with sweat. In the aftermath, Faber told McGregor, 'For not being emotionally invested you sure seemed emotionally invested. I think you need to show up to morning practices from now on out. Help these guys out, this is their opportunity.' For the first time since he burst into the MMA mainstream, McGregor was speechless. The interim featherweight champion of the world stared into the distance, reluctant to make eye contact with Faber, but managed a mumbled, 'Yeah.' It was brief, and it wouldn't happen again for a while, but it provided a moment of true reality amid the bluster and flim-flam of 'reality TV'.

While the rivalry was the selling point of the show, it was rarely anything but good fun as the two traded playful barbs. McGregor repeatedly touted his opulent lifestyle to Faber – a very successful businessman outside mixed martial arts – who laughed and pointed out that McGregor was only renting his exorbitant cars and accommodation. Faber jested about McGregor flashing 'the McGregor roll', a roll of bank notes with a hundred dollar bill on the outside and padded out with singles. In reality McGregor was attempting to portray the opulent lifestyle that was shown by the kind of boxers and rappers who soon bankrupted themselves through horrible investments on products with rapidly depreciating value. Yes, McGregor was renting his extravagance, but in reality it would have been daft not to. But as the cameras rolled and the season wore on, it became hard for the two fighters to hide the fun they had in ribbing each other and that they seemed to enjoy each other's company. When the two met backstage at fights after the season, their interactions seemed heartwarmingly affectionate. There was no question of the nearly forty-year-old bantamweight Faber actually pursuing a fight with this featherweight at the peak of his craft. But the McGregor effect seemed to work briefly: the season premier saw a 21 per cent growth in average viewership over the previous year.

CONOR MCGREGOR LLC

No single moment showed the power of the Conor McGregor rub quite as well as the UFC's 'Go Big' press conference in 2015. But before we turn to that event, it is important to understand just what 'star power' is. Casting agents desperately search for it, impressionable young women are told that they have it by skeezy photographers, and half the time when a high-flying executive thinks they have found it, they have not. For every Rihanna there are a hundred next-big-things that you have never even heard of. Some of it is 'the look' – the idea that people at home simply want to see people more attractive than them. As the young, trendy and incredibly image conscious McGregor continued to draw the public eye, and Ronda Rousey's star continued to ascend, Dana White and the UFC brass realised something: sexy people sell fights.

In creating content for its new online service *Fight Pass*, the UFC developed a series called *Dana White: Looking for a Fight*. The premise for the programme was that White and two companions would travel to local MMA shows, scouting talent. The pilot episode was essentially one big advertisement for a young fighter by the name of Sage Northcutt, whom White believed could be a star. Northcutt had been a minor celebrity for his martial arts as a child, appearing in karate competitions as an infant with a bulging six pack and upper body. Much was made of his seventy-seven 'world karate titles', which really only drew attention to how little 'world karate champion' means in a sport where anyone can make up their own world title. The same is true of kickboxing: there are almost as many world champions as there are professionals. But the nineteen-year-old's incredible body, raw athleticism, good looks and frosted tips were supposed to be enough to get the fans going, so Northcutt was signed to the UFC for a ridiculous $40,000 to show and another $40,000 to win. This was a slap in the face to far better fighters who had come in on the old 'eight and eight' contracts and had to fight out those contracts before any chance at negotiating a better one.

Northcutt's opposition, not unusually, were specifically picked out for him from the lower end of the UFC's talent pool, or even brought in from outside the UFC, giving him the best chance to look outstanding on a UFC card. Even in his victories, however, Northcutt looked fairly unimpressive. For his first two fights, he appeared a reasonable prospect, but fans quickly came to the conclusion that they were being presented with an incomplete fighter packaged as a world-beater. Northcutt soon lost to Bryan Barberena, an opponent he was supposed to run through, and his potential was capped in the minds of many. Yet the UFC kept Northcutt around, on an offensively large contract, even though he continued to look only so-so against mediocre, hand-picked opposition. It encouraged nothing but resentment among the fighters and disinterest among the fans.

Conor McGregor, on the other hand, had captivated the imaginations of every MMA fan and plenty of those who wouldn't think of themselves as followers of the sport. The way he talked, the way he acted, he seemed to have the answer and that intangible 'star power'. When the UFC dragged all of its champions and the biggest booked match-ups on stage for the 'Go Big' press conference, McGregor dominated the time on the microphone, picking fights with anyone and everyone. 'Go Big' was the UFC's new marketing campaign; the previous one had been 'The Time is Now' a year earlier. The latter was a hilarious dumpster fire as the UFC teased a huge announcement for weeks up to the presser; then, when Dana White got on stage, he immediately turned it over to press questions and seemed disappointed that the first one was about the much-touted big announcement, conceding that 'We didn't get it done in time.' Now, clearly, was not the time. At the 'Go Big' presser, however, José Aldo was forced to leave early as he had flown in on the day of his sister's wedding and he would be flying back to be the best man. This left McGregor free to accuse Aldo of running and to go on to pick fights with every single person on the stage, from the already beaten Chad Mendes to the lightweight Donald Cerrone. It went on for the best part of an hour, but for now it was still fairly fresh and the fans couldn't get enough of it. It was here that Conor McGregor announced that any fighter lucky enough to be matched against him should be grateful to him for turning their 'bum life' around. The Irishman continued that a fight with Conor McGregor was a cause for celebration: 'When you fight me it's a cause for celebration. You ring back home, you ring your wife. "Baby, we done it! We're rich, baby! Conor McGregor made us rich! Break out the red panties!"' A trademark on 'Red Panty Night' was quickly filed by former UFC middleweight and public relations genius, Chael Sonnen, who began selling shirts with this phrase on.

McGregor talked over everyone at the press conference until Dana White whispered in his ear, after which he became slightly less abrasive. The most salient point of the entire spectacle was McGregor's assertion that 'everyone else up here would take the fight against me if it was offered, regardless of belts or any of that shit. I'm the money fight in the male shit at all weight divisions so fuck everybody else.'

THE FIGHT

In the dying days of 2015, the mixed martial arts world waited on tenterhooks for some disastrous news to destroy the most anticipated fight of the year for a second time. On the eve of 12 December, everything was still in place and it seemed as though the Aldo–McGregor fight would finally take place at UFC 194. Fans finally dared to begin unravelling the riddles of the match-up in their heads. If Mendes had taken down McGregor with such ease, would Aldo be able to do the same? Could Aldo take the left hand that had crushed every one of McGregor's opponents except Max Holloway? How would McGregor's brand rebound from a loss that would show him to be just a good featherweight and not the best featherweight?

One final example of a UFC approach became evident

before the fight even started. The UFC had just signed a deal with Reebok in which they sold the rights to provide 'uniform' for the fighters exclusively for the next few years. This not only took away the fighters' ability to acquire their own sponsors and wear those sponsors' gear, it also raised some important questions about the fighters' rights, as they were 'independent contractors' but being required to wear uniforms. José Aldo stood in his corner in the drab black Reebok shorts that were part of the 'champion kit'. Every fighter under the new Reebok dress code was to wear either white shorts with black, or black shorts with white – making it almost impossible to tell two bald, white men of the same size apart by their shorts. Conor McGregor stood in his corner wearing bright green shorts made especially for him – and only him – by Reebok.

A tense Aldo and a sprightly McGregor sprung forward at the bell. McGregor shot in a left straight that glanced Aldo, and ducked out anticipating a return. Then, McGregor threw a low line side kick to Aldo's lead leg. Aldo squared up and rushed in, drove through a counter left hand, and smashed McGregor's face with a left hook of his own. McGregor's head was forced upwards and as his eyes reopened and searched for his opponent, McGregor found him on the mat. The counter left hand had stiffened Aldo's legs and sent him to the floor, Aldo's left hook had struck McGregor on the way down. José Aldo was done. Referee John McCarthy leapt in to stop the fight at just thirteen seconds into round one. It was the fastest title victory in UFC history and it had come over the greatest featherweight who ever lived.

José Aldo had begun his rivalry with Conor McGregor showing nothing but disdain. He wasn't scared of the screaming and the antics, and he would laugh in McGregor's face when the two met. Throughout the world tour, Aldo seemed disinterested, then bored, then peeved. By the time the fight came around, something had changed. He was furious. The main criticism of Aldo had always been that he sat back and coasted. He fought conservative. He wasn't bothered about finishes – he would fight his own fight and wouldn't let an opponent touch him. Yet that same man came out and rushed at McGregor, leading with his face and desperate to land the hardest blow that he could. Fighters are always keen to dismiss the effects of trash talk, and the best fighters in the world don't get there without being able to ignore what is said to them, but over the weeks and months Conor McGregor had ground away at Aldo. The objective is not to make a fighter scared or worried, it is to make him fight *harder*. Make him want to win so badly that he doesn't fight smart, he fights on emotion. And fighting on emotion against a top-quality counter-puncher, against whom feints and ringcraft will always be key, will get a fighter knocked out more quickly than anything else.

A grand tradition in the UFC had been that of the immediate rematch. If a long serving champion lost unexpectedly he was always given the chance to win the belt back a few months later. When Anderson Silva lost the middleweight belt he had defended an unprecedented ten times, he was immediately granted a rematch. When BJ Penn lost to Frankie Edgar he was given the same. For a while it was quite a nuisance; to win a belt you effectively had to win a best-of-three series. José Aldo had dominated the featherweight class for a decade, made one mistake to lose the title, and was never granted the rematch that most fans believed he deserved. But this wasn't because

Conor McGregor was the star to make the people care about the featherweight division, no, McGregor was moving on to better and bigger things. As former heavyweight fighter and pundit, Brendan Schaub put it moments after the knockout: 'Is this real life? Well, ladies and gentlemen – there's your biggest star in UFC history.'

6

AN UNEXPECTED RIVAL

From his very first mainstream interview with Ariel Helwani on *The MMA Hour*, ahead of his UFC debut against the largely unknown Marcus Brimage, Conor McGregor was convinced that he was a two-weight world champion. He had won belts at both featherweight and lightweight in Cage Warriors, after all. It was Sean Shelby, the UFC's lower weight division matchmaker, who contracted McGregor as a featherweight in order to add some more talent to that division. Shelby was in charge of the UFC's featherweight division and below, while the UFC's longest serving matchmaker, Joe Silva, was in charge of the roster at lightweight and above. For Shelby, McGregor had proven a nice addition for a still relatively young division – though he could never have known just how many eyes McGregor would bring to the weight class. Joe Silva had never been stuck for world-class fighters at lightweight, though: 155lb was the richest and deepest division in the game. At featherweight, Dustin Poirier's eight victories was the record for the weight class, but at lightweight, fighters could put together streaks of six wins over opponents in the UFC and still not break the top ten of the division. It was a completely different kettle of fish.

THE DIRTY AND DANGEROUS BUSINESS OF DEHYDRATION

One thing was becoming abundantly clear from his talk of challenging the lightweight division: Conor McGregor was tiring of the cut. The brutal loss of weight that he undertook to get to 145lb each time he competed at featherweight. Weight cutting has become one of the most controversial issues in mixed martial arts and combat sports generally. It is telling that in a discipline where a fighter can be quite legally beaten to death in front of a crowd of spectators – murdered for sport – the weight cut is generally seen as perhaps the most dangerous part.

The institution of weight classes was a good idea to begin with. In the days of bare-knuckle pugilism, the sport was dominated by the big men. When mixed martial arts came along and promised no weight classes, the tournaments came to be dominated by the giants. Of course, there were exceptions – Daniel Mendoza's new scientific method of boxing allowed him to beat much larger, more powerful opponents at just 160lb, and Royce Gracie's knowledge of the ground game before it was commonly understood allowed him to win the early UFC tournaments with substantial weight disadvantages. The field soon caught up, however. Secret knowledge and science can mitigate a weight disadvantage to a degree, but once everyone is singing from the same hymn sheet, the bigger men win. That said, if we didn't have weight classes then

Sugar Ray Robinson, Roberto Durán, Floyd Mayweather, Conor McGregor and just about every top-level fighter you've seen inside a ring or a cage wouldn't exist. Good as they are, they could not consistently beat heavyweights with even a fraction of the ring science that they possessed.

The invention of weight classes was a noble idea to give everyone a chance to compete. You sign up to a fight or a tournament under the understanding that you and your opponent will be the same weight on the night. The cracks started to show almost immediately, though, due to the fact that the professional fight game arranges for its combatants to weigh in the day before the fight. It works for the promoters: they get another press event and if a couple of fighters shove each other that can result in a quick spike in interest before the fight the next night. With a full day to recover from the agony of weight cutting, fighters do not need to concern themselves with getting to a healthy weight that they can maintain for the fight. This is why you will hear fight fans talking about 'walking around weight'. Weight is not lost through loss of fat, as it would be for the average dieter – it is lost in water. Much of this is sweated out in the sauna, or even on the treadmill or exercise bike inside a plastic sweat suit. Baths with Epsom salts are also used to dehydrate the fighter; according to John Kavanagh, this is McGregor's preferred method. In August 2014, long-time UFC bantamweight champion, Renan Barão was forced to pull out of the main event of UFC 177 after fainting and striking his head on the rim of the bathtub during this form of weight cutting. The effects of draining the body of water can be severe and it is clear that most fighters could not fight at all if they had to weigh in on the night at the weight they regularly cut to.

Why do fighters endure such ordeals? The more water a fighter can drain, the heavier he will be when he rehydrates and the more he will have beaten the system by. Pure weight in itself is a tremendous advantage: a man with 10lb of weight on you can benefit in every clinch just by leaning on you. But more than that, the more water is drained the higher the percentage of that fighter's contractually specified weight is muscle mass – he is not wasting pounds on the scale with water weight. It is not unusual to hear of fighters weighing as much as 25lb more on the night of the fight than they did on the scales. Some fighters actually relish this and take the opportunity to send out photos of the digits on their own scales on social media just hours after the weigh-in, demonstrating that they are far from their contractually obligated weigh-in figure.

The majority of world champions in mixed martial arts are considered 'big for their weight'. It's a nonsensical phrase that could only make sense in the bizarre world of professional fighting. It is certainly true that the most successful fighters in the UFC's history have been proficient in the weight-cutting game. Some of them have been downright prolific and this often turns the fans off. Jon Jones, the long-time light heavyweight champion, carries such height and reach advantages over his opponents and cuts so much weight that fans accuse him of being a heavyweight who beats up light heavyweights. Conor McGregor received much of the same criticism because he carried such significant height and reach advantages in many of his bouts and seemed to tower even over José Aldo, himself a severe weight-cutter who had suffered from kidney stones at a very young age – an ailment which is often due to aggressive weight cutting. But the weight on the scale was the same for

Jones and his opponent, and for McGregor and his opponents. Neither can be blamed for following his contract to the letter, and certainly weight cutting itself is an art.

When Conor McGregor stepped on the scale for his bouts, he looked almost unrecognisable. His ordinarily pale skin was a pallid, translucent grey and his cheekbones, while defined, were more akin to those of an internment camp survivor than Grace Jones. His eyes were sunken into their sockets as the skeleton of his face pushed forward through his skin. While the muscle could not disappear, his usually bulging shoulders, triceps and thighs were pressed flat to the bone, silently pleading to be watered. On the night of a weigh-in, McGregor looked more like a homeless man whose clothes had been removed to be washed by a kindly stranger than the finest fighter in the world. The worst of these occasions came in the weigh-in for his fight against José Aldo. After the months of build-up and hype, with McGregor bringing energy and movement to every staredown and confrontation, he seemed like a different person altogether when he took to the scale.

Shuffling out to the stage, tripping over his shoes as he removed them, Conor McGregor was visibly nervous as he shuffled onto the scale and relieved when he made the weight. Immediately gulping down half of a large bottle of water, he moved off to the side of the stage and blended into the background as José Aldo jogged out to weigh in. While Aldo was active and playful during the staredown, McGregor seemed slow and lethargic. When he was brought the microphone and asked about the fight by Joe Rogan after the staredown, he had no clever quips, he couldn't even bring himself to shout; he stumbled monotonously over his words, thanked the Irish fans and then simply wandered off. It became a tradition that after McGregor's weigh-ins the mixed martial arts community would remark on the state he appeared to be in and suggest that this was the one – this was the weight cut that would be too much for McGregor.

McGregor himself played into this by being one of the few fighters to give interviews immediately after the weigh-ins. This is when most fighters are desperate to drink, eat and lie down alone. Weight cuts play havoc with the hormones and emotions of fighters, and a particularly arduous but successful weight cut can move even a toughened world beater to tears. But Conor McGregor would stand with Ariel Helwani and answer questions in a slower state of mind than his usual self, because he recognised the value of staying in the media and that this was half the work in the fight game. To fight fans, every single action at the press conference – the weigh-in, the staredown – is pounced upon as an early indicator of the outcome. Fans would leap upon McGregor's malnourished appearance and slower manner as further evidence of how draining the cut must have been for him: he was in for a pasting. It never turned out that way, though. Like the great boxer Harry Greb, who would make sure to be seen by newspapermen 'drunk' with a pair of women the night before a fight, McGregor's pre-fight appearance was no indication of what was to come under the ring lights.

If a fighter can effectively starve himself of water and balloon up after the weigh-in, but never actually misses weight at the weigh-in, that is his decision. There have been some famously poor weight cutters in MMA, though. In September 2016, John Lineker, a 'flyweight' (125lb), managed to miss weight in the UFC a record-setting five times. The last of these came after the UFC insisted Lineker fight at bantamweight

(135lb), but with ten extra pounds of weight to play with he still weighed in, exhausted and stark naked, half a pound over. Fight companies typically do not like to work with fighters with spotty weigh-in records. A fighter who misses weight is fined 20 per cent of his purse and that is awarded to his opponent, but the fight can still go ahead. Missing weight for a title fight, by either party, means that the title is no longer on the line. This leaves the fight in a strange limbo: even if the challenger wins, nothing changes. The sole famous example of this in the UFC is Travis Lutter, who missed weight in a shot at Anderson Silva's middleweight title, lost that fight and was cut from the UFC not long afterward.

Aside from being a pain in the rear for the promotion when done poorly, weight cutting is much more importantly a dangerous practice for the fighter's health. While weight cutting does exist in boxing, some critics blame the influence of wrestling on weight cutting in mixed martial arts. One often hears tale of wrestlers spitting into buckets to get that little bit more water out of their systems. In the United States in 1997, three collegiate wrestlers from different states died from the effects of hypothermia brought on by attempting to 'sweat out' weight in multiple layers of clothing. These three deaths were all within a month of each other and gained widespread media attention, but weight-cutting culture has not changed much and in many cases has got worse. UFC veteran Cody McKenzie was once set to fight Brock Larson in Tulsa, Oklahoma, but missed the welterweight limit by one-and-a-half pounds. Rather than risk sweating it out, McKenzie opted to draw blood. An uncomfortable example of what fighters are willing to do to themselves to be competitive for even a mediocre payday.

In September 2013, a young Brazilian fighter named Leandro Silva, from the Nova União team, received the call to take part in the Shooto Brazil 43 card as a flyweight. As José Aldo's story attests, in a camp full of killers the opportunities don't trickle down to the lesser fighters that often; you have to be ready to go when opportunity knocks. The only problem was that Silva was walking around at 160lb and would have to cut a quarter of his bodyweight to reach the 125lb limit. Brazilian commissions are generally far less stringent in drug testing (though even Nevada, the 'best' commission in combat sports, is limited and predictable in its mandatory testing), and it is speculated that Silva used diuretics in his attempt to make the weight. Whatever the case, he suffered a stroke and died just hours before he was due to weigh in. Some tried to argue that the event had been a rare exception, pointing to the dangers of diuretics and the speed at which Silva cut his weight, but such talk didn't make the uneasy state of affairs in MMA any less awkward. Weight cutting is, to all intents and purposes, mandatory for anyone hoping to compete successfully in mixed martial arts. It is also an extremely dangerous practice.

Conor McGregor had given every indication that he was a fighter whose mind was on his health. The goal of any fighter with an ounce of concern for his well-being is to get in, get rich and get out before the effects of a career in trading blows to the head catches up with them. Very, very few fighters actually accomplish that. Most have no chance of getting to the 'rich' part of the flow chart, but even the fighters who achieve that will usually struggle to hang it up. One more fight, one more pay day; they keep attempting to rediscover the old magic while taking more and more damaging losses. From McGregor's references to the diminishing nature of the chin and the peaking of fighters, it is reasonable to believe that he had his health on his mind despite his bravado and braggadocio. Knowing the long-term effects of weight cutting and actively feeling the drain on his body, McGregor must have felt the same thing that every other fighter has: 'I wish I didn't have to do this part.' The difference is that most fighters only move division when they are experiencing diminishing returns in their current one; they pack on some muscle or they cut more weight to be bigger on fight night and they feel stronger for it for a while. McGregor had conquered the featherweight division and was ready to abandon it at the peak of his powers. This was almost unheard of.

Perhaps McGregor felt that the lightweight division would be a challenge; perhaps he just hated the weight cut but he had already been setting up matches at that weight. Things had been getting heated with Donald Cerrone for a while, and the bitterness between the two ate up much of the time at the 'Go Big' press conference. Yet Cerrone wasn't alone. Everyone wanted a piece of McGregor. He was the greatest star the UFC had seen in years at this point and, as he put it, a fight with Conor McGregor could turn your 'bum life' around. The man who was gifted 'red panty night'? Rafael dos Anjos, the UFC lightweight champion. This was no feeling-out process, where most fighters will dip their toe in a new division to test their stamina, strength and overall feeling in the weight class, then begin campaigning towards a title shot. McGregor was able to declare that he would only fight for the title.

RAFAEL DOS ANJOS

Rafael dos Anjos did not have the near-decade of unanswered brilliance that made José Aldo so iconic to the mixed martial arts fan. In fact, until relatively recently dos Anjos had been something of an also-ran in the UFC's most talent-rich and competitive division. From 2008 to 2011, the prospects for his future in the fight game did not seem all that bright. After making it to the big show, he was knocked out in his first UFC appearance, lost his second and by 2011 had put together a less-than-impressive record of four wins and four losses. Then, slowly, dos Anjos began to turn it around.

Dos Anjos had come to the cage as an awkward 'circle-and-wait' kickboxer, throwing out the odd strike and then allowing his opponent to do the same in tit-for-tat exchanges. The Brazilian began to turn it around in Rafael Cordeiro's hard sparring gym: Kings MMA. Conor McGregor was outspoken against regular hard sparring and 'gym wars', instead preferring to work on timing and technique, but there is something to be said for it. It forces awkward, timid strikers to realise the importance of getting on offence and denying their opponent the opportunity to do the same. In the case of many fighters, such as Fabrício Werdum or Wanderlei Silva, that means wild and flailing flurries that eventually see a knockout loss by way of a well-timed counterpunch. But dos Anjos was an anomaly. Rather than simply swarming his opponents and attempting to overwhelm them, he developed a pressure fighting game. He cooked opponents.

Pressure is about a fighter's presence and is more about the threat of punches than the ones that are thrown. Much of the pressure fighting approach is down to ring cutting, something that Conor McGregor himself is rather well versed in, often forcing his opponents to the fence with his footwork alone. Dos Anjos, another southpaw, would walk his opponents down and make them work to get away from the fence. He loved to pound in powerful round kicks to the arm and body when the opponent circled to his left. When his opponent pumped out a punch or two, trying to stifle the crushing pressure just for a moment, dos Anjos would move his head and start punching the body and the head, rolling behind his shoulders when the opponent threw back. Where Werdum or Silva were there to be hit but had to keep swinging to keep the opponent's hands up and head down, dos Anjos was always directly in front of his opponent, waiting for them to open up, and then couldn't be hit with a handful of rice when they did. Conor McGregor is a fighter who moves forward and cuts the ring, working offence until the opponent lashes out and then gives ground to counter. Rafael dos Anjos advances menacingly until the opponent lashes out, then stays in the pocket and counters from there. 'Retreat' is not in dos Anjos's lexicon.

This style of fighting is often referred to as offensive counterpunching. It looks a lot like swarming, in terms of its effects on the opponent, but it is more reactive than proactive. The fighter is working on the counter, but advancing the entire time. It is about goading the opponent into picking poor times to throw punches just to keep the pressure fighter away from them, then using these opportunities to get in on exposed ribs and the jawline. It is one of the most difficult styles to learn and carries tremendous dangers, but it is probably responsible for more knockouts and finishes against high-level boxers, kickboxers and martial artists than any other approach. The finishes can be a product of the crisp counterpunches or simply through outright fatigue.

There was just one flaw in his game, one that was going to be as much of a pain for McGregor as it was for dos Anjos himself: he couldn't sell a fight for love nor money. Aldo spoke no English, but he was witty and had presence. All dos Anjos could do was fight. In press conferences, McGregor might as well have been trading barbs with a wooden mannequin.

On 20 January 2016, the UFC held a press conference for UFC 197 with Rafael dos Anjos and Conor McGregor present; they were joined by women's bantamweight champion Holly Holm and her challenger, Miesha Tate. Rumours were swirling that McGregor was pulling power plays with the UFC management. It was starting to sound like the brass had reared a bigger beast than they could keep a leash on. McGregor the company man was now signing his announcements 'McGregor Promotions', in a manner that implied he was co-promoting with the UFC, though this was obviously not true. He arrived at the press conference late, just as Dana White was awkwardly answering a question about his absence and was interrupted by cheers and whoops. Sporting a garish short-sleeved silk shirt that was open all the way down to the solar plexus, a pair of cream slacks and a new buzz cut, McGregor was looking bulkier than usual. Noting his increased musculature, most members of the audience would have recalled John Kavanagh's snappy pre-fight line: 'You've seen Conor on salads... Now watch what he's like on steak.'

Dos Anjos was always a quiet and respectful champion, but that was no protection from McGregor's cutting lines. McGregor announced that he was happy to fight whoever was put against him, but was only interested in belts. He added, 'This man across from me has a title. He has nothing else but that. This is a free TV fighter, he has nothing else to offer me except that gold belt.' McGregor batted off the challenges of top featherweights such as Frankie Edgar as 'desperate' and doubled down on slating dos Anjos by calling him a slower José Aldo. Conor had a point regarding dos Anjos – as exciting as he was in the ring, he was not gifted in or even interested in promoting a fight. In fact, dos Anjos was so uninteresting in his reply that McGregor worked a new angle, pointing out the lightweight champion's move to California and claiming it was a betrayal of his people. McGregor insisted that when José Aldo got off a plane in Brazil, win or lose he was greeted by crowds of his countrymen. But dos Anjos? 'He is, in Brazilian lingo, a gringo.' Sensing that he might be able to cause some controversy, McGregor continued to insist that dos Anjos had given in and learned 'the language of the oppressor'.

The fight was set to go off as the main event UFC 197 on 4 March 2016, but the fight gods had other plans. On 23 February, Rafael dos Anjos was forced to withdraw from the fight with a broken left foot. There was no question of an interim title being made up for the Irishman this time. No matter how personally let down he felt by another barrier being put between him and his dream of a second world title, McGregor understood that UFC 197 was still the Conor McGregor show if he wanted it to be. He had sold the fight, the fans were tuning in for him, and he would only get paid if he got in the cage and fought. As McGregor always insisted, he was there to whoop ass for piles of cash, belt or no belt. The UFC scrambled to find McGregor a replacement opponent, understanding that any featherweight bout would be off the cards just a couple of weeks out from the fight. The men in suits decided on a long-time UFC veteran and MMA bad boy, Nate Diaz.

THE BILLION DOLLAR MAN AND THE STOCKTON SLAPPER

It seemed a strange choice. Nate Diaz had been in an ugly public spat with the UFC over his contract for some time. Diaz had knocked out the ailing Gray Maynard in November 2013 and had then sat out a year in a contract dispute. Despite being one of the UFC's most exciting veterans, and having the most finishes (knockout or submission) in UFC history, Diaz was reportedly only being paid $20,000 to show and another $20,000 to win: an insulting figure for a fighter who had been with the organisation since 2007. Additionally, the UFC's deal with Reebok had hacked away at the revenue of those fan favourites who could make up for their limited UFC payout by procuring numerous sponsorships. Heavyweights such as Fabrício Werdum and Brendan Schaub complained of losing up to $150,000 in sponsorship alone, in return for as little as $2,500 from Reebok's sponsorship deal with the UFC.

During his absence from competition, the UFC announced that Diaz would be fighting Matt Brown at welterweight, a weight that he no longer competed in, and then pulled Diaz from their own rankings. Diaz returned to the cage in December 2014 against Rafael dos Anjos, but came in overweight and looked nothing like his usual self. Diaz finally got back to his usual form with a victory over lightweight up-and-comer Michael Johnson. Diaz, a well-known marijuana enthusiast, was famous for his rambling post-fight speeches, giving shout-outs to seemingly anyone and everyone he had met in the months since the last time he fought, but after he defeated Johnson he gave the crowd something more visceral. In the UFC's programming deal with Fox they have had to be more careful about profanity than they would on their pay-per-views. For some reason, TV audiences are deemed to be too sensitive to hear curse words between the blood and battery of professional fighting. This made for television gold when the UFC's Joe Rogan asked Nate Diaz what he thought of his own performance and Diaz responded with a filth-laden, emotional tirade into the camera lens:

> Fuck that! Conor McGregor, you're takin' everything I worked for, motherfucker. I'm gonna fight your fuckin' ass. You know what's the real fight, the real money fight: it's me. Not these clowns that you already punked at the press conference. Don't no one want to see that. You know you beat them already, that's the easy fight. You want that real shit, right here.

At this point, Joe Rogan had to remove the microphone before more profanity spilled over it. 'Unfortunately we can't talk like that on Fox!' said Rogan, a devout fight fan who was struggling to contain his excitement at the notion of a Diaz–McGregor meeting and his laughter at the daftness of the broadcast team allowing him to interview the notoriously foul-mouthed Diaz on live television. But the seed had been planted, the fans began to wonder about the possibility of two smack-talking finishers meeting in the centre of the ring to goad each other and trade blows. It seemed like something to file away for down the road: there were too many moving parts for that fight to happen when Diaz called for it – he was getting back into the division and Conor McGregor was working on bigger things. Yet that is the way the fight game works: you sign a contract, you pay your coaches, you train for weeks with an absolute obsession on one man – and it can all be pulled out from under you if he gets hurt doing the same.

Nate Diaz stepped into the limelight in accepting the McGregor bout, but he had long been considered the lesser of the Diaz boys. His elder brother Nick Diaz was in the UFC back in 2003, leaving the promotion in 2006 to fight around the world. Nick came to rest in the Strikeforce promotion, where the wily promoter Scott Coker put him to good use as the welterweight champion. Coker realised that Nick Diaz was the most exciting fighter in the world when his fights remained standing. Despite being a jiu-jitsu black belt who came to the boxing game later, Diaz would walk forward eating blows and throwing what appeared to be half-power shots of his own until suddenly his opponent tired. From then on, the remainder of the fight would be Diaz throwing ten-punch combinations against a winded, reeling opponent until they fell. So Coker fed Nick Diaz striker after striker, never making the elder Diaz face the wrestlers who had troubled him in the UFC and who made up most of the welterweight top ten. Meanwhile, Nate Diaz fought his way into the UFC through an early series of *The Ultimate Fighter* and achieved a far more mixed record than his brother, leading to belief that he was the lesser fighter. The difference was that Nate Diaz was fighting the wrestlers, being tested against a varied crop of fighters and growing in the process.

A cult of personality had grown around Nick Diaz. Aloof, stand-offish and socially awkward, he was still capable of some of the most lucid insights and criticisms in the fight game. He was also more quotable than almost any other fighter in mixed martial arts. 'Don't be scared, homie,' has become a standard call out in the MMA world but was born with Nick Diaz. Throughout his career, Diaz has had to deal with numerous suspensions due to his consistent marijuana use and failed drug tests. When asked whether his recreational indulgences threatened to get in the way of his career after his victory over Takanori Gomi was overturned, Diaz responded: 'On the contrary, my fighting career is getting in the way of my marijuana smoking.' Nate, the younger Diaz, idolised his brother and this only helped to keep him in Nick's shadow for much of his career.

A press conference was hurriedly put together for Diaz and McGregor at a UFC gym and McGregor immediately attempted to get under Nate Diaz's skin by referring to him repeatedly as 'Nick's little bro' and speaking to Nick Diaz, who was on the sidelines: 'Relax, Nick, he's doing good up here. He's okay, Nick.' The Irishman carefully repeated anything he had prepared beforehand to make sure that the press got it down, most noticeably, 'He makes gun signs with the right hand and animal balloons with the left hand.' Another line that the featherweight champion ran into the ground was his assertion that Nate Diaz was 'skinny-fat'. Safari imagery also cropped up frequently: McGregor repeated over and over again that Diaz was heavy on his lead leg like a 'wounded gazelle'. McGregor foreshadowed the bout's conclusion beautifully when he stated: 'I'm a lion in there and I'm going to eat you alive. Your little gazelle friends are going to be looking through the cage watching your carcass getting eaten alive and all they're going to say is "We're never crossing this river again."'

Diaz might not have been McGregor's most eloquent opponent, but he seemed the least fazed by the featherweight's antics and the partisan crowd. He simply retorted, 'Fuck you' or 'I don't give a fuck' in any break in McGregor's stream of prepared lines. The presser often devolved into a back and forth of 'I don't give a fuck', 'I don't give a fuck either!'

Nate Diaz had Conor McGregor reeling for a second, however, after declaring that he didn't 'give a fuck' about belts. When McGregor replied that he didn't either, Diaz asked why he was carrying his everywhere with him – and was met with a moment of incredulous speechlessness. It was true: McGregor had been carrying the belt constantly, even when he was just the interim champion. Clearly, he did give a fuck. But Diaz was left speechless himself when McGregor responded to Diaz's assertions that 'everyone is on steroids' by pointing out that of the four members of the famous 'Skrap Pack' – the Diaz brothers, Gilbert Melendez and Jake Shields – half had been caught with banned substances in their system. Two-thirds, if you included Nick's numerous marijuana woes, though those are looked on less stringently than steroid or diuretic use by pundits and fans because it aids the fighter in neither the weight cut nor the bout. Perhaps the most significant insight at the press conference came as McGregor was asked what adjustments he had made to his training to accommodate Diaz's style, which was radically different to that of dos Anjos. McGregor insisted that he didn't prepare for opponents, or any specific set of movements, but for fights. He repeatedly pointed out that the heavyweight Fabrício Werdum had recently turned down a last-minute change of opponent and declared that anyone who did this was a 'pussy'. To McGregor, it seemed, they really were all the same.

At the official pre-fight press conference some days later, McGregor reverted to his usual well-tailored suit, but Nate Diaz wore the same black T-shirt and jeans. Diaz, despite his long tenure as a fighter for the UFC, was not being taken seriously. After answering his first question from the press, an enquiry as to how it felt being in his first main event despite twenty previous fights with the promotion, Diaz was met with a cry of 'Who are ya?' from the crowd, which was met with raucous laughter. When a reporter announced 'Question for the champion, Conor McGregor' the audience applauded and cheered. McGregor dug his fingers into the chip on Diaz's shoulder by drawing attention once again to Diaz's twenty and twenty purse for his last fight, and observing that Diaz's entire purse for a victory was less than a 'Fight of the Night' bonus. Diaz replied that he was a bigger money fight than dos Anjos and that by fighting him McGregor would draw more views. McGregor cut him off swiftly: 'Don't talk about money, you're broke... I could easily switch you up and put you back on that twenty and twenty.' Conor McGregor's ongoing insistence that he chose his opponents and was in a partnership with the UFC was rapidly drawing attention and drew questions from the media in attendance. Many were beginning to see early signs of the UFC creating a monster that it couldn't control. Dana White himself readily admitted that it was extremely difficult to say no to Conor McGregor.

Much of the attention in the press conference was less on the featherweight champion's opponent and more on McGregor's growing star power. One reporter observed that 2015 had been the first year that the UFC's revenue was able to break $600,000 and that McGregor had headlined three cards in that time. It was certainly true that 2015 marked a turnaround for the UFC after a period in which it was thought that the pay-per-view market was dying out – the organisation received less and less revenue through its main means of income year upon year. World Wrestling Entertainment (WWE) had begun moving away from the pay-per-view model on which it had made its billions and had launched its own online service to mitigate the falling popularity of pay-per-view. The UFC's exact buyrates are rarely disclosed and the media mostly works on projections from business insiders such as Dave Meltzer. Most estimates saw the UFC earning around eight million pay-per-view buys through the year, with four cards earning over a million buys.

Those four cards included the first two pay-per-views headlined by Conor McGregor. The other million buy pay-per-view cards were headlined by Ronda Rousey. Her impact on the 2015 growth of the UFC cannot be underestimated, as she transcended the sport of mixed martial arts to become a cultural phenomenon. It helped that Rousey's fights were usually ended quickly, by armbar, and with little blood. She appealed to little girls across the nation. Unfortunately, in November 2015 Rousey had met Holly Holm and had fallen victim to the striking clinic that saw her knocked unconscious in under two rounds. Rousey then disappeared from the UFC, remaining largely silent in the media until the announcement of her UFC 207 return in September 2016. It looked to all intents and purposes as though the UFC had two mega-stars and had lost one of them altogether; McGregor was all that remained. The big dream for the UFC had been to hit the billion-dollar revenue mark, bringing it into conversation with the 'real' sports leagues of America such as the National Football League and National Basketball Association. McGregor, when asked about the viability of the goal, stated, 'I'll hit that billion dollar mark.'

Nate Diaz's response to McGregor's repeated flashing of

cash was: 'Who do you train with?' Diaz asserted that he trained with top ten kickboxers, mixed martial artists and grapplers. Certainly, the Skrap Pack had been floating around the upper end of their weight classes for a long time in mixed martial arts. Diaz also trained regularly with Joe Schilling, one of the United States' best middleweight kickboxers. In Diaz's corner for the bout would be Kron Gracie, the son of the legendary Rickson Gracie and a grappling phenomenon who was threatening a move to mixed martial arts at the time. More than that, Andre Ward – perhaps the finest talent left in the boxing world after the retirement of Floyd Mayweather, Jr – called in Nate Diaz when sparring with southpaws in the lead up to his bout with Chad Dawson. Ward, a defensive genius, would say shortly after the fight:

> He's hard to fight. I mean he's really hard to spar, really. They call it The Stockton Slap. He'll slap you to death, man… Nate helped me get ready for Chad. He always comes in shape, he throws a million different punches from a million different angles.

In terms of training with world-class talent, it was certainly true that Diaz had McGregor pipped. Two Strikeforce welterweight champions, a Strikeforce lightweight champion, an Abu Dhabi Combat Club no-gi grappling world champion all in his camp, and experience sparring the most talented boxer in the world. Meanwhile, Conor McGregor worked with his friends at the Straight Blast Gym in Dublin. Paddy Holohan was making a decent run of it in the UFC flyweight division, but he was not a particularly rounded fighter. A rare blood condition, which hindered the clotting of his blood, would soon force Holohan into a premature retirement in April 2016. Cathal Pendred, the former Cage Warriors welterweight champion had hardly embarrassed himself in the UFC but had scraped some questionable decisions, which saw him become the butt of many jokes among MMA fans. It was thought by many fans that were it not for Conor McGregor's personal influence, Pendred would not have much business hanging around the UFC. Artem Lobov, while McGregor's close friend and travelling companion, was not nearly the same level of fighter as McGregor. Eddie Alvarez would later laugh about warming up in the same area as McGregor and his team ahead of UFC 178:

I remember him bringing in that poor sap, some training partner and Conor just beat the shit out of him for like three hours… I thought it was the funniest shit I'd ever seen… They padded him up with all these pads and Conor just beat the living shit out of this guy, I felt bad for him.

Artem Lobov had a healthier attitude towards his relationship with McGregor than a desire to simply be McGregor's walking heavy bag, but in a candid interview during the Aldo–McGregor world tour he touched on the same issue that Diaz pointed to. The prevailing consensus in the fight world is that a talent can only go so far if he or she is not training with other world-class fighters and sparring partners regularly. Lobov said:

Jiu-jitsu, wrestling, he can do it all and I'm trying to catch up to that level. I think it's almost harder for him because he is better than anyone so you don't know: Where can you go? What is the aim? How far away can you go? How high can you go? How good can you be? Whereas for me, for example, I have a clear target now. There's Conor, I have to catch up to him first and that's been my goal for the last few years.

It is the big fish in a small pond and it had seemed to hold true for much of the modern history of mixed martial arts. Many European fighters such as Alexander Gustafsson and Michael Bisping discovered the sport in their home countries and got into the UFC on their own talents, but made their biggest strides on moving to the United States and training with longer-standing teams of elite professionals. Yet McGregor was happy. He was surrounded by the people who had brought him into the game and who had never failed him. John Kavanagh had talked him around after his first loss, urged him to look at his lengthy rehabilitation as another challenge, and introduced him to all the non-boxing tools that he now loved to practise and utilise. Rolling with grapplers as slick as Paddy Holohan and Cathal Pendred day in and day out had strengthened McGregor's rapidly improving grappling game. But immediate results didn't bother Diaz, who believed McGregor was simply knocking out 'midgets'.

One recent addition to the McGregor team who had raised some eyebrows in the MMA media and fan base was Ido Portal. A skilled gymnast, Portal was one of a new breed of 'movement coaches' who were catching on fast among athletes. McGregor's fascination with human movement was long-standing. Shortly after arriving in the UFC, he had declared that he had a degree in the art of human movement and the art of expressing the body. In an interview with the

Daily Mail in November of 2015, he had declared that he studied 'all types of movement'. Throughout McGregor's career, 'movement' and not 'techniques' have been at the centre of the impromptu lectures he gives in interviews and press conferences. In the same 2015 interview he elaborated:

'I'm fascinated by it so I study all forms of movement, animals because they are graceful and beautiful, I just enjoy movement as a whole. But anyone who is doing anything; I will analyse a man walking down the street to see how they carry themselves. I feel you can tell a lot about someone by the way they carry themselves so I try to move cleanly and efficiently.'

Along with his obsession with movement patterns, another element McGregor was actively trying to implement in his training was a focus on balance, for which he turned to yoga. Speaking to *Muscle and Fitness*, he said: 'If it doesn't involve balance, I don't think it's beneficial. I do yoga every day. I'm perfecting my handstand.' This approach even bleeds through to the weight training he does, which sees him adopt unconventional exercises like a single-legged deadlift to build balance as well as strength and explosive power, and as well as the notoriously crucifying one-legged 'pistol' squat. In the same vein as pistol squats, he also places a high value on any dynamic movements which utilise the body's own weight: pull-ups, muscle-ups and burpees are all grist to the McGregor mill.

Some mixed martial artists such as the welterweight veteran Carlos Condit began working with movement coaches to attempt to minimise their injuries (he had suffered a long-lasting ACL injury, just as McGregor had). This is similar to what many strength and conditioning coaches believe their job is with athletes now: to ensure that the athlete is moving safely through positions where their joints are safely loaded in the hopes of preventing injuries on the field of play. The fight game now incorporates endless gimmicks – such as training masks and breathing through snorkels during cardio – but remains sceptical of change.

For instance, a tradition persists that having sex too close to fight night will drain a man of his 'energies'. Studies have shown that any drop in testosterone after intercourse is extremely short term at most, but tradition is tradition and fighting is a sport where science and old wives' tale meet. While the rest of the fight world focused on High Intensity Interval Training (HIIT) and circuits to boost their cardio, the Diaz brothers competed in triathlons and ironman competitions in-between fights. In many ways they were ahead of the curve, but they had little time for fads. Videos of McGregor and his team performing unusual mobility drills with Portal had been appearing online for months, but Nate Diaz thought it was a waste of time and energy. 'Who do you train with? You got that goofy motherfucker with you... You're playing "touch-butt" with that dork in the park, with the ponytail.'

Things reached fever pitch when the two stared down at the pre-fight press conference: McGregor immaculate in a well-cut suit, Nate Diaz in his standard black T-shirt and jeans. As the two got in each others' faces, posing in their stances, McGregor punched Diaz's lead hand and a tussle ensued. As the camps left the stage, Diaz could be seen shaking his hand off and rumours abounded. While McGregor was unlikely to be trying to hurt his opponent before the fight, an old trick in boxing was to attempt to bruise or damage the opponent's hands on the glove touch before the bout even started. Most fighters leave a hard fight with swollen fists, but damaging the hands early can leave a fighter reluctant to hit with force later in the fight. Some old-timers didn't even engage in the pre-fight glove taps, just to avoid the possibility.

Much was made of the fact that the bout was going to be fought at a catchweight of 170lb. This is the upper limit for the welterweight division, two divisions higher than McGregor's featherweight home. But Diaz didn't consider himself a welterweight, he had made a go of it in that division and had proven too small for the genuine welterweights. The big wrestlers who dried themselves out to make 170lb were just too strong for him. Rory MacDonald – who you will remember for accidentally reinjuring McGregor's knee in training – was able to ragdoll Diaz, hoisting him into the air and slamming him to the mat repeatedly in their bout. But size is a vague term. There is height and reach, and then there is weight. Nate Diaz was not the kind of fighter to make an opponent feel any weight advantage he might have; he didn't hang on to opponents and keep dragging them to the mat, or lean against them on the cage. What became apparent when the two stood at the end of the press conference to have a staredown was that Diaz did have a height and reach advantage, and as a decent boxer he could make great use of both of those.

From the opening bell, McGregor was the fighter on the front foot, advancing on the bigger man and throwing low kicks. Diaz immediately tied up and pushed McGregor to the fence, but did nothing with any real effect. McGregor wasn't immediately struggling with the weight or strength of his opponent, a good sign. Then the left hands started coming in. Diaz would lean back deep into his stance as the left hands came through and seemed to be taking a hellacious beating. He backtracked for much of the first round and by the end of the opening stanza his face was open and the claret was flowing. The amount of scar tissue around Diaz's face made him prone to cutting, a remnant from a youth in less prestigious, bare-knuckle showdowns. But by the end of that first period of action, McGregor had changed from a rounded threat into focusing entirely on his left hand. It happened around the first time Diaz leaned away from a left and timed McGregor with a lead-handed slap as the Irishman was off balance. It was accompanied by a knowing grin. The Stockton Slap: a calling card of both Diaz brothers, it had brought a flush to the cheeks and caused a gritting of the teeth in calmer fighters than McGregor. The hunt was on. All McGregor was concerned with from then on was moving forward and landing left hands. Each time Diaz showed him even a whiff of a jab, McGregor would attempt to slip and counter. This was nothing like the McGregor most fight fans knew.

McGregor at featherweight had dealt in distance, controlling that buffer zone between himself and his opponent and immediately retreating whenever his opponent lashed out at him. Perhaps recognising the range advantage the taller, lengthier Diaz had, he didn't attempt to fade away from Diaz's returns, instead attempting to slip them and close the distance. Leaning well forward of his centre of gravity in an attempt to reach Diaz's head, McGregor was chasing the connections and being met with checking lead hooks and jabs from Diaz. The eyes of the crowd were on McGregor's left hand; it was the most spectacular element of the fight, even when it missed, but Diaz's short connections were disrupting McGregor's rhythm, breaking his concentration and causing him to tire.

When watching a world-class offensive counter fighter in boxing, a fighter who likes to crowd the opponent and counterpunches as they move forwards, you will notice one thing that they have in common: they tend to be moving their head constantly. Think of Mike Tyson or Julio César Chávez. Their head movement was habitual to make them a more difficult target, rather than simply reactionary. McGregor was attempting to react to every punch that Diaz showed him while advancing and this meant that when Diaz feinted with his lead shoulder, McGregor would attempt to slip or duck the punch, only to eat a real one once he had moved his head off line.

Throughout the bout, Conor McGregor's corner were calling for the uppercut. It is reasonable to assume that this was something they had been focusing on for dos Anjos before the last-minute change of opponent. The lightweight champion was a fighter whose head movement in the pocket often brought his head forward of his hips and would make him a good mark for strikes from below. While Diaz was the taller man, he was in the habit of ducking after his engagements in the early going. He would step in to jab McGregor as the Irishman advanced and then duck out. Several booming uppercuts caught Diaz in this bent-over posture in the first round and a lesser fighter might have found himself in serious trouble – as Marcus Brimage had. The more often McGregor went to this punch, though, the harder Diaz's chin went with it. Diaz began to stand upright, sway away in anticipation of the counter uppercut, and to feint McGregor into dropping his hand to begin the uppercut, but jab him in the face inside the attempted counter blow.

In the final moments of the first round, McGregor threw a

lead leg kick, but it was caught and Diaz took him to the mat. McGregor inserted his hooks with his insteps in the inseam of the standing Diaz, catching both feet and sweeping the Brazilian jiu-jitsu black belt in the moments before the round's end. An extremely positive sign for McGregor, whose ground game had always been a talking point among detractors. As the second round progressed, however, McGregor began to tire and his left hands began to fall short far more often than they had previously. Diaz was getting McGregor's timing and reach down, leaning back into his lengthy stance and letting the blows fall short. Diaz's jab and lead hook were still interrupting McGregor's work, but soon he began to land his vaunted one-two. It was by way of the one-two thrown with pinpoint accuracy over and over again that Diaz had outstruck Michael Johnson in his previous bout. Johnson would throw a strike at Diaz, Diaz would lean back with it and return like a Weeble with a crisp two-punch combination. In McGregor's corner Kavanagh repeatedly called for the low kick, and Owen Roddy kept insisting that 'the body's there as well' but McGregor had tunnel vision. He wanted to knock Diaz's head off and he was struggling more and more to connect his power on it cleanly. In the corner Kavanagh remarked to Roddy that McGregor was 'loading up on the left hand' and 'falling in with it and he's just throwing the left'. By the midpoint of round two, Diaz had McGregor's timing and intentions sussed – when McGregor began opening up, he would make sure to be too far away or else get his forearms up and step into McGregor's chest when the shorter man was swinging, crowding him to the point where he could not effectively get his blows through the holes in Diaz's shell.

With two minutes remaining, McGregor unleashed a five-punch flurry and Diaz stepped in to smother it, attempting to slap McGregor as the Irishman exited. As McGregor stepped back to admire his work, Diaz stepped in with a one-two and caught McGregor leaning. McGregor's legs quaked and suddenly Diaz was on the advance. Moments after the UFC had flashed a statistic of each man's 'Time Advancing', which somehow added up to less than 50 per cent of fight time, Diaz had turned the momentum of the contest. Walking McGregor down, all of Diaz's usual habits came to the fore. Slapping McGregor and scoring clean connections with his jab, Diaz threw out his hands and smack-talked the stunned Irishman.

The Stockton slapper rattled off a salvo of blows at the fence and drove into a clinch, pushing McGregor into the cage. A hard knee winded McGregor and the top of Diaz's head came in underneath McGregor's face to pin him to the cage, as Diaz's left hand began to connect unanswered punches to McGregor's head. Pandemonium had broken out in the crowd: McGregor's fifteen-fight winning streak looked to be in dire straits. The fighters were pressed to the fence in front of Diaz's corner and his brother and coaches were in uproar as Diaz pounded in more knees to the midsection. As Diaz broke free of his clinch to let loose with both hands, McGregor began to circle out before stepping in with a flurry of his own to keep Diaz's head down. Diaz waited for a break in the fire and threw out his hands to say 'What?' The featherweight champion stepped in again with a booming left hand and follow-ups, but Diaz leaned back and connected his check hook once more. McGregor dropped his left hand for the uppercut, which had gradually lost all its surprise and was rarely connecting anymore; as his left hand hung low he was stunned momentarily as another one-two hit him clean, and he reeled as a three punch combination glanced him from all angles. The Irishman swallowed his pride and dived for Diaz's legs. The lightweight veteran sprawled hard on McGregor, driving the featherweight face down into the mat underneath him. But McGregor still had hold of one leg, and as he began circling up towards it to salvage his takedown attempt, Diaz snuck a forearm under McGregor's throat and rolled to his back. Trapping one of McGregor's legs to prevent him from advancing, Diaz used his free hand to push McGregor's shoulder away from him in order to sneak the choking arm through in front of McGregor's chest and join his hands. McGregor reacted quickly, as he did against Mendes, rolling his back to the mat to alleviate the pressure and create space to scramble up.

Diaz was having none of it. He was savvier on the ground than Mendes and he stopped McGregor's roll as the Irishman was flat on his back. Diaz slid his right knee across the abdomen of the flattened out McGregor and advanced to mount as if there were no resistance at all. Those years on the ground were paying dividends in seconds on the mat. Diaz sat upright to drop punches on McGregor, who bucked and gave up his back. Diaz began to sneak his right forearm underneath McGregor's chin once again, but lubricated the process with a hard, slapping left punch to the face from behind McGregor. In the moment that McGregor's head was raised by the strike, Diaz drove his forearm through underneath McGregor's chin and there was nowhere left for the Irishman to run. A short, sharp squeeze and McGregor raised his hand to tap Diaz on the arm, 'tapping out' and signalling his submission to the Stockton black belt.

Nate Diaz bounded off McGregor and paraded around the

Octagon, flipping the bird to the fans who had been booing him during his introduction and cheering for McGregor throughout. Flexing his biceps and snarling towards the cameras around the cage, Diaz's face was a mask of blood. To all appearances, it was Diaz who had taken a beating and not the dejected man lying on the mat. Diaz paced the cage, jubilant but still aggressive. As a commission worker laid his hands on Diaz from behind in an attempt to herd him over to his own corner, Diaz turned with his hand cocked and ready to fire.

As the official result was announced, the UFC's Joe Rogan stepped into the cage to interview the victor. 'Nate Diaz, you just shook up the world. How does that feel?' The quieter Diaz leaned into the microphone and took another step out of the shadow of his elder brother, coining the quote that would follow him and McGregor around for the rest of their careers: 'I'm not surprised, motherfuckers.' T-shirts were printed, posters were made, and weeks later a piece of street art immortalised the blood-soaked face of the younger Diaz, flexing his biceps, with the line 'I'm not surprised...' Discussing the details of the bout, and still slowly weeping blood from his cuts (now covered in fresh Vaseline), Nate Diaz remarked that he expected a slow start due to his being out of shape and not being able to get a lot of sparring in for the bout: 'If I had a full camp, I don't think I'd have been touched.' Finally, regarding the finish of the bout Diaz announced, 'I would have a lot more knockouts on my record but as soon as they start getting landed on they start shooting, all of a sudden they're wrestlers.' To end the interview Diaz articulated what had to be a nightmare for the UFC brass: 'There's a new king of this motherfucker now and he's right here.'

Conor McGregor had been pacing listlessly, staring off into the distance this entire time. His hair and beard were dyed in patches with Diaz's blood, where the two had jostled for head position in the clinch and where they had been cheek to cheek as Diaz squeezed on the choke. In bygone eras, an audience would only have access to what was put out through the TV feed, but in 2016 a camera angle that followed only McGregor throughout Diaz's entire post-fight speech was soon released to the public. In this footage, McGregor looked like a man whose entire worldview had crumbled. Fighters who make it to the top of the heap tend to have an unshakeable self-belief that borders on the delusional; those who have this confidence and don't reach the top are typically considered to be mad. Conor McGregor often referenced the self-help book *The Secret* as one of his key influences and was a firm believer in the rule of attraction. His confidence in himself had seemed to be completely justified throughout his UFC run. Indeed, with his predictions of his own knockout victories McGregor had earned the nickname 'Mystic Mac'. To see McGregor lose, a fan would have to scout out videos from small shows back in 2010 or 2008 when he was still very much an incomplete product. For a fight fan it was quite understandable in 2016 to believe that Conor McGregor was near unbeatable based on his results, and that Nate Diaz would be little trouble given his hit-and-miss record. But fighting is about match-ups of individuals and habits, not of records.

As he wandered around the Octagon waiting to be interviewed or allowed to leave, McGregor was met with John Kavanagh. His long-time coach was understandably saddened by the result, but was more concerned with the physical well-being of his friend. In his memoir, Kavanagh would recall promising himself that he would do everything in his power to avoid seeing McGregor absorb such blows again. In calming his charge down, Kavanagh quoted the great Russian heavyweight, Fedor Emelianenko. Emelianenko rarely spoke at length and through his measured responses and his unchanging stoicism even in the middle of a fist fight, the Russian gained a degree of mysticism. When Emelianenko suffered his first real defeat in 2009 he simply remarked that only the man who never stands up can never fall down. Even moments after the bout the loss was just a bump in the road for McGregor and Kavanagh; nothing had changed and nothing had been broken beyond repair.

When Joe Rogan approached McGregor, the latter seemed to be struggling to take the result in. The Irishman remarked that he felt he had been inefficient with his energy while Nate had been efficient. Then he thanked the crowd and ambled off. At the post-fight press conference, McGregor was understated and humble, reiterating his remarks about energy inefficiency and his surprise that Diaz could take the shots so well. When asked what was next for him, McGregor referenced what he had achieved in the featherweight division, gesturing to his ever-present belt, and stated that it might be time to go back down and defend his crown. McGregor also made reference to Diaz's crowding of his combinations: 'In the second round he was coming closer and I was hitting glove. That was kind of draining me.' McGregor was hit with a trickle of sombre questions about his intentions and was visibly irked by a reporter remarking 'now that the winning streak is over', but kept his poise and suggested that he might still want to fight on the UFC 200 card, insisting that he wasn't injured or cut, simply heartbroken.

AN UNEXPECTED RIVAL

Both Nate Diaz and Conor McGregor had arrived at this press conference late, McGregor looking dapper in a light blue suit but lacking his usual sunglasses and allowing the genuine emotion to show in his face. As he entered there was silence from the press. When Nate Diaz arrived some minutes later, in his customary plain black T-shirt and jeans, he was met with a ripple of applause, interrupting another fighter's response to the press. Immediately, Nate was asked what his plan of action was next. He replied: 'I'm at the top, so it's their call what's next. We'll see what happens.'

The fight game often produces its most intense rivalries and its greatest fights seemingly out of nowhere. Not only that, it has a sadistic passion for poetic justice. Conor McGregor submitted to a rear naked choke at the hands of the wounded gazelle. In Portuguese: *mata leão* – quite literally, the 'lion killer'.

7

THE REMATCH

THE GLORIOUS ART OF TALKING BOLLOCKS

When Cassius Clay was taken to a professional wrestling show as a young man, he was lucky enough to see the great heel Gorgeous George in action. In pro wrestling, the performers are either babyfaces or heels. Babyfaces, or 'faces', play by the rules, they stand up for what is right and they overcome the odds and dirty tactics to win. From Hulk Hogan to John Cena, the babyface shifts the merchandise and has the children saying their prayers and eating their vitamins. Conversely, a heel is a coward, looks for every opportunity to get one over on his opponent and will happily cheat or enlist the help of others to win. Many of the greatest wrestlers of all time have done their best work as heels, whipping the crowd into a frenzy. Without a solid heel to build 'heat', a babyface has no interesting matches. It is no secret that many of the all-time greats of professional wrestling have been at their best as heels, from Gorgeous George to Buddy Rogers to Ric Flair. When Gorgeous George came out in his glittering robe, combing his golden locks and talking down to the crowd, he was reviled. But Clay saw the genius of it. He recounted his epiphany in typically rhythmic fashion: 'They hated Gorgeous George, they wanted him beat, but they paid a hundred dollars for ringside seats.'

Cassius Clay, later Muhammad Ali, would become famous for declaring himself 'The Greatest of All Time'. While his accomplishments in the ring eventually made a case for this, and the people came to love and respect Ali, he built himself up on the money and ill will of his detractors. The arrogance of Clay, calling himself the greatest in the history of the boxing game having beaten no one of note! Those who knew the game of boxing couldn't wait for this gangly young braggart to be exposed by Archie Moore. Then by Henry Cooper. Then by the world champion, Sonny Liston. But that moment of comeuppance failed to materialise and Clay kept talking more and more.

There had been braggarts in boxing before Muhammad Ali of course. The morbidly obese slugger 'Two Ton' Tony Galento had talked himself into an undeserved shot at then-heavyweight world champion Joe Louis simply by being an outrageous and unlikeable character. When asked what he thought of being matched with the world heavyweight champion, all Galento had to say was 'Never hearda him' and 'I'll murder the bum.' Before that, Jack Johnson had become the first black heavyweight champion of the world – and rather than pretend to be someone that he wasn't, he exaggerated all the parts of his personality that the average white fight fan hated. An adept clinch fighter, Johnson stalled out many of his opponents by tying them up and tiring them out over many rounds. Late into a boring fight, Johnson was once heckled by a fan in a ringside seat: 'Why don't you fight, you big nigger?' To this Johnson responded over his opponent's shoulder: 'Why? I've already got your ten dollars.'

Conor McGregor's behaviour, attitude and popularity with the casual fan drew many comparisons to Muhammad Ali in the press. When asked about the idea of being an Irish Muhammad Ali at the official UFC 196 press conference, McGregor was unusually humble, replying seriously, 'I cannot accept a comparison like that' but that he was 'honoured to be put in that bracket by some people'. It was doubtless a comparison McGregor appreciated, though: from the declarations of his greatness to his predictions of the rounds in which his opponents would be stopped, McGregor was a fighter in the Ali mould of promotion from top to bottom.

Every example of successful promotion in the history of combat sports has relied on one of three factors: the heat from a smack-talking heel, a reputation for brutal knockout victories, and national (or occasionally racial) pride. Conor McGregor – the trash-talking, concussion-dispensing Irishman – had all three going for him. The problem is that Muhammad Ali imitators are a dime a dozen in combat sports. Anyone can write a couple of lines about their opponent beforehand and repeat them to make sure the press get them down. But if you have a hit-and-miss record, no one will care. The smack talk only matters if the people want to see the fighter eat humble pie. There were plenty of people who tuned in to see Floyd Mayweather, Jr's beautiful boxing technique, but there were plenty more who tuned in each time believing that whichever flavour of the month fighter he was fighting this time might be the one to catch Mayweather out and give him the whooping he deserved. Mayweather himself concisely summarised the importance of a fighter in promoting his own bouts when he said, 'Closed mouths don't get fed.'

'SHUT HIM UP'

The genius of trash talking is that it sells fights but can also affect the opponent. The prospect of making the other man eat crow can cloud the mind of even the most experienced fighter, to the point that he will rush or make mistakes or abandon the game plan that he has spent the previous few months training to apply. The attention brought to the fight by the opponent suddenly becomes popular pressure on him to do a public service and knock the guy out. Henry Cooper recounted that he used to have people approaching him on the street to encourage him for his fight with Cassius Clay and imploring Cooper to 'Shut him up!' Sonny Liston was the victim of Clay's most prolonged and extravagant campaign of verbal abuse and was clearly riled up by the challenger's comments. Liston declared that he had a secret punch he'd been working on called 'The Lip Buttoner'. But if that was true, it mattered little: Liston was never afforded even a chance to land it, as Clay danced around him beautifully for seven rounds before the fight was waved off.

Yet once the fighter is forced to eat crow, once he has to admit he isn't the best in the world, that interest is gone. The danger that Conor McGregor now faced was that he had suffered the crushing defeat that had always served as the teaser to buy his fights. Every quip he made or phrase he coined could be countered with, 'Remember when Nate Diaz choked out Conor McGregor?'

It didn't help that so many of McGregor's disdainful pre-fight remarks about his opponents had come back to haunt him. The Irishman had insisted that once his opponents felt his left hand, they suddenly turned into 'panic wrestlers'. The sound bite was brilliant and when overlaid with the footage of the finish could match up perfectly with Nate Diaz's left hand wobbling McGregor to his feet, and the Irishman shooting a takedown attempt to escape trouble. Hardly something to be scoffed at, McGregor did exactly what every good fighter should do when hurt – he attempted to close the distance and tie Diaz up either in a clinch or on the mat in order to evade further strikes and clear his head. But that is the nature of trash talk: if you talk a big game the moment that you cannot back it up, it will be turned against you. Another remark that resonated with the audience was McGregor's assertion that Nate Diaz taught children's jiu-jitsu classes on a Sunday morning. Naturally, as soon as McGregor had been submitted by the Stocktonite, images of McGregor's face photoshopped onto kids in BJJ classes started to do the rounds.

One loss was more than enough for the people to stop caring about the British boxer Naseem Hamed. His career had been marked by trash talk and incredible knockouts until he met Marco Antonio Barrera, who picked the slugger from Sheffield apart. Hamed took another fight, boxing smartly over the distance to take the IBO title from Manuel Calvo, seemingly to prove that he didn't just need the knockout, but he was booed throughout for not being the cocky knockout artist of old. It just wasn't the same and he retired shortly afterward. For most great trash talkers, there is a chance to rebound, though, as long as they can argue that they'd simply made a mistake when they were defeated, or had

had an off night. The thing that no trash talker can do is accept that he has lost to a better man – if he does so, he risks becoming just another fighter in a competitive division. There is no joy to be gleaned from watching a pretty good fighter lose. The best he can hope for at that point is that he becomes a sympathetic figure.

A fighter can talk all the witty, cutting trash in the world, but he won't get the crowds interested if he can't win the fights. For confirmation of that, one need only look at the career trajectory of Chael Sonnen (who you will remember attempted to trademark 'Red Panty Night'). He became one of the UFC's biggest stars by means of his terrific wit, the larger-than-life character he portrayed, and a heap of homages to professional wrestling's greatest heels. A Chael Sonnen promo might contain lines from 'Superstar' Billy Graham, Scott Hall and Ric Flair, with the names of his rivals inserted where relevant. After giving the middleweight champion Anderson Silva the hardest fight of his UFC career, Sonnen failed a drug test and was handed a lengthy suspension. Following a successful return to the cage against Brian Stann, Sonnen was approached for an in-cage interview by Joe Rogan. Ignoring the question he was asked, Sonnen cut a promo:

Anderson Silva, you absolutely suck. Super Bowl weekend, the biggest rematch in the history of the business. I'm calling you out Silva, but we're upping the stakes. I beat you, you leave the division. You beat me, I will leave the UFC forever.

It was clearly ridiculous. With Sonnen's brand soaring, the UFC would never have allowed him to leave, even if he lost to Silva. Yet the fans gobbled it up! The post-fight interview received more attention than Sonnen's submission victory and overshadowed the rest of the card. The rematch between Chael Sonnen and Anderson Silva drew almost a million pay-per-view buys, a break from the UFC's continually declining buyrates, and drew $7 million at the gate alone. Sonnen lost far more decisively than in the first match (helped by the fact that a number of flagrant fouls by Silva went unpunished) but he had done exactly what he set out to do: he made the biggest rematch in the sport.

But as the losses began to add up, Sonnen did himself no favours by becoming a comic character rather than a detestable heel. After losing to Anderson Silva, Sonnen opted to go a bizarre route. Rather than give the fans the 'I just made a mistake, he got lucky and it won't happen again' style line they were after, he repeatedly joked that he was the real middleweight champion. 'I am the middleweight champion... and I am willing to give Anderson a shot at the true belt, the linear belt, the people's belt.' After each loss, he would claim to still be undefeated. It was funny and self-effacing and charming, but self-deprecation doesn't make people want to watch you fight.

UFC 200 – MCGREGOR VERSUS LESNAR

Conor McGregor was not Chael Sonnen, though. He had the chance to rebound. In the depths of his post-UFC 196 melancholy the featherweight champion had hinted that he would take a step back and return to featherweight to defend his world title, but he had also hinted that he would like to take part on the UFC 200 card. UFC 100 and UFC 200 had little reason to mean anything as anniversaries, as the UFC had hosted far more than that number of cards and there was even a UFC 37.5 and two cancelled pay-per-views to throw the numbering system off entirely, but they took on that role in the minds of the general public. UFC 100 on 11 July 2009 had sold an amazing 1.6 million pay-per-views, the most of any card in UFC history.

UFC 100 was a significant event for the '100' number, but it was also headlined by Brock Lesnar, the biggest star in the history of the sport. How was Lesnar so successful? This is where we see that cross-over with professional wrestling once again. Lesnar was literally a professional wrestler. Having gone into professional wrestling straight from an outstanding amateur wrestling career, Lesnar had been one of the biggest stars in WWE for some time. His size and athleticism was the main appeal – a near-300lb man who could perform backflips and high flying manoeuvres as well as the big slams and suplexes. When Lesnar wanted to try his hand at mixed martial arts, the UFC brought him on board quickly and he was able to win the heavyweight title on a short path through the mediocre division.

Conor McGregor's desire to be the greatest attraction in mixed martial arts likely had something to do with his desire to headline the UFC 200 card. He was a genius of self-promotion, and one of the few fighters to appreciate fighting as a business; plus, he was laser-focused on prize money and buyrates. McGregor had to know that while his success was an anomaly in an era of declining pay-per-view sales, he was not on Brock Lesnar's level as a PPV attraction. The first four pay-per-views Lesnar headlined with the UFC broke one million buys, and two of them came closer to two million – the magic number that the UFC has never been able to reach.

But Lesnar also had something that McGregor lacked: freak appeal. Cutting weight to make the UFC's upper weight limit of 265lb, Lesnar was a terrifying figure in the largest weight class in the sport. The heavyweight division has always had that absolute appeal, while the lighter weight classes have been the business of the fight connoisseur. To put McGregor's pay-per-view accomplishments in perspective, consider that José Aldo's last title fight before Conor McGregor, a hotly anticipated rematch with the surging Chad Mendes that turned into a fight-of-the-year candidate, managed just 180,000 buys. When the UFC doubled up, placing the bantamweight champion Dominick Cruz and José Aldo in different fights on the same card, they managed 230,000. As an asset, McGregor was worth several times what most other champions were to the UFC.

While Conor McGregor might have threatened to defend his featherweight belt, he, Dana White, and Lorenzo Fertitta all had to know that the biggest fight they could make in the sport right now was the Conor McGregor–Nate Diaz rematch. It was risky: a second loss to Diaz might kill the McGregor momentum altogether. All the trash talk in the world can't interest people in a fighter who is just good. Brock Lesnar's pay-per-view numbers were built on his being an unstoppable monster and were split in half after he lost the UFC heavyweight title in convincing fashion. Yet there was little hesitation: just thirteen days after McGregor had seen his winning streak shattered, Ariel Helwani reported that negotiations were in the works for McGregor–Diaz II. Twelve days later, it was made official by Dana White, who added that the first fight at UFC 196 surpassed UFC 100's record buyrate. An incredible feat, which begged the question: was

Diaz right when he said he was a bigger money fight than dos Anjos? Or was McGregor's star power alone enough to draw the largest pay-per-view audience in UFC history?

Tickets for UFC events come with an important piece of fine print: 'card liable to change'. No sport is affected by injuries in quite the way the fight game is. If you go to watch a team game, you might not get to see your favourite player but the team will show up and the match will go ahead. If you go to watch a day of tennis or golf, you will still see plenty of stars in the tournament, even if your favourite player is sidelined. But in the UFC, where whole cards are sold on the attraction of one or two fights or fighters, fans can sometimes get the worst of it. Usually, the UFC will stack its big events to the rafters with strong, relevant fights, perhaps with a couple in the same weight class as the main event so that if the worst comes to the worst they can bump a fighter up the card and into a spot vacated by injury.

After months of speculating over whether the UFC was putting all its eggs into the McGregor basket, and whether they gave McGregor too much leeway, the fighter himself decided not to attend a press conference to advertise the Diaz rematch. This was where the conflict between the act of fighting and the business of fighting emerged in one of the greatest practitioners of both. Conor McGregor had flown to Iceland to prepare for what was clearly the most important fight of his career. For him, there was no time to fly back and forth, changing locations and missing training sessions or having to substitute them with sessions with Artem Lobov under less than optimal conditions. The featherweight champion was putting his fighting first, but both he and the UFC understood that his fighting was just one aspect of his worth. Where

McGregor made the money was in the press conferences and interviews, giving outrageous and funny quotes that got people riled up and rooting passionately for him to win or lose. McGregor made it clear that he was not going to fly to the USA to shoot a commercial or take part in press events for this fight. Previously the UFC had proven to be as hard line on its media commitments as it could, cancelling the hotly anticipated fight between Georges St-Pierre and Nate Diaz's older brother Nick, because the latter no-showed a press conference in 2011. The two parties were at an impasse.

IRELAND'S RIGHT TO FIGHT

On 19 April 2016, Conor McGregor sent the MMA world into panic with a thirteen-word Twitter statement:

I have decided to retire young.
Thanks for the cheese.
Catch ya's later.

This was the first that most in the MMA world had heard of the tensions surrounding UFC 200 and the organisation's officials were bombarded with media requests and questions from fans via social media. It seemed unthinkable for a man at the peak of his craft, making increasingly impressive payouts and achieving more and more recognition in the mainstream media, to quit the game so abruptly. To most, it appeared as though this was simply a stunt to shock the public and demonstrate McGregor's worth to the UFC. Even Straight Blast Gym's head coach John Kavanagh joined in with the poking of the bear, using Twitter to send out the message 'It was fun while it lasted.'

Yet there was some reason to believe that Conor McGregor was serious. On 12 April, just weeks after his loss to Nate Diaz and seven days before his alleged retirement, the mixed martial arts world was shaken by the death of Joao Carvalho. A Portuguese fighter, Carvalho was competing in Ireland under the banner of Total Extreme Fighting in Dublin's National Stadium. His opponent was Charlie Ward, a Straight Blast Gym representative and one of Conor McGregor's training partners. John Kavanagh was in Ward's corner and McGregor was ringside for the first major tragedy that mixed martial arts in Ireland had faced.

Not being recognised by Sport Ireland, mixed martial arts had no legal standards or regulatory body. Boxing in most first-world nations has benefited enormously from enquiries into deaths and the strict regulation of bouts with minimum standards for post-knockout care. Mixed martial arts in Ireland was still the Wild West. Not illegal, but completely uncontrolled by a governing body. Even as John Kavanagh and others work towards getting mixed martial arts recognised by Sport Ireland and forming a national governing body, organisations such as the Irish Martial Arts Committee are keen to denounce the sport as 'pornographic, sadistic and voyeuristic to its core'. Whether or not Total Extreme Fighting's post-knockout care was inadequate is a matter that should be looked into by a sanctioning body, but the alarming part for a fight fan was that the bout itself was nothing unusual. In the third round, Carvalho took a hard blow and stumbled backwards onto the fence, traded punches with Ward and then fell to his knees. Ward was able to ride the side of Carvalho as he was turtled and throw in nine good punches, which warranted a stoppage as Carvalho was deemed to be not intelligently defending himself. He later died in hospital of a brain haemorrhage.

While Conor McGregor had achieved superstar status in Ireland, the sport of mixed martial arts was still taking a kicking in the court of public opinion. The passing of Joao Carvalho allowed many in the press to get on their soap boxes, but the longer the rants continued it became clear that many who wanted it banned had no idea of the details of the situation. Comparisons to the gladiatorial contests of Rome were standard, as were the observations that MMA fighters are stripped to the waist and locked in a cage – as if they have no say in the matter.

This ignores completely the fact that professional mixed martial artists are engaged in an occupation they chose and enjoy, and are getting financially compensated for their performance. Charles Barron, a member of the New York State Assembly, attempted to turn professional fighting into a race issue right off the bat by declaring: 'Firstly, as an African American we have been in cages fighting on the plantations.' Barron apparently felt strongly against legalising professional mixed martial arts because it was akin to making two slaves fight, conveniently ignoring the fact that amateur mixed martial arts was already completely legal in New York. It would have been interesting to hear Barron explain to black New Yorker and top-tier bantamweight Aljamain Sterling that he could not be paid to fight in New York because that was something like slavery, although he would be more than welcome to compete as an unpaid amateur. Barron stirred things up even further by referencing the case of Eric Garner, who died from compression of the neck after being held down by police, insisting, 'You know how we feel about the chokehold in New York City.' The scaremongering regarding MMA can be outright hilarious, but the saddest thing is that any MMA fan could probably make a better case for banning the sport than anyone who gets to vote on these things.

Returning to the Emerald Isle, *The Irish Times*, in a story titled 'Death of Carvalho is an Inevitable Outcome of Mixed Martial Arts', insisted that 'in MMA the rules give license to attack opponents, who may already be brain damaged' and gave a poorly thought-out comparison with boxing where 'a knock down, or potential brain trauma, stops the fight [...] The referee inspects the boxer, who either takes a mandatory 10-second count or is told that his fight is finished. In MMA a knock down, or brain trauma, represents opportunity. It is an invitation, an opening for the dominant fighter to secure victory by inflicting more punishment on an opponent.' The argument that the standing-eight count makes the sport of boxing safer is as vacuous a case as you could make with little to back it up. A boxer can take a knockdown blow, suffer a concussion, be given time to recover his senses, and if he can stand under his own weight he can still beat the count twice to continue taking punishment. The nature of mixed martial arts, as brutal as it is, is that it doesn't give a fighter breathing room to pretend that he is okay. Far, far more fights in mixed martial arts are stopped as a result of the first knockdown and an attempt to follow up, than on the first knockdown in boxing.

Many criticisms of mixed martial arts are wildly inaccurate. A remarkable number of the most vocal opponents of the sport regularly refer to kicking downed opponents, something that is illegal under the Unified Rules of MMA, which all major Western promotions use. Joe Duffy, a radio host for Ireland's national broadcaster RTE, and a moaning reminder of the good old days that never actually existed, conducted an entire episode of his radio show discussing the death of Carvalho wherein he and countless others offered little but despair and controversial comment. It started off well, as Duffy seemed upset that the two men were not wearing headgear or 'foot protection', but he expressed his greater incredulity that there were women in the audience holding pints. A handful of calls came in from various parts of the country decrying MMA and summing up perfectly the lack of understanding of the sport. Numerous callers insisted that 'they' should at least make the fighters wear headgear, one caller actually saying 'at least then the brain will be saved'.

Research over recent years has shown that headgear does little to stop trauma to the brain – in fact, the additional weight of the headgear in boxing or helmet in American football can simply provide more weight to the head as it is knocked around. Headgear, like the use of gloves, simply lowers the likelihood of cutting the skin. Many laymen equate less blood with less brain trauma, but that is unfortunately not true. In fact, the padding over the skin and bone leads to many NFL players diving head-first into collisions that they would never dream of attempting without a helmet. One such study, published in the March 2011 issue of *The British Medical Journal*, came to the conclusion on headgear and mouthguards that there was 'no good evidence that they can help prevent concussion, and paradoxically, they may even encourage players to take greater risks'. But studies don't change the public perception of brutality. When headgear was dropped for the boxing in the 2016 Rio de Janeiro Olympics (curiously, only for men), many boxing publications applauded the decision to respond to the increasing amount of research on concussions and headgear. Yet *Newsday*, in an article titled 'Without Headgear Boxing is Bloody Again' treated the decision as one to appeal to more fans though 'the sight of blood on a fighter's face and chest is common – and an undeniable part of the sport's primal lure'. The great difficulty in getting combat sports accepted – or at least tolerated – is trying to cut down on the blood to appease outsiders without covering the fighters with unnecessary padding that only serves to add weight to impacts and increase the likelihood of brain damage. The greatest irony of all is that gloves only protect the puncher's hands: in a bare-knuckle fight, blows to the head are used more cautiously, less frequently and with less force, as the bones of the hand are far more brittle than those of the skull.

Conor McGregor himself came under fire simply for being present and for his success. RTE's Joe Duffy laid into the UFC featherweight champion by playing an interview from after the fight, before anyone was aware of the extent of Carvalho's injuries, wherein McGregor said that he was happy for Ward and that he thought it was a great performance. In Duffy's opinion, anyone who had been ringside for the 'nine digs to the side of the head' that concluded the fight 'could never use the words "awesome, great fight, great performance"'.

Amid the argument between supporters and the critics of the sport, Conor McGregor, John Kavanagh and every fighter in Ireland ruminated on the uncomfortable truth. It is something that every fight fan has to accept eventually too: death *is* a possibility in combat sports. The miracle is that combat sports have managed to keep their death rates as low as rugby or American football or even football, despite violence being the prime intention in combat sports and somewhat extracurricular in other sports. There are deaths in the fight game that could be prevented and are truly harrowing. The sight of Emile Griffith savagely beating the unconscious Benny Paret, as the latter was held up by the ropes and the referee was late to intervene, is shocking. Or to witness Gerald McClellan's bizarre behaviour through his bout with Nigel Benn – which should have seen his corner, the doctor, or the referee questioning his well-being, but concluded in his collapse after the fight. McClellan survived but lost his vision, hearing, and ability to walk. The problem is that plenty of the deaths in combat sports happen in largely unremarkable fights. There have been a thousand late stoppages that have produced no fatalities. In fact, the footage of the Charlie Ward–Joao Carvalho bout is abhorrent for the usual reasons to those who don't know the sport (a man being held and hit while turtled), but to the regular fight viewer with no knowledge of the aftermath it was completely unremarkable aside from being a hard-fought bout. The stoppage was not particularly heinous, the referee did not seem to disregard Carvalho's safety or fail him at any point, and yet that fight ended in tragedy while far uglier, more gruelling fights have left the competitors perfectly healthy. Well, perfectly healthy on the outside except for a little bruising.

The other aspect of fighting brought home by Carvalho's death was that of cumulative damage. This is an idea that every fighter knows is not just a risk but pretty much a guarantee, given his career choice, yet it is treated as the word 'Macbeth' is in the theatre. It is rarely spoken about for fear of jinxing it or having to openly accept it as an inevitability. A fighter competing in a combat sport – in fact, an athlete competing in any contact sport – is going to receive his fair share of knocks.

That is why the mantra always repeated by everyone in the fight game, from fighters to trainers to managers to journalists, is 'get in, get rich, get out while you are young'. As these knocks accumulate, the signs of *dementia pugilistica* start to show through. Colloquially termed 'punch drunk', this condition is routinely manifested in older boxers who display a slowing of speech, a slurring of words and in more serious cases memory loss. Like combat sports fatalities, we know exactly what causes it but it seems largely random in its severity. Jake LaMotta, the inspiration for Martin Scorsese's brilliant *Raging Bull*, fought 106 professional bouts and is still lucid and sharp as a knife in his nineties. What's more, he was famous for his tremendous chin and ability to take a punch, something you don't typically get famous for if you can avoid the blows. Meanwhile, Jerry Quarry had half as many fights in a terrific career, taking on Joe Frazier, Muhammad Ali, Earnie Shavers, Ken Norton and Floyd Patterson. Quarry retired in 1992 and by 1995 was being cared for by his younger brother, unable to dress himself and barely aware of his surroundings. Quarry's younger brother gave this heartbreaking quote to the *Los Angeles Times* in October 1995:

> We've lived in this house for four months, and he can't find the bathroom or his bedroom. He's walked out and we've had to call the police to find him. He'll leave at 5 o'clock in the morning, so he has to be watched 24 hours a day. If he gets milk out of the refrigerator, he can't remember where it goes back. He's not violent. He's happy. He lives in a small world... My father has to take responsibility, but he won't. He has to take responsibility that it was him that put us in boxing, him that made us not be quitters and take more punishment than was necessary.

And yet George Chuvalo, one of Quarry's peers, who fought many of the same men and took hellacious beatings – including the blows of George Foreman – is still eloquent and clear-thinking in his seventies. The degree of symptoms suffered seems not to reflect the nature of the fights these men are in. That is perhaps the most terrifying part for a fighter or spectator of this sport: no one escapes without taking blows to the head and yet there seems to be no consistency in how these strikes will manifest themselves in later life.

John Kavanagh was certainly hit hard by the death of Carvalho. One of the driving forces for the growth of MMA and its regulation in Ireland, Kavanagh lost sleep over the bout and even questioned his involvement and future in the sport. Thankfully for MMA in Ireland, Kavanagh moved past the tragedy and continued to push Sport Ireland to recognise and regulate mixed martial arts. Conor McGregor, meanwhile, was acutely aware of the dangers of repeated strikes to the head. In the first UFC 196 press conference with Nate Diaz, McGregor was asked about the possible opponents he had been offered to replace Rafael dos Anjos and the conversation got around to José Aldo. McGregor asserted that after being knocked out like that he should take at least ten months off. The crowd, having been enjoying a standard McGregor press conference up to that point, chuckled. McGregor seemed genuinely irked by this: 'You can't bounce back into a fight. And that's no joke! Everyone laughed there! You can't take head trauma and bounce back into the gym and spar.' The idea that fighters who can limit the head trauma will get away with a clean bill of brain health has proven to be another incorrect assumption. When the promising Bellator MMA fighter Jordan Parsons was killed in a hit-and-run accident, the autopsy report turned a tragedy into a stark and startling warning about head trauma. Parsons had just thirteen fights on his record and had only suffered one knockout loss, yet his brain was suffering from chronic traumatic encephalopathy (CTE). A handful of fights, a single knockout loss, and this twenty-five-year-old prospect was already suffering from a degenerative brain disease. To John Kavanagh's enormous credit, in December 2016 he announced: 'For 2017 ALL SBG fighters, both amateur and professional, will be getting a one off brain scan to make sure there's no underlying issues that would preclude them from competing. It is not yet a requirement to get this done to compete on shows but it will be a requirement to represent SBG.'

Fear of absorbing punishment is one thing, but Conor McGregor held one of the highest knockout ratios in UFC history – knockout ratio meaning the percentage of a fighter's victories that came by knockout or technical knockout: a big selling point for fighters. Not only did McGregor have to contend with a stark reminder of his own mortality, he also had to acknowledge that he was probably inflicting brain damage on other athletes. His official statement after the bout read:

Terrible news regarding Joao Carvalho. To see a young man doing what he loves, competing for a chance at a better life, and then to have it taken away is truly heartbreaking. We are just men and women doing something we love in the hope of a better life for ourselves and our families. Nobody involved in combat sports of any kind wants to see this. It is such a rare occurrence that I don't know how to take this. I was ringside supporting my team mate, and the fight was so back and forth, that I just can't understand it.

Conor McGregor's later remarks in an interview with fitness periodical *Men's Health* reflected the pressure he felt as the face of mixed martial arts in Ireland – and as a name mentioned in every criticism of the sport through the Irish press. 'How do I feel?' he asked. 'How would you feel? [...] It's fucked up. I wasn't just watching that fight. I helped train a guy to kill someone, and then someone wound up dying.'

Unlike stars in other major sports, fighters receive no salary. They fight for a purse and a win bonus, which is usually equal to their 'show money'. Victory in combat sports can be taking food off the other man's table, cutting his payout in half with the bonus of handing him brain trauma. This made the UFC's 'Knockout of the Night' bonus even more bizarre and the company recently made the move to drop this in favour of 'Performance of the Night' bonuses – usually given for knockouts but not openly incentivising brain trauma in a way that could look bad in the future, when more fighters have had their brains autopsied. While it seemed as though McGregor's desire to stay in Iceland to train was the crux of his threatened retirement, Ariel Helwani speculated on the significance of the death and the general feeling in the SBG camp. In a discussion with Luke Thomas for MMAFighting. com, Helwani stated:

I don't think that we can just brush that aside. Based off of the discussions that I've had, and knowing Conor like I do, the idea of going to Las Vegas and promoting a fight and just pretending like all's well in the fight game after witnessing something like that first hand. It's a tough, tough thing for a young man to swallow, at least one in his shoes. And I believe that's perhaps one of the reasons why he wasn't willing to go to Las Vegas to promote this fight.

THE DEBACLE

Regardless of how much Conor McGregor was shaken by the death of Joao Carvalho and negative press bombardment of his career in Ireland, his timely retirement seemed a clear response to the UFC's insistence that he attend press events and shoot the commercial for the pay-per-view in the United States. Hours after McGregor's retirement, Dana White appeared on the ESPN television show *SportsCenter* to announce that McGregor was off the UFC 200 card. Nate Diaz was flown into Las Vegas to negotiate an alternative fight and the hunt was on for a new main event. The UFC proceeded with the press conference, making the bizarre decision to have an empty chair opposite Nate Diaz in place of Conor McGregor.

Despite his public announcement that the Irishman was off the card, Dana White was immediately asked about the absence of McGregor. Even when he wasn't there, McGregor seemed to be the star attraction of the event. The overwhelming view of the crowd seemed to be that White should make an exception and let McGregor compete on the card without his media commitments. In one of his most candid moments, White turned down every attempt to talk him around with the simple observation that it wouldn't be fair:

Anybody who is sitting up here and anybody who has fought for the UFC in the last sixteen years knows that we try to give as much leeway as we can on things, but you have to show up to promote the fight. You have to show up to the press conferences and shoot the commercials... These guys all came, they have better things to do and they're here... We gave Conor every opportunity in the world to get here too.

Pushed again, White posed a rhetorical question:

Is that fair? [...] I don't know if you guys remember the last time Conor was fighting José [Aldo]. José's sister was getting married and he was sitting right here. José flew in for that press conference... It's part of the job, it's the one thing that you have to do.

But this wasn't just about fairness. This was the UFC's own monster turning around and biting them. They had given McGregor every favour they could and now he was in danger of growing bigger than the brand itself. Dana White said:

We get criticised a lot for bending too much for Conor, and we do. Conor is a guy who has stepped up and fought in big fights on short notice, and I respect Conor very much as a fighter, and I like him, but you have to show up and do this stuff.

While White insisted that Nate Diaz would be found another opponent, Diaz immediately sank the idea when asked if he had an opponent in mind:

I came to fight Conor McGregor and I don't have too much interest in anybody else. I don't have an interest in fighting at all, but I thought we were going to do it... I didn't ask for that fight, but he asked for it and he wanted it. If that ain't going to happen I'm going on vacation.

Helwani pushed Diaz, knowing that the Diaz brothers both had a distaste for press conferences themselves. Would Diaz still fight McGregor at UFC 200 if Dana White would let him? Diaz understood McGregor's disinterest in the press conference, but nonetheless jibed the absent Irishman by noting: 'He's got a lot of catching up to do so he ain't got time for all this shit.'

Dana White's bald head was beginning to flush as he was showered with boos each time he had to reiterate that yes, Conor McGregor was definitely, finally and absolutely off the UFC 200 card. After Diaz had said that he would still fight McGregor, Helwani pushed the issue and played to the crowd by asking White that if all parties still wanted the fight, why not make the fight? White was crystal clear: 'The fight's still three months away. That's why we do it this early so that we try not to interfere with their training and their lives and everything else.' He continued, asking rhetorically, 'We're spending ten million dollars on marketing this fight and we can't even shoot a commercial with the main event?'

Dana White assured everyone that a new main event for UFC 200 would be found and the crowd left unhappy. It seemed as though the empty chair had fans expecting a sudden walk-on by McGregor to reveal that the card was still going off as it was originally intended. Unfortunately, that would be a little too contrived, a little too much like professional wrestling. McGregor, having watched the press conference from Iceland, again took to Twitter for a minimalist comment on the current state of affairs: 'Everyone flew in. Respect. But not everyone up there made the company 400 million in 8 months.'

The UFC 200 event proved to be a continuing disaster for Zuffa LLC. The parent company of the UFC was in the process of selling the Ultimate Fighting Championship to William Morris Endeavour Entertainment (WME-IMG) for the unfathomable sum of $4.2 billion, but the signatures were not on the paper yet. This was without a doubt the highest-profile, most important event in UFC history and they had lost their biggest star due to behind-the-scenes bickering. The UFC salvaged the card on paper when it signed light heavyweights Jon Jones and Daniel Cormier to the main event to unify the light heavyweight title. Cormier was the champion, but Jones had never lost the belt – rather being stripped of it due to his continuingly irresponsible behaviour outside the ring and his run-ins with the law. News broke on 7 July, just two days before the show, that Jon Jones tested positive for oestrogen blockers and could not be allowed to compete. In desperation, the UFC did something unprecedented – they called in all the favours they could and borrowed a talent from World Wrestling Entertainment.

The man to replace Conor McGregor? Brock Lesnar. The gigantic heavyweight returned to face knockout artist Mark Hunt at short notice. It would technically be the co-main event with a women's title fight going on last, but everyone knew that Lesnar was there to shift pay-per-view buys. Grinding out an ugly but still impressive decision victory over his top-ten-ranked opponent after almost half a decade away from the game, Lesnar was paid a disclosed $2.5 million for his troubles – then promptly failed a drug test. UFC 200, the UFC's big anniversary show packed to the rafters with top talent and with two title fights on the card, managed an impressive 1.2 million buys. But Conor McGregor and Nate Diaz had already outsold that with few special measures taken by the company to ensure that everyone knew how big the card should be.

Whatever the case, the UFC scraped together a passable marquee fight at the last minute and on 11 July, two days after UFC 200, the UFC was sold for $4 billion in the most expensive purchase of a sporting league in history. Ultimately, Dana White's absolute on press conference attendance was undermined just months later, in December 2016, when Ronda Rousey was coaxed back to headline UFC 207. Rousey, increasingly media averse since her crushing loss to Holly Holm a year earlier, was allowed to skip all media commitments.

THE REMATCH

In the days after Conor McGregor's removal from the UFC 200 card and 'retirement', speculation ran rampant. Many looked for McGregor's next move. Would he go independent and make his own McGregor Promotions an actual organisation, as many top boxers have? Perhaps he would go to the UFC's biggest competitor, Viacom's Bellator MMA. Certainly, if he threatened to, he would have tremendous leverage against the UFC in negotiations. Or maybe he would take up one of the many boxers talking about him. Amir Khan or Canelo Alvarez? Surely the most sensible fight to make if he were getting out of the MMA business would be that billion-dollar fight with Floyd Mayweather, Jr? Could he go to Japan or the Netherlands and join one of the big kickboxing companies as a work around to his UFC contract for mixed martial arts competition?

Unfortunately, none of those were feasible options for Conor McGregor. Anyone who understood the UFC's contracts knew that McGregor wouldn't have a leg to stand on if he attempted to compete elsewhere. The UFC's contracts prevent fighters from competing in other combat sports, such as boxing or kickboxing, because it would be daft to let fighters take brain trauma for money while the UFC benefited in no way. Any money made from a boxing match with Floyd Mayweather, Jr would likely then be lost in a lawsuit with Zuffa. The UFC has generally been more lenient regarding pure grappling competition, which can cause broken bones and torn ligaments, but generally isn't a huge money business. Moreover, it is unlikely to hurry a fighter's shelf life along as it is essentially the kind of sparring most fighters do every day. Many MMA fighters will take grappling matches with major events such as Metamoris or Polaris during their downtime while recovering from hard fights or suspended for medical or legal reasons. Occasionally, top UFC fighters such as Georges St-Pierre, Benson Henderson or Fabrício Werdum will be allowed to compete in the ADCC no-gi championships, which are held every two years and are considered the most prestigious event in the no-gi grappling world. But these are side projects. There is little money in professional grappling, and no grappling organisation could offer McGregor the reported multi-million dollar paydays he had been making recently.

The UFC's contracts are generally strict regarding activities that are likely to get fighters hurt and affect the timing of events. Funnily enough, it was the injury-prone José Aldo who prompted a review of the 'dangerous activities' when he was forced out of a fight by a motorcycle accident in 2012 and left the UFC stumbling to put together a last-minute main event for UFC 153. In fact, the UFC has an interesting history with motorcycles all of its own. Back in 2004, the UFC was struggling to prop up its mediocre heavyweight division while the Japanese PRIDE FC threw money at anything over 230lb. The man keeping the UFC division alive was the bone-crunching submission artist Frank Mir. Then, in September 2004 Mir, the heavyweight champion, suffered a motorcycle accident that put him out of action until 2006 and left the heavyweight division in a shambles. It was even stranger when you consider that, while sponsored by Harley-Davidson, the UFC would give the winner of each season of *The Ultimate Fighter* a motorcycle – which they would subsequently be encouraged not to ride!

No, Conor McGregor was locked in with the UFC until he fought out his contract or until they didn't want him anymore. As he had stated in the pre-fight press conference for the first Diaz fight, he was set to be with Zuffa until the day he hung up his gloves. The UFC had also always been sharp on getting contracts renegotiated before they expire. A fighter had to go out of their way to not renegotiate before reaching the end of their contract and, once it had been established that a fighter would be testing his worth in the free agent pool, he might suddenly find his matches appearing lower down the card in less celebrated spots. Or worse, he might find himself in with a stylistically horrible match-up.

These are the subtle things that fight companies occasionally seem to do to reduce the promotion they give to a fighter who will probably be working for a competitor in a few months. A fighter could ask for his release publicly, but this has worked on less than a handful of occasions for athletes who, in the grand scheme of things, didn't matter much to the promotion. The great José Aldo had won an 'interim' featherweight title at UFC 200 and was going to be denied another crack at McGregor while the Irishman tested the waters of lightweight once more. Aldo asked for his release publicly and was rebuffed. The UFC was never going to just let the most accomplished featherweight of all time walk away. Of course, with the amount of money that McGregor was bringing in through his extra promotional work and his active schedule, it was in the UFC's interest to come to terms with him amiably. But they certainly couldn't afford to allow it to appear as though McGregor was running the show.

Yet behind all the politicking and match-making strife, McGregor was as focused as ever, revamping his training to come back faster, stronger, sharper – a whole new physical animal, built to stand up to another Diaz onslaught in the Octagon. After physically tying up against Diaz the first time around, McGregor realised that he needed to be fitter to carry the extra muscle through the rounds, and began a more scientific approach. He attacked a new cardiovascular programme – a combination of classic road work, bikes, rowing machines and inclined treadmills, but concentrating on training within certain heart-rate intervals to avoid the possibility of over-training but increasing his tolerance to the lactic acid build-up which haunts athletes who are operating in their 'red zone' during intense exercise. Both non-impact sports, rowing and cycling allowed him to train at the required capacity without stressing the old knee injury he had sustained previously. As a result – in terms of VO2 max and lung capacity – McGregor was approaching the showdown in the best cardiovascular shape he had ever been in.

Going a step further, McGregor restructured his day, banishing the late-sleeping and nocturnal training. Instead, he would divide his day into two blocks – a technical skills session in the morning and a strength and conditioning session in the evening. Whilst he still incorporated body-weight movements and some weightlifting, he suggested that the bulk of his strength gains were coming 'from groundwork and jiu-jitsu'. The reason for the split, as he would sagely point out, was because 'from a neuro standpoint, the athlete is sharper and fresher earlier in the day. For the second session, the athlete doesn't feel like he needs to hold back in the conditioning training. You don't have to worry that, if you get tired, someone will get you in a guillotine choke!' And with a submission loss chalked up against Diaz, excelling in the technical sessions – and in particular the groundwork – was something both McGregor and Kavanagh were regarding as a key training element.

Their hard work and diligent preparation were to pay off: the UFC and Conor McGregor agreed terms and in June, before UFC 200 had actually taken place, a rematch with Nate Diaz was announced as the main event of UFC 202. Reportedly, McGregor had missed out on as much as a $10-million pay day on the UFC 200 card, so when it came to crunch time the Irishman realised that the extra couple of dates in the diary where he would have to fly Stateside would be more than worth it in the long run. Certainly, the idea of holding the biggest rematch in UFC history without the usual build-up was not particularly well thought through. While it should be the job of the promoter to promote and the fighter to fight, that is not usually the case. Conor McGregor was living proof of this: he was worth the big bucks for his mouth, not as just another top-notch fighter.

Yet McGregor knew the power of controversy and speculation, and he loved to get the last word. As the pre-fight press conference for UFC 202 began, Dana White stood centre stage, while Nate Diaz and the co-main eventers, Anthony Johnson and Glover Teixeira, flanked him. But the empty chair was there again. A curt White asked for questions and, without the microphone that was traditionally passed around to the press at these events, someone immediately shouted 'Where is Conor?' White insisted McGregor was on his way and fielded the first official question. It was the same again: was White at all concerned that McGregor was late after the UFC 200 debacle? A noticeably frustrated White interjected midway through the question: 'We're starting without him. He has to start respecting people's time, man. Yours, theirs, mine, everybody's.' Another question along the same lines and White snapped: 'Listen we're having a press conference. If it's over before he gets here then it's over. Do you have any questions other than Conor being late?' When Diaz was asked about McGregor's lateness, he was far less concerned. 'Nah. I don't care,' he said then added with a chuckle 'It's rude.'

These were evidently not mind games with Diaz but an attempt to prove a point with the UFC's management. To cancel another fight at this stage just to punish McGregor would be madness. When McGregor finally turned up, fifteen minutes into the press conference, it was to rapturous applause. Asked about his lateness, McGregor was coy, insisting that he thought the conference started later, and that traffic was heavy, but adding that he was just happy to be there. As he answered his second question, Diaz got up and walked out, flipping the bird at McGregor as he left with a crew of hangers-on and team mates. The Irishman berated him over the microphone. Stopping as he got to the door, Diaz propelled the bottle of water he was holding at McGregor. McGregor responded in kind, and then the two teams began a blistering exchange of ballistic beverages. McGregor ran along the front of the press conference desks and collected a handful of Monster canned energy drinks as Dana White shouted desperately, 'Conor, no, not the cans!' before the Irishman pelted them at the Diaz team. While a pre-fight brawl is par for the course at many boxing press conferences, and is an easy way to build interest in a fight, White seemed furious. No sooner than McGregor had whipped the first can, a dejected White announced: 'Okay, shut it down.' UFC executive Dave Sholler held on to McGregor as he continued to shout abuse at the Diaz team and White spoke into the microphone: 'Sorry folks, see ya Saturday.'

The contracts for the bout revealed another act of McGregor stubbornness. It was to be fought at 170lb again: welterweight. Nate Diaz wasn't a real welterweight. He had fought a couple of bouts at welterweight and not had much success. The exaggerations about Diaz's weight by Dana White and others had become laughable in the aftermath of the first bout. Diaz himself brought it up at the presser, saying, 'All of a sudden I've got thirty pounds on him and they're making excuses [...] I don't know how I suddenly became this monster, this heavyweight against Conor McGregor just 'cause I won the fight.' After Nate Diaz was interviewed on *UFC Tonight*, footage was released of him speaking to hosts Kenny Florian and Michael Bisping during a break in which he said: 'And now I'm trying to do the fifty-five [155lb] thing because I'm like: "I don't want to hear it no more." I'm a lightweight and everyone is backing him up on this.' When asked outright at the presser about the obvious exaggeration that he had got up to 200lb by fight time, Diaz wryly replied: 'Yeah, I'm like one-seventy-five, two hundred pounds, something like that.'

The unbridled stubbornness displayed by Conor McGregor in insisting the rematch be fought at 175lb demonstrates once again how his mind works. It was becoming a familiar theme by this point: when faced with adversity McGregor would double down, put in the hours and prevail in a way that perhaps wasn't even necessary. He had hit rock bottom after destroying his anterior cruciate ligament in 2014, but when encouraged to view it as a challenge by John Kavanagh, he became consumed with beating Georges St-Pierre's recovery time for the same injury. The fight had been fought and lost at 170lb due to it being put together at short notice; now McGregor wanted Diaz at a proper, planned, lean 170lb with a full camp ahead of him. Diaz had insisted that with a full camp he wouldn't have even be touched; the pressure was as much on him as it was on McGregor.

The hyperbole over Diaz's weight became clear at the weigh-ins. McGregor took to the stage first, draped in the tricolour and wearing his usual sunglasses. Shedding his shirt and wearing no shoes, McGregor looked more muscular than ever as he stepped onto the scale but clearly had no trouble making the weight, coming in at just 168lb. When Diaz took to the scale, he weighed 170.5lb, just within the pound of leeway given in non-title fights – but kept his shoes and shorts on. This is almost unheard of at a regular weigh-in, where fighters shed every ounce of clothing they can while maintaining their modesty. Often, fighters will weigh in naked with a towel held in front of them if they are struggling to hit the numbers. When the stunning Gina Carano did this, she drew more publicity for her fight than any weigh-in brawl could, and Oscar De La Hoya's trainer famously dropped the towel deliberately, knowing that his charge was a sex symbol and that he could get some easy press. Neither man was a real welterweight; men such as Tyron Woodley and Rory MacDonald were drying themselves out to scrape the upper limit of the welterweight class. But the weights didn't really matter. This bout was not for title, or for any position in the rankings. This was a rivalry that came about by accident but in which the fight world had struck gold. There was no need for hyperbole on the eve of Diaz–McGregor II: it was genuinely the most anticipated fight in MMA history.

THE SWEET SCIENCE
THE HABITS OF NATE DIAZ

Nate Diaz had proven to be Conor McGregor's kryptonite, but he was far from an enigma in the fight game. Diaz had lost many fights and had plenty of flaws that could be readily exploited. The difficulty was more that sticking to a game plan against Diaz required remarkable discipline. Nate Diaz and his elder brother Nick fought with different styles but they shared most of their key attributes and flaws, and succeeded on the same principles. Both were avid endurance athletes, regularly competing in triathlons, marathons and ironman competitions. Nick Diaz boasted the unusual accomplishment of having swum from San Francisco to Alcatraz twice. Sharing 90 per cent of their genes, it seemed as

232

though both brothers were lucky enough to receive something in their make-up that gave them the gift of a great chin. Not only could the Diaz brothers take the shots, but they would take the hardest punches and show complete disdain for the man who had thrown them. There are countless photographs of both throwing their hands out, imploring the opponent to stand and fight or to throw more punches. Whether it was Nate Diaz pointing and laughing at a reeling Michael Johnson after catching him with a beautiful counter left straight, or Nick Diaz lying down in the middle of the cage like a *Playgirl* centrefold against Anderson Silva, the Diaz brothers had proven themselves a gift that kept giving to the young business of MMA photography.

Every fighter learns from a very early point in his training that if you hit the other man and he cracks a smile, you hurt him. Yet to watch a Diaz fight, neither seems to be a 'try hard', or desperate to hide the fact that they got hurt. The flipping-off of opponents, the constant trash-talk even between taking punches, the goading-on of opponents – it all seems to serve one purpose. The genuine desire of both Nate and Nick Diaz seems to be to turn the 'bout' into a 'fight'. Their ability to take a shot, and the high pace that they push, means that if a fighter begins trading blows with Nate Diaz or Nick Diaz, he stands a good chance of tiring himself out. Nate Diaz set the UFC record for most strikes landed in a three-round fight by landing 258/314 strikes against Donald Cerrone in 2011. That works out at Nate Diaz landing more than 80 per cent of his strikes against one of the tallest, longest, most efficient strikers in the history of the lightweight division.

Nick Diaz preferred to swarm on opponents, walking them to the fence and digging in body shots, while Nate Diaz was the more defensively savvy of the two and did most of his best work with straight blows. In a combined seventy bouts, no opponent had ever got the better of a Diaz brother by simply standing in front of them and trying to hit them as hard as possible. Conor McGregor is as proficient a knockout artist as ever entered mixed martial arts, but he threw everything he had at Nate Diaz in their first fight and soon – it is always sooner than is expected – the short, partial punches that Diaz was landing began to add up. Then, McGregor began to swing harder and harder to compensate, each time landing less cleanly and eventually struggling to hit anything but air. Finally, McGregor, usually a precise and picky striker, began swinging at Diaz's forearms and guard and, as the Irishman himself put it, being 'inefficient with his energy'.

While they shared many merits, the Diaz brothers had plenty of common flaws, though. Chief among them was that the two had difficulties with footwork. Their long, bladed stances made lateral movement far more difficult. In mixed martial arts, stances don't tend to be the long type familiar in boxing. Squarer stances are required to deal with the threat of round kicks, particularly to the legs. To check a low kick, the targeted leg must be picked up and turned so that the shin faces the shin bone of the opponent. The higher on the leg a fighter can take it, the more solid the surface that the opponent is kicking, but the longer a fighter's stance, *a la* Diaz, the slower he is to pick up his lead leg.

The brothers fought with their lead foot turned in and their lead shoulder well forward of their rear one in order to maximise the reach of their jab and take their centre line away from the opponent as a target. The downside is that with the lead foot turned in under rules that allow kicking, the tender hamstring is exposed to the standard low kick, and 'low-low kicks' can be thrown at the back of the calf and ankle that will sweep the lead leg out in the same direction

as the toes. Nate Diaz's long, side on stance is heavy on the lead leg, just as McGregor had asserted before their first bout (*Fig 1*), and kicked hard enough by men such as Benson Henderson and Josh Thomson, Nate Diaz would almost turn his back to his opponent. Conor McGregor would make full use of this in their second meeting.

Figure 1

THE FIGHT

As the two men came together in the centre of the cage for the referee's instructions, they were further apart than at their previous meeting. Held away from each other by six large commission officials, they were scarcely close enough to touch gloves. That was all right, though, because neither wanted to. The two backed into their corners as the commission workers left the cage and the doors were shut. The call for action came and the bout was underway.

Conor McGregor came out kicking at Nate Diaz immediately at UFC 202, pounding in low kicks and stepping off line when Diaz came at him. It was the textbook game plan for beating a Diaz. But more than that, it removed the range disadvantage that McGregor had suffered. Diaz was taller and had a longer reach – if they went punch for punch, Diaz would always have a far greater effective range than McGregor. But by attacking a closer target – Diaz's lead leg rather than his head – with a longer weapon (kicks), McGregor was able to hit

Diaz from outside his opponent's preferred range. Suddenly it was as though Nate Diaz was the shorter man, trying to close the range. He reached out ahead of himself with a jab and attempted to step in on McGregor, but his long jab was always met with a left straight down the pipe. A minute-and-a-half into the bout, McGregor had Diaz by the fence and was shellacking in kicks to the lead leg. Diaz, awkwardly trying to pick his leg up and failing, lashed out with a jab. McGregor parried the jab with his lead hand and shot back a left straight that put Diaz to the mat for the first time in their rivalry.

The cross parry is a technique that you won't see all that often compared to other defensive methods. Since the bare-knuckle days of Daniel Mendoza in the eighteenth century, the simplest truth in defensive boxing is that your defence is a mirror to your opponent's offence. If he punches with his left, you parry or block it with your right. If he punches with his right, you parry or block it with your left. In this way, a fighter avoids having to block across himself and tie his arms up in confusion. The cross parry flies in the face of this principle.

It is only a possibility in a closed stance match-up, and thus was something new from McGregor for the Diaz fight. The difficulty in landing the rear hand against a good boxer is due to the lead shoulder obstructing the line to the jaw and being easy to duck down behind, whereas southpaw McGregor could find the chin, temple or even neck of his orthodox opponent as his power hand was on the opposite side to their lead shoulder.

As Diaz hit the mat, McGregor advanced as if to dive on the downed Stocktonite, but the Irishman's corner screamed at him to back up. Nate Diaz could take a swing from a baseball bat and still submit many top fighters from his back on instinct. McGregor swallowed his pride and backed off, beckoning Diaz to get up and try again. The featherweight champion immediately returned to kicking the leg. He had scored a knockdown blow, but he was not going to get carried away with it as he did last time. Reducing himself to a pure boxing match with Diaz was the way to give his opponent back all of the physical advantages he had on the 'tale of the tape'. As the low kicks continued to land, Diaz began limping pronouncedly. He lashed out with the body jab that had doubled McGregor over in their first fight, but was cut off mid-thought with a left straight to the temple each time he attempted it.

Fans realised that this was Conor McGregor in his comfort zone again. The principle was just the same as with the squat Dennis Siver. The 'Notorious One' was working from beyond Diaz's range and maintaining the distance accordingly. He was visibly frustrating Diaz and the American was opening himself up to clean counters as a result. And McGregor was careful not to get into the habit of simply kicking and running; often as Diaz attempted to catch up to McGregor, the Irishman would use the chance to close the distance with a lead hook to the body and another left straight upstairs – a classic combination and a favourite of the great 1940s world heavyweight boxing champion Joe Louis.

Nate Diaz became visibly frustrated, just as he had been when Benson Henderson, Josh Thomson and Rafael dos Anjos had kicked his lead leg and out-manoeuvred him. Dropping his hands to his sides, Diaz stopped following McGregor and walked off in disdain. As McGregor stopped retreating and came towards Diaz, the latter met him with the exact same lead hook to the body and rear straight to the head. Throwing out his hands and egging him on, Diaz traded punches with the Irishman and it seemed for a moment as if McGregor was falling into the trap. Trading punches with a Diaz had never been a good idea. Bigger punchers than McGregor had tried it and every single one had failed. But he came to his senses and got back on his bicycle. Five more low kicks thudded in between periods of circling and back-pedalling, while Diaz landed nothing of any note. The raucous Vegas crowd drummed up an 'Olé, olé, olé' chant as McGregor played the matador. Another hard low kick connected as Diaz was lunging in for another body jab and buckled his leg inwards.

As the final seconds of the first round wound down, it was apparent to everyone present that Conor McGregor had his man's number. Nate Diaz tried to throw out some kicks of his own, but McGregor was simply never there to take them. Diaz threw out his hands in frustration, hoping to instigate another trade, then lunged in with a jab only to eat the same cross-parry counter on the right eye that sent his head rocking backwards, and was followed by a right hand that smacked across his nose before the round ended.

John Kavanagh concluded his instructions to McGregor between rounds by saying, 'That's the technical difference between the two of us, and that's what it's going to be for the next four rounds.' Keeping McGregor calm and focused was crucial. Diaz was the wounded tiger, at his most dangerous when hurt. Nate Diaz's corner, meanwhile, screamed to him as they were ushered out of the cage to begin the second round: 'No free kicks, Nate!', desperately imploring their man to not sit on the end of McGregor's kicking reach. The Diaz brothers had always shown disdain for low kicks, which was fine when they were able to step in and make the opponent pay for every kick thrown, but was a blueprint for disaster if the kicks were taken free of charge.

A low kick connected early to start the second round, but after that Diaz began to pick his lead leg up and even tried to kick back. Nate Diaz is not a gifted kicker, though. His entire set-up is against it: the long, side-on stance, does wonders to facilitate his boxing but is not conducive to free and swift kicking. That is why you do not see many side-on fighters excelling in forms of kickboxing that allow low kicks. Twenty seconds into the round, McGregor feigned a kick along the fence and Diaz lifted his lead leg in anticipation. As his opponent stepped in again, Diaz picked up his leg to check just the same way, but instead McGregor flashed the jab and swung in an overhand left that sent Diaz to the mat for a second time. This was the second effect of the low kick – having to deal with it meant picking up the lead leg; to do that, Diaz's rear leg had to be underneath him to hold his weight. In the first bout, McGregor had wasted enormous amounts of energy as Diaz leaned far back into his stance and rolled with the shots or was caught just on the end of them as they ran out of steam. Standing on one leg, with his rear leg directly underneath him, there was nowhere for Diaz's head to go.

The Irishman had scored two knockdowns on the iron-jawed Diaz, but he hadn't learned to punch any harder between fights. This was the fistic science at its most pure: attacking openings, forcing adaptations and striking again into the unguarded spots left by these defensive adaptations. The Straight Blast Gym representative advanced towards Diaz on the mat, gripping both of Diaz's ankles in preparation to pass Diaz's guard. McGregor had been working with the brilliant grappler Dillon Danis in preparation for the bout; he had to feel confident. Much of McGregor's identity is built on proving people wrong: his parents, his doctors, even the man behind the counter who gave him his dole. But whatever thought he had of pouncing on Diaz and finishing the fight there was quickly pushed from his mind. Kavanagh and his corner were screaming to let the staggered American back up.

As Nate Diaz got to his feet, the familiar early bleeding was present on his face, and he looked dazed and confused. McGregor kept him close to the fence and Diaz ate a couple more hard left hands as he attempted to punch his way out of trouble, with a pounding left low kick in between for good measure. For McGregor, there was no point chasing the finish – why risk getting tied up on the ground when he was near untouchable on the feet? The chances of Diaz standing up to five rounds of a performance like this were becoming increasingly slim. McGregor pumped the jab several times, a technique that had been largely absent through their first meeting and rarely appeared through most of his career as he took on mainly orthodox opponents. Diaz began reaching to parry the jab and then McGregor tapped him with a lead hook and shot a left straight down the centre. The old one-three-two: a classic set-up for the straight that succeeds when an opponent is drawn into focusing on parrying and blocking with their rear hand against lead-handed attacks coming in from different angles. The left straight was picture perfect: no extra motion, no wind-up, no overextension; in fact, it would have looked rather lacklustre if it hadn't found the mark perfectly and crumbled Nate Diaz's legs for a third time. Diaz had four minutes left to survive in the second round.

Then something happened that changed the direction of

the fight entirely: Nate Diaz stopped reaching for McGregor. Those long, desperate jabs that McGregor had been picking off, or pulling away from and uncorking a left hand in retaliation, became less frequent. Instead, Diaz put his forearms up, forming a wedge in front of him with his elbows about chin height, and began walking McGregor down. Covering up can be a terrible defensive strategy, because it gives the opponent opportunities to pour on combinations and work the body and head, up and down. But for the most part, McGregor wasn't fighting in combinations – he was picking his shots and stepping off line before Diaz could follow up. Throwing combinations would mean staying in range for longer. McGregor kept back-pedalling and Diaz kept trying to walk straight into McGregor's chest as the blows smashed against his forearms. The clean openings were not there for McGregor and rather than the occasional burst to close the distance, Diaz was now just walking forwards constantly. Each time McGregor stopped to fire, his blow would graze off Diaz's guard and Diaz would begin to throw back three or four shots. With ninety seconds left in the round, Diaz ducked a jab and came up with the infamous Stockton Slap. The sting of it invited McGregor to abandon his game plan, but McGregor stayed resolute and continued to dance, with Diaz getting closer and closer each time McGregor fired at him.

The crowd began to turn. McGregor backed up as Diaz stuck to him doggedly, firing another jab at the American that was deflected and answered with a four-punch flurry, the last of which was a left straight that turned McGregor's head around. The audience had realised that McGregor was starting to puff. Had he punched himself out? Was the pace that Diaz was putting on him too much? Midway through the second round was exactly where Diaz began to rally on a slowing McGregor in their first fight. McGregor turned and ran to circle out from Diaz.

Diaz, bloodied up and bruised, knew the momentum was turning. He began to throw his hands out, to mock McGregor, and to invite the punches, getting his guard up in time to deflect the shots. As McGregor fired a crisp left, Diaz caught a hold of him behind the head and got off an ugly uppercut and attempted a knee. This was quickly turning into the fight Diaz wanted and one that McGregor's coaches dreaded: a tit-for-tat brawl. Owen Roddy and John Kavanagh were calling for Conor to 'shell up' and to keep moving and get his breath back. Just as McGregor returned to the kicks, he was caught on one leg and a combination of punches and pushing sent him stumbling onto the fence. Six punches clipped him against the cage as he moved his head and attempted to gather himself; as he slipped under the seventh, Diaz pressed into him and the two were grappling on the fence for the first time. It was here that Diaz began to do his best work, driving the top of his head in underneath McGregor's, using it to stand him up along the fence, and freeing his hands to throw two-fisted combinations at the Irishman. The round ended with McGregor eating shots along the fence but moving his head and looking for an opportunity to break away.

John Kavanagh was a vision of calm under fire in the corner: 'This is why you did all the training. This is why you pushed yourself every day. Recover, recover. He's got one more round in him. That was his last flurry there. You know you can shell up when you're getting pressured like that. We don't have to use any more energy – shell up, they'll bounce off your forearms, you can work in an underhook. Relax, beautiful. Three rounds to go. Save the left hand – less left hands in the round. Jab, kick, if you want to work into the clinch: head position. We're up two rounds. Let's go!'

The Diaz corner was far less orderly than McGregor's. Throughout the round they had been screaming over each other. Any time Diaz did something that worked, Gilbert Melendez would shout, 'I like that! I like that! I like that!' But when Melendez got into the cage to talk to Diaz between rounds, he was calm and astute with his coaching: 'Don't be scared to block, I like when you block. Dirty boxing is what we want. Get into that clinch. Block, block, clinch.'

Conor McGregor was still breathing hard as the third round opened and while Nate Diaz's face looked as though it had been dragged the length of a city block along the pavement, he was as fresh as he had looked in the opening round. 'Chop and move,' shouted Owen Roddy as the first hard kick dug into the meat of Nate Diaz's thigh and McGregor darted off the line of attack immediately afterward. But within ten seconds the movement was not nearly so sprightly, and Diaz was looking to step in on the kicks and catch McGregor on one leg. McGregor fell back on the jab, but all it did was bounce off Diaz's forearms or forehead.

In the Burmese sport of Lethwei, which is the bare-knuckle cousin of Muay Thai and permits head butts, the strategy that Nate Diaz employed is termed the 'bull guard'. The fighter advances with his arms high and his head down, and any punches taken on the top of the head and the forehead are more likely to break the opponent's hands than cause a loss of equilibrium in the receiving fighter. It is not conducive to the long-term health of the fighter, and in gloves the hand injuries are less likely (though KJ Noons broke both of his hands on Nick Diaz in their second fight), but if walking through blows is the desired end, the bull guard is a viable, if primitive, means of doing so.

As McGregor puffed, he attempted to sidestep out, but ate a slap across the face as he did so. The featherweight champion jogged around to the other side of the cage while desperately trying to keep Diaz off him. A smile broke through on Diaz's face. With four minutes left in the round and McGregor sucking air, Diaz pointed at McGregor and laughed before unleashing a slap and a left straight down the pipe. In a curious move, McGregor overhooked Diaz's left arm and leaned back against the fence as Diaz took the wrestling position that he wanted.

And so the infight began, and it was gruelling. The infight is not pretty and can be hard to appreciate without some experience of wrestling against the will of another man. The classical infighting position of boxing – before referees became overly concerned with two fighters' heads touching and began breaking any semblance of a clinch immediately – was with the head underneath the opponent's chin or on their sternum. Once against the ropes or fence in this position, the man with his head on 'inside position' can force his opponent into an upright posture, with his feet directly underneath him, from which he cannot effectively generate power. The man on the inside, though, can readily hit the body of the man on the ropes or fence with some force.

With a single underhook, Diaz began to work to get his head underneath McGregor's and then, without looking, would begin punching over his own head to hit him.

But McGregor's work along the fence in the third round

was excellent and through the use of an overhook, wrapping over one of Diaz's arms, and pushing away Diaz's other arm at the biceps, he was able to stall out Diaz's favourite holding-and-hitting position – the same position from which he had taken so many unanswered blows in the first fight. Apparently, taking the clinch as Diaz moved in and hoping to recover some wind had worked, because McGregor soon cut an angle, began circling off the fence and cracked Diaz in the brow with an elbow as he exited, following with a salvo of head-turning punches afterwards. Diaz stuck out a couple more jabs and ate sharp counterpunches as a result.

At the two-minute mark, McGregor began turning and walking away again. It was clear that he was content to work in bursts, and it was certainly apparent to Diaz, who made sure to move in immediately whenever McGregor had finished hitting him. The Stocktonite began talking to McGregor, always advancing, and as he jumped in to slap McGregor across the face, his opponent fired back a left hand. But Diaz rolled with it perfectly. He threw his hands out to the sides and shook his head, then dropped his hands and walked straight at McGregor. The Irishman had slowed and Diaz had his timing down. A body shot along the fence saw McGregor turn his back and jog around the cage to avoid Diaz. The latter, never a gifted ring cutter and easy to frustrate, resorted to pointing at McGregor as if this appeal to McGregor's masculinity would make him stand and trade.

The last two minutes of the third round were spent along the fence and they saw McGregor in deep waters. This was the closest to being stopped by strikes that McGregor had ever been in his career. Unable to hold and hit effectively, Nate Diaz dug his head underneath McGregor's and freed both hands. With McGregor momentarily pinned to the fence and both hands uninhibited, Diaz dug in shots to the body and head. So successful was he in doing this that McGregor was even raising his knees to try to stop the shots coming into the body. On one leg and eating blow after blow, McGregor was in dire straits. As Diaz poured on the shots, half against McGregor's guard and half seeping through, his corner screamed for Diaz to take McGregor down. Amid the barrage, Diaz grabbed a double collar tie, both hands on the back of McGregor's head, and slammed a knee home into McGregor's face. McGregor went back into the fence and ate half a dozen more shots on the chin as he tried to slip and evade them. In an instant, the Diaz corner changed from, 'Take him down!' to 'Finish him!' McGregor rode with the shots and tried to keep up with Diaz's withering pace of output, desperately seeking an opening to escape as the klaxon sounded the end of the third round.

As Conor McGregor returned to his corner, John Kavanagh attempted to reassure him. 'You're winning the clinch every time. When your back's against the fence, hands up and catch them on your arms. You can slip, and catch them on your arms. They're slaps. Just recover, loads of time.' 'Slaps' was what fighters had been calling them for years. The Diaz brothers had wilted dozens of fighters this way, because disdain is not armour and ignoring blows won't stop them from connecting. Joe Calzaghe, the great Welsh boxing world champion, changed his style to focus on volume after his hands had become brittle from years of power punching and knockouts. When branded 'a slapper' by the American power puncher Jeff Lacy, Calzaghe threw a thousand punches over twelve rounds and battered Lacy with sheer volume. Taking to the microphone afterwards Calzaghe jeered: 'Not bad for a slapper, eh?' At the end of the third round, the volume of Diaz's strikes was catching up with McGregor: in those few moments of activity along the fence, Diaz had landed almost as many blows as he had in the first two rounds put together.

Owen Roddy had been calling for McGregor to 'shell up' and get his arms up each time he was getting hit throughout the last two rounds, but McGregor never did. As the break between rounds wound down, Kavanagh reminded McGregor that it was time to go into the championship rounds – the fourth and fifth five-minute rounds, which McGregor had never been taken to in his professional career. Cardio had to be a concern, and Kavanagh advised McGregor to instigate the clinch and use the chance to get his breath back as he had successfully at points in the previous rounds, but McGregor still had few answers for the flurries when Diaz could free both hands along the fence. As the corner was ushered out of the Octagon, Owen Roddy chimed in once again: 'Hands high, Conor!', advice that it seemed unlikely McGregor would (or could) ever obey.

Diaz's corner was once again the less organised of the two. Richard Perez, Diaz's boxing coach, screamed from outside the fence that Diaz should put McGregor to the cage, work the uppercut and bang the body. The others in Diaz's corner were happy to simply cheerlead. 'He can't stay on your pace, Nate!', 'He's tired, Nate!', 'He's drowning!' Gilbert Melendez, the member of the team inside the cage with Diaz, once again cut through the disorder to reinforce the one principle that had clawed Diaz back into the fight: 'Walk him down with your hands up and counter.' All of McGregor's best work had come on the outside; Diaz's only meaningful work was in the ugly, inside fight. But when Diaz was pressing McGregor to the fence and couldn't get his hands free, all he was doing was giving McGregor chance to recover. As the fourth round began, Melendez said to the Diaz team: 'I think we're winning 2-1, we're going to finish his ass.'

BREAKING THE BULL

Conor McGregor was sprightly for the opening seconds of the round, as always, but Diaz was not showing many openings to counter through. As McGregor's feet slowed, Diaz's corner called for their man to 'drop the left' on him. Diaz knew he was having the most success in the clinch and being picked off on the outside, but things had got drastically worse. In the third round, McGregor had been using a slashing left elbow each time he broke off the fence. The unpadded bone of the elbow, when thrown at a particularly bony point of the face, is used to open gaping gashes in an opponent's head that look as though they could have been made with a blunt axe. One of the strange truths about fighting is that often glancing elbows are more likely to open cuts than smashing, full-on connections.

Nate Diaz was always prone to cutting. From a misspent youth of bare-knuckle fights against grown men, he had accumulated a good amount of scar tissue that reopened in almost every fight he had, no matter how little he got hit. But McGregor's elbows had connected around his right eye socket. The bones of the orbit are among the easiest on the face to break and can often end a fight, but around the eye and the brow the meat of the face is the thinnest and can be opened up more easily. Punching the top of the head and forehead is generally bad for the hitter – when using fists, an ideal connection that most aim for is on the jawline. Elbows, conversely, are used almost exclusively higher up on the head – firstly, because the skin is thinnest around the brow, but also because cut placement makes the difference between a fight-changing cut and just a mild annoyance.

A laceration below the eye is rarely a problem, but a laceration above the eye will bleed into the eye itself, obscuring the fighter's vision. The thinly covered bone around the eye is most prone to severe injury if hit with an elbow, and while the blood had been mopped off Diaz's face between rounds and Vaseline had been smeared over his cut, a couple of left hands came in and within the first minute of the fourth round he was reaching up to wipe his own blood from his face between every exchange. Often the role of a jab is simply to obscure the opponent's vision, by either flicking him in the eye or just filling 90 per cent of what he can see with the lead hand while the rear hand is lined up. Once a fighter is bleeding into his own eye, his vision is being obscured with no further effort required from his opponent. With that eye obscured he will struggle to see blows coming from that side, and will usually develop a blind spot off to that side. It just so happened that Nate Diaz was being blinded on the side that McGregor's corking left hand came in, and that McGregor would jog off line into each time Diaz attempted to step in on him.

Nate Diaz's 'bull guard' had protected him from McGregor's power and pinpoint accuracy on counters, but in the fourth round, seemingly without the advice of his corner, McGregor had sussed it out. Diaz's exaggerated elbows-high, head-down guard protected him from his opponent's left hand; McGregor couldn't knock a man down when he was punching exclusively forearms or glancing connections on the top of his head. But now the Irishman showed the adaptability that had not been present in the first fight. He abandoned the left hand and the head hunting. Instead, he dug in shots on Diaz's exposed midsection. A front kick to the solar plexus early in the round sent Diaz stumbling back, to the evident concern of his corner. By protecting one target above all others, Diaz was leaving his midriff completely exposed. McGregor went back to the low kicks and as soon as Diaz picked his leg up to check, McGregor stepped in and hammered Diaz's body with punches while the American was on one leg.

Finally, McGregor went to the elbows out in the open. Diaz wanted to advance with his hands on his head? McGregor pinned them there. Extending both hands to check or trap Diaz's hands in position, McGregor would fold over into an elbow across the top of Diaz's head. A favourite technique of UFC light heavyweight great Jon Jones, and a mainstay in Muay Thai and Lethwei, folding elbows are especially valuable because both hands can be used to occupy or check the opponent's, and the fighter can still attack effectively from a position that in boxing would be completely defensive: tying up both his hands.

Two minutes into the fourth round, Diaz was able to duck an elbow and drive into the clinch along the fence. The two battled for control and traded hard elbows, before McGregor was able to break his hips off the fence and escape out the side again. McGregor capitalised with a flurry of blows, but Owen Roddy and John Kavanagh screamed at him for 'Just the jab! Jab!', as Diaz returned fire with a four-punch combination ending in a left hand that knocked McGregor off balance. McGregor kept stepping in with flurries and Diaz would return in kind. Kavanagh and Roddy were well aware that this would allow Diaz back into a round that McGregor had started so promisingly: 'Don't fall for his shit, Conor!' 'Stay on your job! Chop at the leg!' But Conor McGregor was in a world of his own. He pounded the body, snicker-snacked in elbows across Diaz's brow and scored hard counterpunches when Diaz opened up. While Kavanagh called for McGregor to back up, kick the leg, and get his breath back in the last minute of the round, McGregor stood directly in front of Diaz, looking to land hard blows instead.

The stools came in with the corners for the break between the fourth and fifth rounds. Conor McGregor had made it through his first championship round. In McGregor's corner, the message was clear: just five more minutes. John Kavanagh insisted 'You can do anything for five minutes!' In the Diaz corner, Gilbert Melendez maintained that they needed the finish. Nate Diaz's face was hanging open like an old shoe and the damage control between rounds was barely holding back the blood for the first few seconds of each round. On his own stool, the Irishman was bruised up but uncut, though he was covered in Diaz's blood. Each time the two battled in the clinch, each time they jostled for head position, each time Diaz threatened a takedown, his claret was painted across McGregor, shading the designs on the Irishman's chest and colouring his short blond buzz cut a not unpleasant hue of pink. McGregor had seemed to gain his second wind in the fourth round, but he was still breathing heavily as his team was ushered out of the cage ahead of the final five minutes. This was it: he was faced with an opponent whom he couldn't just blast out in under two rounds. A fighter who could take his power and keep moving forwards and a fighter who didn't give a damn about being dropped on his arse. Diaz flew in the face of McGregor's belief that no man could take his left hand. This was Conor McGregor's chance to prove to the world that he was not just a front runner but a true champion who could rise to the occasion and overcome an opponent with the height, the reach, the grit, the courage and the heart to take everything McGregor had – and spit it back with disdain and a smirk.

McGregor breathed through an open mouth and a face of stern determination in his corner as the seconds left the cage, but Diaz marched back and forth, flexing to the crowd. McGregor had to be ready: the old adage held that the Diaz brothers never lost, they just ran out of time. Diaz would be coming for McGregor like a bat out of hell in this last round and McGregor didn't have much left in the tank. Diaz immediately pressed in on McGregor and the Dubliner jumped into a flying knee that saw him pushed to the fence. As McGregor tied up Diaz's arms once again, the American ground his face along McGregor's in a struggle to attain dominant head position, painting a two-inch-wide stripe of blood along McGregor's right cheek. As McGregor broke free from the fence, he performed a half lap of the cage, turning his back to Diaz and looking at the clock. Things were looking bad for the Irishman as Diaz pushed forward again and drove McGregor to the fence, this time dropping down in an attempt to pull McGregor's legs out and dump him to the mat. Diaz set his grips and stood to hoist McGregor up, but McGregor stayed on balance. Diaz tried again – and again McGregor stopped the takedown.

'Work! Work! Work! Work!' screamed Diaz's corner, concerned that their man was wasting time forcing failed takedown attempts. Now Diaz freed his hands and flurried on McGregor with a solid three-punch combination, working the body up and down. Diaz culminated this with a slap across McGregor's face as the Irishman turned his back to run off the fence again. McGregor walked all the way to the other side of the cage with his hands on his hips, panting and looking at the clock on the big screen. There was no hiding it, McGregor was trying to run out the round. Rather than urgently cut across the cage and herd McGregor into the fence again, Diaz swaggered towards McGregor with his hands down, pointing at the Irishman. As McGregor continued to jog away from Diaz, his opponent turned his hand around and flipped the middle finger. It was vintage Diaz, and magnificent television, but it was doing him nothing to win the round on the judges' scorecards. McGregor put on another burst of offence against Diaz's guard and Diaz pushed him to the fence once more. Freeing his hands, Diaz dug to the body, and – hanging on the back of McGregor's head – pounded in a couple of uppercuts to the shorter man's face. Then, pushing McGregor away by the throat, Diaz smacked a hard right elbow across his noggin.

With a minute left in the round, McGregor turned Diaz onto the fence and hit a trip that briefly sent Diaz to the mat. It was completely unexpected, given the result of the first fight, but a masterful use of the unexpected and, additionally, a way to eat up seconds in the waning round. As Diaz rose from the floor, McGregor cracked him over the back of the head with a left elbow and Diaz ate the illegal strike like it was a Tic Tac. The two traded more grips and short strikes along the fence and as they waltzed along it, Diaz hit a trip that sent McGregor spiralling to his back, with Diaz landing on top. With less than ten seconds to work, Diaz stacked up in McGregor's guard and dropped elbows and punches on the face of the Irishman. As the final klaxon sounded, Melendez screamed from the red corner, 'Yeah, yeah, yeah! We got that! We got that round! That's three rounds, baby!'

As the fight was waved off, Diaz stood from inside McGregor's guard and offered his hand. McGregor didn't hesitate for a second, taking the help of the American in standing up. Smiling, they embraced and exchanged affectionate back slaps. Drenched in claret, both men returned to their corners, happy with their output and anticipating the judges' decision. Not only was it a show of mutual respect, it also reflected that the two were simply playing the game. It is very hard to hate another person when the smack talk you exchange is going to make both of you filthy rich.

In a frank moment with Gilbert Melendez, an exhausted Nate Diaz gasped: 'Did I win that shit?', to which Melendez could only offer encouragement and say that he thought Diaz had won three rounds. Three rounds, 'that's all we needed. That was a fucking war.' In the Straight Blast Gym corner, John Kavanagh had been completely unconcerned in the final moments. As soon as Diaz took McGregor down, the crowd had erupted, but Kavanagh had simply said, 'It's over.' Even a flat-out, exhausted McGregor could stall Diaz out in his guard for seven or eight seconds. The final push had come too late.

As the two men came to the centre of the cage, the scorecards were read out. McGregor had won the fight 48-47 on two cards: a single round separating it. The third card had scored it a draw. A majority decision.

Taking to the microphone afterwards, Conor McGregor assessed his performance. To the Irishman's way of thinking, he had proven that he was in another class to Diaz through the early going, but Diaz's toughness had clawed the Stocktonite back into the fight. McGregor reiterated John Kavanagh's mantra, saying that he would win or learn, and that the first fight was a learning experience. One thing was for certain: both McGregor and Diaz wanted a third fight. In a solo press conference afterwards, a sincere McGregor made it clear how much this fight had meant to him. He seemed genuinely concerned with the opinions of those in the public and the media, who had counted him out in this bout. Repeatedly, he asserted that Nate Diaz had to be close to 190lb and that the American had about 30lb on him, something Diaz had been insisting was untrue from the start. When asked about the embrace at the end of the fight, McGregor remarked that 'Respect is earned through battle, for me and for them. This battle was won. We'll regroup, we'll go our separate ways, see what happens, and we'll gather up for another battle. And then we'll be right back where we started.' Insisting that he wanted to get his six pack back, McGregor stated that he was done mucking around at 170lb and would be going back to 155lb for his next fight.

Clearly, this was not the easy victory many had expected once McGregor had prepared specifically for Diaz. The latter had been there for the whole fight and never stopped being a threat – in fact, he had become more dangerous as the fight went on. McGregor had limped into the press conference on crutches. Immediately questioned on this, the featherweight champion replied, 'My shin. I kicked his knee about forty times and it's fuckin' hurting me.' When queried about the effect of the leg kicks on the fight, McGregor laughed. 'I tell you what,' he replied, 'fuck leg kicks. Me leg is in bits after that. I don't really throw leg kicks. In my whole career I've thrown about three [...] But this time you have to hit the legs on him, so I practised leg kicks and I'll tell you what, he's got pretty good at checking them. He's not what he was. He's able to handle the leg kicks now, he's a lot more seasoned with them. But I just kept kicking.'

Nate Diaz was more like his usual self following the fight. After the decision was read, he announced to the arena that 'they can't have a motherfucker like me winning' because he was too 'real'. In the post-fight press conference, Diaz reverted to the line that both brothers often used: if they lost, it was because their opponent was running and their opponent should have been docked points as a result. Morally, as far as he was concerned, the Diaz brothers remained undefeated.

Vaping from a pen full of CBD or cannabidoil during the presser, Diaz espoused the product's healing benefits to the members of the media present. Cannabidoil is a banned substance 'in competition' in Nevada, and the 'in competition' window extends until six hours after the fight. Yet Diaz was sitting there puffing it, just minutes after his bout. Following the incident, the UFC's additional testing body, USADA, announced that they would be launching an official investigation, though if Diaz had done his post-fight blood work before vaping the CBD, it looked as though he would get off scot free in spite of the video evidence.

Conor McGregor had found a rival out of nowhere and suffered an embarrassing loss after inviting Nate Diaz to get up to 170 lb if he needed it. In the rematch, the obsessive McGregor had made sure that everything was the same, fighting Diaz – a 155-lb fighter – at 170 lb once again. By sticking perfectly to the game plan, McGregor was able to dominate Diaz through the early going, but found himself in as much trouble in the middle rounds as he had been in the first fight. As many questions were raised by the performance as were answered, and it seemed as though the rubber match, the final installation of the trilogy, was inevitable. But it would have to wait, because something a little more pressing was on McGregor's agenda to see out 2016. He had to pick up where he had left off before Nate Diaz even appeared on his radar.

8

THE TWO-WEIGHT CHAMPION

Nate Diaz had proven a significant bump in the road. The idea that Conor McGregor was just going to waltz into the lightweight division and continue racking up easy wins as he had at featherweight seemed to have been swiftly shot down. Even though a more thoughtful McGregor had gotten the better of Diaz a second time around, it was far from decisive. McGregor promised a trilogy, but had bigger fish to fry. It was a smart decision to move on before the rubber match – not only did he have more momentum with that hard-earned win under his belt, but a second loss to Diaz could have killed the McGregor gravy train for good. He would then be just another fighter.

Rather than sign the rubber match with Nate Diaz, the UFC opted to return to the way things had been before Rafael dos Anjos pulled out of UFC 196. Conor McGregor would get a shot at the lightweight title and a chance to become a two-division champion – the title he had been set on claiming since before he joined the UFC. But there was a new dog at the head of the pack now: Rafael dos Anjos's incredible streak of victories had been broken. Not just broken, but shattered in emphatic fashion by an American named Eddie Alvarez.

THE UNDERGROUND KING

The UFC's lightweight division was dead in the water when Eddie Alvarez started out in mixed martial arts as a welterweight in 2003. After BJ Penn and Caol Uno fought to a draw in a match for the vacant UFC lightweight title, the promotion put the belt on hold for three years and many of the best lightweights in the world jumped ship to the Japanese PRIDE FC. Alvarez spent his early years in the game fighting as a welterweight for smaller promotions such as the now defunct BodogFight and ShoXC. In 2008, Alvarez got his big break: 12-1 and having finished everyone he beat, he was entered into the DREAM lightweight tournament. DREAM was another Japanese organisation that was set up in 2008 to take the place of PRIDE FC when the original Japanese MMA powerhouse went under. DREAM was able to secure the talents of numerous world-class lightweights and the competition seemed to be the most legitimate in mixed martial arts. Tournaments are rare in the United States and are usually much diminished because most commissions have a limit on the amount of time that a fighter can be in the ring on one night. For this reason, any tournament on US soil that hopes to have fighters compete multiple times in one night must make concessions on the number of rounds. The abysmal Yamma Pit Fighting competition demonstrated this by having the quarter-final and semi-final contested in one-round fights, five minutes each. This was not enough time to get anything meaningful done, so the man who got the first takedown simply held until the end of the round and thus the end of the fight.

But Japan had a proud tradition of mixed martial arts competitions, whether it was the K-1 kickboxing Grand Prix, the PRIDE FC Open Weight Grand Prix, or DREAM's comical 'Super Hulk Tournament' – effectively an open-weight grand prix with more gigantic freaks and undersized gimmick fighters than genuine world-class competitors. Sometimes the final was on a different night, or the qualifying round, but in most cases successful fighters ended up fighting twice or more in one night. Terrific entertainment and completely unpredictable. It is one thing to prepare for an opponent for a couple of months – eating, sleeping, and training with them and their habits constantly in mind. But in a tournament, no one knows what will happen between unpredictable results, injuries and reserve fighters being kept on hand to take the place of drop-outs. The best fighter in the world is not always the best tournament fighter in the world and vice versa. It is a different terrain altogether from the usual tradition of one fight, one opponent, every few months.

Though he had already won welterweight titles in Reality Fighting and BodogFight, Alvarez was the dark horse of the DREAM lightweight tournament. He was in with many huge names of the lightweight division. In the tournament, there were numerous other champions from various promotions who had proven themselves among the world's best at lightweight. K-1 Heroes champion Gesias Cavalcante was a ferocious knockout artist with a 14-1-1 record. Also present were many PRIDE FC veterans and Shooto champions.

Tatsuya 'The Crusher' Kawajiri was a smothering wrestler and ground 'n' pounder, Shinya Aoki was a rubber-limbed submission artist, and Joachim 'Hellboy' Hansen was a Norwegian MMA pioneer. All three had owned Shooto titles and fought on the big show in PRIDE FC. The belts of Alvarez, the 'Underground King', didn't mean all that much here.

Alvarez scrapped his way through the tournament but suffered an eye injury in the course of knocking out Tatsuya Kawajiri in the semi-final and was unable to compete in the final later that night. He was replaced by Joachim Hansen. Known as 'Hellboy' Hansen, this Norwegian scrapper with unorthodox grappling techniques and the ability to intercept any takedown attempt with a knee to the dome, had contested what was arguably the fight of the year with Alvarez in the quarter-finals. Alvarez missed out on the belt that he probably deserved to win, but had made his name as one of the most exciting and explosive fighters in the lightweight division. His porous defence and incredibly heavy hands meant that he was always just inches either from being dropped and having to rally, or from knocking his opponent out cold.

While he was never able to claim the DREAM title, Alvarez moved on to bigger and better things by becoming one of the first stars for Bellator MMA. A promotion in the United States, Bellator was able to move into the recently vacated position of second best MMA company in America after the UFC bought out Strikeforce. With a televised spot on Spike TV, Bellator used a tournament format to determine its champions but did not insist the participants take part in multiple fights on one night. Submitting the three lightweights placed in front of him, Alvarez won the Bellator Season One Lightweight Tournament and became the Bellator lightweight champion.

As Eddie Alvarez got more fights under his belt, his hands became crisper. Always a heavy hitter and a strong wrestler, his boxing was blossoming into a more creative and economical science. While he remained undefeated through seven fights from the moment that he joined Bellator, only allowing the technically brilliant Pat Curran to survive to the final bell, Eddie was also gaining a reputation as a strangely slow starter. It was becoming a theme that Alvarez would come out slow, get dropped with a punch, and only then pull ahead with his science and power. He was one of those fighters who needed to taste his own blood to realise that he was in a fight. Alvarez's sole loss under his Bellator tenure came to the powerful wrestler Michael Chandler, who came out and threw caution to the wind – stunning the champion multiple times with blows and securing a rear naked choke to win the fight after four terrific rounds of war.

Alvarez quickly rebounded from the loss and stopped Shinya Aoki with a beautiful counter right hand, and Patricky Freire with a brutal head kick that left the Brazilian limp. Having fought out his Bellator contract, it was apparent that Eddie Alvarez planned to go to the UFC. The UFC recognised Alvarez's ability and value to Bellator and were willing to throw money at him to bring him over. Like any smart fighter, Alvarez was keen to get the most exposure and money; the sole factor holding up proceedings was Bellator. Bjorn Rebney, the president of Bellator MMA, made full use of the right to match offers from competition, which was apparently stipulated in Alvarez's contract. Rebney and Alvarez began legal action against each other, but finally came to an agreement that Alvarez would return to Bellator. Alvarez bested Chandler in another fantastic barnburner, scraping a split decision on the judges' scorecards. While a third fight was on the horizon and would have been nothing but good news for Bellator, when Rebney was ousted in favour of new CEO Scott Coker, the latter made the decision to comply with Alvarez's original wishes and tear up his contract, allowing the fighter to go to the big show.

Eddie Alvarez's first opponent in the UFC was a rough one as he drew Donald Cerrone. Alvarez was billed at five-foot nine but in reality was scarcely an inch taller than his long-time training partner, the five-foot-six Frankie Edgar. Cerrone was a towering lightweight at six-feet even. Furthermore, Alvarez did his best work with his hands, while Cerrone excelled with long kicks and intercepting knee strikes. Alvarez had a vast distance to close in order to get to work with his hands, and in the first round he was able to do this, stunning Cerrone, grabbing the lightweight giant by the back of the neck, and whaling away with right hands. Cerrone rallied, however, and by connecting knee strikes as Alvarez advanced he was able to wind the former Bellator champion. Alvarez got trapped out at long range for longer and longer periods, ate low kicks, and limped to the end of the third round to lose a unanimous decision on the scorecards.

It was an ugly start to the UFC career of Eddie Alvarez. In his next fight, against the last Strikeforce lightweight champion Gilbert Melendez, Alvarez edged a decision on the feet. Then, against former UFC lightweight champion Anthony Pettis, Alvarez stuck to his opponent on the fence and wrestled his way to an ugly and uninteresting decision victory. Anyone who had not seen Alvarez outside the UFC was now convinced that he was a boring staller who was scraping past top competition. For many, it was a foregone conclusion when Alvarez was announced to be the next opponent for Rafael dos Anjos: Alvarez was going to get smoked by the best lightweight alive.

Conor McGregor was tied up in his unexpected do-over with Nate Diaz, so dos Anjos took the next logical challenger at lightweight. Even if Alvarez's victories hadn't been impressive, they were over big names in the division. Dos Anjos began the fight with his usual advance across the ring and herding his man towards the fence. He wanted to put Alvarez in the pressure cooker just as he had with all the others. But each time dos Anjos closed in along the fence, Alvarez would clip off a counterpunch, move his head and avoid the return, then circle out to a new position and dos Anjos would have to follow. With two minutes left in the round, Alvarez flashed a jab as he came off the cage and threw a wide right hook that arced behind dos Anjos's left hand and clacked off his chin. Never has fighting been more obviously a game of inches, as dos Anjos's guard was just a hair's breadth out of position to stop the blow. Dos Anjos stumbled and Alvarez, smelling blood, went berserk swinging wild with both hands. In a post-fight interview, Alvarez would remark: 'That's the old me. Don't bring out the dog in me!' So wild was Alvarez's swinging that he tripped to his hands and knees amid his flurry, while dos Anjos desperately clung on. Alvarez leapt into a flying knee and wound up underneath dos Anjos before scrambling up to continue firing. Dos Anjos swung like a rag in the breeze as Alvarez rained a tempest of blows against his guard. Dos Anjos's face was catching two for every one deflected by his arms and finally the bout was waved off. Alvarez was the lightweight champion.

Eddie Alvarez had fought his way through every second-tier

organisation in mixed martial arts, beaten the best fighters in each, and even been tied up in legal proceedings from Bellator while the UFC pursued him. He wanted a money fight and so, at the post-fight press conference, the new champion remarked that as he had bested Gilbert Melendez, Anthony Pettis and Rafael dos Anjos, so he deserved a softball:

> I'm not taking on Top 15, so I would ask Dana White to give me an easier fight like Conor McGregor. I deserve that, I've been fighting the best guys, so I would like a gimme fight, so Conor, I more than welcome that.

A HEARTFELT APOLOGY

The bout was scheduled for UFC 205 in November 2016, in the UFC's first event in New York City. New York had been a nightmare for the UFC, as they had seen every effort to legalise professional mixed martial arts in the state fail. Finally, in 2016 the New York State Assembly stumbled its way through an awkward debate, in which both sides seemed completely inept and clueless as to the details of mixed martial arts and the contents of the bill, and professional MMA was finally legalised in New York. The UFC booked out Madison Square Garden and a few months later the pieces fell into place for McGregor versus Alvarez. With the biggest star in the sport fighting for his second world title in the most famous venue on earth, the UFC was set to make history.

In the weeks up to the meeting at UFC 205 on 12 November 2016, the UFC pushed the hype into overdrive by billing this as McGregor's chance to make history and become the first simultaneous two-weight champion. The word 'simultaneous' was important, because there had already been two other two-weight world champions in the UFC – BJ Penn at welterweight and lightweight and Randy Couture at heavyweight and light heavyweight. It was also a touch contentious, though, because McGregor hadn't fought at featherweight since January, the fight with Alvarez would be his third since winning the featherweight title and he hadn't even planned to defend it once. The problem of tying up two titles was the reason that the UFC hadn't let any other champions shoot for a second title in another weight class. At UFC 200, José Aldo had defeated the number one contender at featherweight, Frankie Edgar, and been awarded an interim featherweight title in McGregor's absence, but it seemed increasingly unlikely that McGregor would come back down to featherweight after proving competitive at lightweight without the arduous weight cut.

An announcement regarding Conor McGregor was teased in the run up to UFC 205 and it had the MMA community speculating wildly. The match-up with Floyd Mayweather, Jr? A run at the welterweight title? The most reasonable guess seemed to be that Dee Devlin was pregnant and that McGregor would be taking some time off after this fight regardless of the result. At the pre-fight press conference, Alvarez came out with a line about McGregor's announcement, joking that the news was that McGregor was expecting two children, but that Devlin wasn't having twins. A funny line, but the delivery fell flat. For McGregor's part, the wit of his early press conferences was largely absent. He fell back on lines about his 'big Irish balls' and pretending to lunge at Alvarez, who was completely unfazed. Just as José Aldo had pointed out during the Aldo–McGregor world tour, McGregor threatened to start a fight at the press conference every time, knowing that he would be held back; it never actually meant anything. Seeing that Alvarez wasn't bothered at all as Dana White held McGregor back, the Irishman lifted a chair overhead and acted as if he intended to throw it, which again no one bought. McGregor did redeem himself with the line, 'I wonder how much a chair would cost me.' This was a reference to the Nevada State Athletic Commission's reported decision to fine him the absurd sum of $150,000 for his bottle-throwing incident before the Nate Diaz rematch. The commission's executive director, Bob Bennett, later explained that the sum was to be only $75,000, but McGregor still intended to avoid paying it. 'Good luck trying to get it,' he famously quipped.

The sole interesting point about the UFC 205 pre-fight presser, which simply ticked all the 'easy fight hype' boxes, was Conor McGregor's choice of outfit. Something that McGregor seldom drew attention to, but seemed to enjoy, was playing dress-up. For his press conference with Rafael dos Anjos, McGregor had picked out a hideous Versace shirt in the style of the infamous drug lord 'El Chapo' Guzmán. At an autograph signing leading up to UFC 205, McGregor turned up in a $600 sweatshirt reminiscent of that made famous by Biggie Smalls. And for the UFC 205 press conference, the UFC's first main event in Madison Square Garden, McGregor paid homage to the Fight of the Century by turning up in a white mink coat over the top of a red turtleneck sweater, as Joe Frazier had forty-five years earlier before handing Muhammad Ali his first professional loss.

Having realised just how easy it was to create hype for any fight he should take in the future, McGregor spent much of the time backstage at UFC 205 squaring up to seemingly anyone he might possibly sell a fight with in future – welterweight champion Tyron Woodley and lightweight contender Khabib Nurmagomedov included – with someone always on hand to film it on their phone and upload it to the Internet.

Many of the questions about Conor McGregor's form at lightweight were answered emphatically when the cage door was locked. Eddie Alvarez came out pounding in low kicks to McGregor's long, bladed stance. These knocked McGregor's lead leg out of position and troubled him. The first kick that went in sent McGregor to his hands and knees. After a minute of cautious fighting and feinting, Alvarez gritted his teeth and shot in at McGregor with the right hand. The distance that McGregor had been maintaining was vast, and he was always ready to drive off his lead foot and create some more. As Alvarez lunged, his punch due to connect just on the extreme end of his reach, McGregor slipped his head off line and the blow flew harmlessly over his shoulder. McGregor returned with a left hand and a quick second and Alvarez was on the mat at the one-minute mark. McGregor walked his wounded opponent to the fence and teased him with strikes, springing back ready to counter each time Alvarez tried something of his own. At the two-minute mark, Alvarez lunged in again and was quickly dropped to his knees as McGregor slipped and returned the left hand. Alvarez was dropped three times in the first round, pounded with front kicks to the body and had no success of his own.

Alvarez returned to the game plan for the opening moments of round two, scoring with kicks again. With Alvarez fighting cautiously, McGregor did something very rare in combat sports and placed both his hands behind his back. Of course, McGregor was safe from harm because his defence was being done entirely with his feet – as long as he controlled the distance, Alvarez couldn't touch him – but it was an invitation for Alvarez to open up or face further jeers from the crowd. Alvarez began to throw punches and McGregor resisted the temptation to counter, finally taking one right hand on the chin before clipping him with the counter left and sending him stumbling once again. Alvarez summoned up the courage for another charge with two minutes remaining in the second round, and was hit with the same counter left as he dived past McGregor, but this time it was followed by a right hook, another left hand, and a second right hook that sent him to the floor. This time, McGregor was directly on top of him as he fell and the fight was waved off.

After a brief embrace with the fallen Alvarez, it was back to *kayfabe* (a professional wrestling term for things done 'in character' as part of the storyline) and McGregor began setting up the next pay day. In his post-fight interview, McGregor declared, 'Listen, I've spent a lot of time slating everybody in the company. Backstage I'm starting fights with everybody. I've ridiculed everybody on the roster. And I just want to say from the bottom of me heart, I'd like to take this chance to apologise...' here McGregor paused for effect, 'to absolutely nobody! The double champ does what the fuck he wants!'

NO WORLDS LEFT TO CONQUER?

After winning a second UFC title at a second weight, it was unclear what was next for Conor McGregor, but he cleared that up with a simple statement at the post-fight press conference. When quizzed as to his big announcement McGregor had unusual difficulty getting it out, but finally announced that he was going to be a father early in 2017, adding, 'I'm crapping me jocks.' When asked about the due date, McGregor said he thought it was March, before someone off stage (presumably Dee Devlin, who would be the most qualified to comment) corrected him that it was May, which was greeted with much laughter and applause. Conor McGregor, a man who had adapted to celebrity as naturally as a duckling to water, was adamant about one thing: he did not want his family growing up in the shadow of celebrity and so for the time being he was taking some time off.

There were many who figured that McGregor was untouchable now, having won titles in two divisions, but the thing that has kept his career fresh is that there are still so many unanswered questions. The Irishman won the lightweight title, in the UFC's deepest division, with a record of 2-1 against world-class lightweights. Any fight made at that weight brought its own fascinating stylistic questions. Top of the heap was the American wrestler Tony Ferguson. Nicknamed 'El Cucuy' after the Mexican equivalent of the bogeyman, Ferguson was a gangly fighter for the weight class with loopy boxing form but terrifically accurate hands. Most importantly he drove a frenetic pace. As a tall fighter for the class, he specialised in the snap down, pulling opponents forward by the head and slapping on the front headlock from which he would attack with his favourite D'Arce choke. Ferguson was so effective with this choke that he owned almost a quarter of all D'Arce choke submissions in the UFC's twenty years of fights. Shortly after UFC 205, Ferguson defeated the former champion Rafael dos Anjos in a convincing five-round beating, cementing himself as a worthy challenger for the lightweight title.

Then there was Khabib Nurmagomedov, the Dagestani wrestler who had been considered the number one contender for the better part of a year but had been forced out with injuries. In the course of negotiating the McGregor–Alvarez fight, Nurmagomedov was apparently sent a contract to fight Alvarez for the lightweight title, which was then revoked when McGregor–Alvarez came together. The stories were different from all sides, but whatever happened Nurmagomedov came out of the experience bitter and resentful towards the UFC. Fighting on the UFC 205 undercard against top ten lightweight Michael Johnson, Nurmagomedov put on a clinic. So powerful and able was he as a wrestler that he was able to plough through Johnson, get him to the mat, pin one hand behind the American's back or under one of his own legs, and beat Johnson senseless. For two-and-a-half rounds Nurmagomedov held the desperately squirming Johnson in place, battering him with punches and elbows, and talking to him between blows.

In a clip shared extensively on social media immediately after the fight, Nurmagomedov could be heard saying to Johnson mid-fight, with one hand around his throat, 'You have to give up.' Punching and elbowing the prone Johnson with the other hand, Nurmagomedov continued in his thick Russian accent: 'I have to fight for the title. You know this. I deserve this.' In between rounds, the embittered Dagestani ignored his cornermen in order to chat to UFC president Dana White through the fence from his stool. Ordering White to not send him any more 'fake contracts', Nurmagomedov warned, 'Be careful, I'm going to smash your boy.' The 'boy' referred to was clearly Dana White's promotional favourite, Conor McGregor. Nurmagomedov was a wrestler, but more than just the basic takedowns, he was a man who could suplex even the most skilled wrestlers in the division on their head, and who could pin the hands of the best fighters in the world behind their backs like an older brother.

At featherweight, José Aldo had dominated Frankie Edgar to pick up the interim title at UFC 200 and was desperate for the rematch with Conor McGregor, threatening to leave the UFC if he wasn't given the match. He even asked for his release from the organization at one point when it became clear that McGregor had moved on to the lightweight division. Of course, Aldo, being a champion for almost a decade and losing entirely because of a loss of composure in the opening seconds of his bout with McGregor, would have received an immediate rematch under any normal circumstances. But he had been a vocal dissenter and a poor pay-per-view draw, and McGregor was a superstar and a company man (at the time, at least), so the UFC let McGregor carry on and leave the featherweight division behind. More recently, though, Max Holloway had been cutting a swathe through the featherweight division. A 7-2 prospect when McGregor had taken a convincing decision victory over him, Holloway had since run his record up to 16-3, banging out a staggering ten victories in a row over world-class featherweights and finishing the vast majority of them. Clearly, there were still a great many options open for Conor McGregor, and that was important. Floyd Mayweather, Jr had been a terrific draw in the boxing world, delaying the mega-fight with Manny Pacquiao until near the end of his career. After that disappointing Pacquiao bout, no one had any more questions about Mayweather and his final pay-per-view drew a pretty mediocre 400,000 buys. Questions and doubts are what keep people – even the most ravenous fans and detractors – tuning in.

Conor McGregor had pulled off a fantastic coup, though.

The UFC had always avoided letting a fighter tie up two titles at the same time before because they sell pay-per-views based on belts and slapping two on one fighter means one is always going to be out of the running. Things got even more interesting when McGregor announced at the UFC 205 post-fight press conference: 'I want the ownership now. If we're going to keep doing this, let's talk, but I want an equal share. I want what I've deserved, what I've earned.' The UFC had always sought to keep the company bigger than any one star, but they had allowed McGregor to grow bigger than the promotion and perhaps even the sport. Then, on 26 November 2016, just days after McGregor had won his second belt and been billed as the UFC's first simultaneous champion, the UFC announced that he had relinquished the featherweight belt. 'Relinquished' was the official term, but many questioned this. Aldo's title was solidified and a second interim title was immediately made for Max Holloway and Anthony Pettis to fight over at UFC 206, because it seems that there has to be a belt on the poster even if the card is good enough without it. (Interestingly enough, if Pettis, a former lightweight champion, had won this title, he would have been the fourth man to hold belts at two weights just weeks after McGregor achieved it – something that the UFC didn't push nearly so hard.) Holloway went on to win that belt in emphatic fashion. After having relinquished his belt, whatever the circumstances, McGregor remained quiet for a few days and then it was announced that he had been granted a boxing licence in California.

The MMA media went into overdrive speculating wildly over the Floyd Mayweather, Jr match up. Of course, it is never safe to say 'never' in the fight game, but the obstacles to that fight seemed completely insurmountable. Not only was Floyd Mayweather, Jr thirty-nine years old and retired. He was exceptionally proud of his 49-0 record and his many, many wins over world-class boxers. Moreover, 49-0 was held to be a meaningful number for Mayweather because it tied him with the great Rocky Marciano. Why would he get back into the boxing ring just to take a fiftieth win over someone with no professional record and no great accomplishments, even as an amateur? Some would say he'd do it for the money, which was always Mayweather's number one concern, but McGregor was granted a boxing licence in California. Floyd Mayweather, Jr hadn't fought outside Nevada since 2005 because the tax laws were so favourable there. Even the allure of Madison Square Garden's bright lights couldn't get him out of Nevada, because as McGregor had just found out, the taxes on a prize fighter in New York are harsh. In fact, this was something that McGregor would likely have to confront soon, as he could not compete in Nevada and enjoy these lower tax rates until he had paid his outstanding fine for the bottle-throwing incident.

Then there would be all the complications at McGregor's end – even if he could work out some kind of loophole in his UFC contract, or appeal through the Ali Act in California now that he was a licensed boxer, the UFC and the new ownership WME-IMG could certainly make life hell for him in court with months or years of legal fees even without winning the case. As Fox Sports host Colin Cowherd pointed out in a rare moment of genuine insight when McGregor was in a stand-off with the Fertittas over UFC 200 back in April 2016: 'Millionaires don't get into whizzing matches with billionaires.' Oddly enough, the one reason that most thought the fight would never happen – that no commission would sanction it – seemed the least likely to prevent the fight. Time and time again, it has proven far easier to sign a mismatch than fight fans would like to think.

It seemed as though the UFC would never agree to risk having their top star embarrassed in the boxing ring. Make no mistake, as a boxer Conor McGregor is not even close to the level of the most middling opponents that Mayweather has beaten. And Mayweather, in turn, seems very unlikely to agree to a mixed martial arts or kickboxing match against McGregor. At the time of writing, it seems, for the most part, just the flapping of gums to draw attention. And it worked a treat in getting McGregor into the headlines, even while he was on a supposed ten-month hiatus.

CHANGING THE GAME

Whatever happens after UFC 205, whether he goes on to fight for ten more years or retires upon the birth of his first child, Conor McGregor has already accomplished things that no one else in the history of mixed martial arts has been able to. A good amount of that came from becoming a 'company man' in the eyes of the UFC, but that in turn came from his willingness to fight anyone and everyone, even at short notice. A fighter is well within his rights to turn down a last-minute change of opponents, but McGregor has always gone with it and, in all but one instance, he has won. He also realised that while it should be the job of the promoter to promote, a fighter who can do the advertising for himself is far more valuable than a dozen quiet, humble, world champions.

Conor McGregor has become one of the first fighters to get the million-dollar pay days, and certainly the first featherweight to do so. He attracted interest to the lower weight classes in a way that no one else had managed. In the UFC, the numbers have always been a secret and there is a great deal of talk about 'locker room bonuses' and unofficial payouts, so no one in the media ever really knows what they are working with. The most contentious issue has always been the revenue split between fighters and the promotion – if Conor McGregor could be paid $2 million or more for performances, why couldn't others? The revenue split between league and athletes – which is publicly available for the NBA, NFL and other major sporting organisations – is kept secret by the UFC. Shortly after McGregor won his second title in the biggest fight the UFC had ever held, a new mixed martial arts athletes association – the Mixed Martial Arts Athletes Association (MMAAA) – was formed, headed by some of the sport's biggest stars: Georges St-Pierre, Donald Cerrone, Tim Kennedy, TJ Dillashaw and Cain Velasquez.

Then there is style to consider. McGregor came into mixed martial arts as a power-punching boxer, but rounded out his game taking elements from every element of the martial arts. Capoeira and taekwondo were as readily visible in McGregor's game as the more common Muay Thai. This is a fighter who took inspiration from everywhere, and the bits that worked stuck around in his game after he had tested them out. Low line side kicks – the sort Bruce Lee was preaching about in the 1970s – jumping switch kicks of the kind you would see in Olympic taekwondo matches. McGregor even noted in one interview with Ariel Helwani before the Holloway fight that he had been watching a lot of kyokushin karate and wanted to try a 'rolling thunder'. Sometimes called *kaiten-geri* in Japanese, this is a forward flip where the heel of one foot is brought down as in an axe kick as the feet follow through on the tumble. It is a technique that is more at home in *Street Fighter* than the cage, but at the end of the first round with Max Holloway, McGregor leapt into a rolling thunder as promised.

While some detractors have decried McGregor as just a left hand, he bridges initiatives beautifully. Where the sport's most famous counter fighters, Anderson Silva and Lyoto Machida, were passive and asked their opponents to come forward, McGregor moves forward and throws heavy blows at his opponent until they return at him, whereupon he hits his money counters. That kind of comfort on the lead and on the counter, and being able to switch between the two in an instant, rather than making a change of plans obvious with a change of behaviour, is extremely rare in mixed martial arts.

Meanwhile, the Straight Blast Gym has gone from strength to strength from the moment that Conor McGregor found his feet in the UFC. John Kavanagh and his team were able to move once again to a new facility on the Naas Road, Dublin, which was large enough for multiple matted areas, a ring and a full-sized cage – things that were unimaginable for Kavanagh when he started out in his 'shed'. Young prospects such as James Gallagher and Charlie Ward have quickly been snatched up by the UFC and Bellator, whereas in the past they might have toiled on the regional circuit for many years before getting the call-up. McGregor truly has kicked in the door for the Irish.

Conor McGregor has gone from having little and throwing away his only paid gig to having enough money to buy the cars, suits and gifts that he wanted for himself, his family and his friends. The plumber, who quit after the first year, has become one of the most famous athletes on the face of the earth, has been pastiched in *Saturday Night Live* skits and had his Vince

McMahon-style strut imitated by celebrating athletes at NBA and football games. McGregor has won RTE's sportsperson of the year, beating out the great Katie Taylor and many others, won the *VIP* 'Most Stylish Man of the Year' award, and was nominated in the same category in *GQ* magazine. In a sport that is often erroneously called 'Ultimate Fighting' – even by a young Conor McGregor and Tom Egan – McGregor has come to overshadow even the brand name. It seems that, at the present time, there was Conor McGregor, and then there is MMA. Fans can go back and forth all day about whether he believes the hyperbole he spouts in interviews, or whether he can be a 'real champion' until he defends a belt, but one thing cannot be disputed: Conor McGregor is most certainly 'Notorious'.